Topics in
Cognitive Development

Volume 2
Language and
Operational Thought

Topics in Cognitive Development

Marilyn H. Appel, Editor-in-chief
Medical College of Pennsylvania, Philadelphia

Volume 1 **EQUILIBRATION: THEORY, RESEARCH, AND APPLICATION**
Edited by
Marilyn H. Appel, *Medical College of Pennsylvania*
Lois S. Goldberg, *Glassboro State College*

Volume 2 **LANGUAGE AND OPERATIONAL THOUGHT**
Edited by
Barbara Z. Presseisen, *Research for Better Schools, Inc.*
David Goldstein, *Temple University*
Marilyn H. Appel, *Medical College of Pennsylvania*

A Continuation Order Plan is available for this series. A continuation order will bring delivery of each new volume immediately upon publication. Volumes are billed only upon actual shipment. For further information please contact the publisher.

A Publication of the Jean Piaget Society

Topics in Cognitive Development

Volume 2
Language and Operational Thought

Edited by

Barbara Z. Presseisen
Research for Better Schools, Inc.
Philadelphia, Pennsylvania

David Goldstein
Temple University
Philadelphia, Pennsylvania

Marilyn H. Appel
Medical College of Pennsylvania
Philadelphia, Pennsylvania

Plenum Press · New York and London

Library of Congress Cataloging in Publication Data

Main entry under title:

Language and operational thought.

    (Topics in cognitive development; v. 2)
    "All the papers in this volume were presented at the third and fourth annual symposia of the Society."
    "A publication of the Jean Piaget Society."
    Includes bibliographies and index.
    1. Cognition in children—Congresses. 2. Children—Languages—Congresses. 3. Piaget, Jean, 1896-   —Congresses. I. Presseisen, Barbara Z. II. Goldstein, David. III. Appel, Marilyn H. IV. Jean Piaget Society. V. Series. [DNLM: 1. Language—Congresses. 2. Thinking—Congresses. W1 T0539LI v. 2/BF455 L287]
BF723.C5L37   155.4'13   77-20977
ISBN 0-306-33002-4

© 1978 Jean Piaget Society

Plenum Press, New York
A Division of Plenum Publishing Corporation
227 West 17th Street, New York, N.Y. 10011

Printed in the United States of America

Contributors

Roger V. Burton   State University of New York at Buffalo, Buffalo, New York

Michael J. Chandler   University of Rochester, Rochester, New York

J. A. Easley, Jr.   University of Illinois, Urbana–Champaign Campus, Urbana, Illinois

Linda Chapanis Fox   Department of Health, State of Hawaii, Honolulu, Hawaii

Jeanette McCarthy Gallagher   Temple University, Philadelphia, Pennsylvania

Carol Gilligan   Harvard University, Cambridge, Massachusetts

Bärbel Inhelder   University of Geneva, Geneva, Switzerland

Annette Karmiloff-Smith   University of Geneva, Geneva, Switzerland

Robert Karplus   AESOP, Lawrence Hall of Science, University of California at Berkeley, Berkeley, California

William Kessen   Yale University, New Haven, Connecticut

Lawrence Kohlberg   Harvard University, Cambridge, Massachusetts

Eric H. Lenneberg   Late of Cornell University, Ithaca, New York

E. A. Lunzer   University of Nottingham, Nottingham, England

Katherine Nelson   Yale University, New Haven, Connecticut

Hildred Rawson   The Ontario Institute for Studies in Education, Toronto, Ontario, Canada

H. J. Sinclair   University of Geneva, Geneva, Switzerland

Preface

This is the second volume in a series that records the official Symposium Proceedings of the Jean Piaget Society. Like the first volume, this work includes theoretical, empirical, and applied aspects of Jean Piaget's seminal epistemology. The focus of this publication is the intricate interplay of language development and the development of operational thought.

All the papers in this volume were presented at the third and fourth annual symposia of the Society. The authors are a formidable group of scholars from around the world who are working in Piagetian theory in many fields of endeavor. Their work shows the breadth and depth of Piaget's studies, as well as the richness of his ideas over time.

The Jean Piaget Society was founded to provide a forum in which scholars and educators could examine and explicate the concepts of genetic epistemology. In many cases, the papers presented at the annual symposia raise many more issues than they resolve. That they generate discussion and further research is self-evident. Such activity is a tribute both to Professor Piaget and to the Society.

Further volumes in this series will record the research presented at later symposia.

Barbara Z. Presseisen
David Goldstein
Marilyn H. Appel

Contents

Introduction

The breadth and richness of research and application stimulated by the theory of Jean Piaget and his colleagues is clearly exemplified by the breadth and richness of topics covered in this volume. Indeed, the four topics in language and operational thought included here are merely a sample of the vast range of topics examined and influenced by the Genevans.

The four papers on language development collectively emphasize the necessary role of cognitive development in the acquisition of language and underscore the recent move by developmental psycholinguists away from claims of a priori linguistic knowledge and toward a truly developmental perspective.

The semiotic function, described by Inhelder and Karmiloff-Smith as "the capacity to represent sensorimotor actions through signifiers that are differentiated from their significates," is seen as the key to an understanding of the interdependence of cognitive development and language development. An important distinction is drawn between two types of signifiers: the symbol, a subjective and personal signifier, is the mode of representation in symbolic play, deferred imitation, and mental images; and the sign, which is conventional and communicable, is the mode of representation in verbal utterances. Inhelder and Karmiloff-Smith point out that language development proceeds from a stage at which a child's utterances are a combination of signs and symbols to a stage at which the utterances form a highly structured system of signs. Thus, the development of the child's ability to represent objects and events not immediately present, or occurring in terms of signs rather than symbols, makes possible the child's ability to communicate verbally in a nonegocentric manner.

Hermine Sinclair examines the relationship between Piaget's early work on language and thought in the child and work currently being conducted by psycholinguists, such as Klima and Bellugi, Susan Ervin, and herself. In particular, the focus of this paper is on the manner in which an understanding of the nature of children's questions leads subsequently to a better understanding of how children view the world. As Sinclair points out, the major difference between the approach that she, Klima and Bellugi, and Susan Ervin take and that taken by Piaget is the relative degree of emphasis placed on syntactic and semantic aspects of children's questions. While Sinclair chooses to study syntactic regularities in children's questions, Piaget was concerned with the content of their questions.

In their paper, Kessen and Nelson consider two apparent contradictions in early development: (1) while the infant is finely tuned to certain stimuli (presentations), he is insensitive to many aspects of his surroundings, and (2) the infant is concurrently creating particulars and general categories or concepts. Issues discussed by Kessen and Nelson in relation to these apparent contradictions are fine tuning and the inherited categories, the construction of figure, the move from schememes to schemes, the categorization of particulars, and the importance of unfinished forms of the infant's thought. Kessen and Nelson's approach differs from that taken by Piaget in that they are concerned with the irregular, complex, and unfinished aspects of the infant's cognition.

Lenneberg and Chapanis Fox examine the importance of neuropsychological evidence to an understanding of the role of sensory and motor integration in the construction of spatial and temporal organization. While the focus of their research is on brain dysfunction, Lenneberg and Chapanis Fox perceive a relationship between the characteristics of behavioral disintegration and its initial development. Their evidence for the existence of cross-modal extinction—the masking of a stimulus in one sensory domain by the simultaneous presentation of a stimulus in another sensory domain—in stroke patients has practical implications for physical therapy and the treatment of dyslexia.

Current approaches to the problem of formal operational thought are among the most complex and controversial in the cognitive literature. The three papers in the following section explore numerous alternatives, some of which are critical of the Piagetian approach.

Lunzer begins his analysis of formal reasoning with a historical look at both concrete and formal thought. He questions whether past definitions are currently adequate, including Piaget's explanation of the development of formal thought in the context of the INRC group. Two features of advanced thinking are stressed and analyzed in Lunzer's reinterpretation of formal thinking: acceptance of lack of closure (ALC) and multiple interacting systems (MIS). Important research and experimentation, even beyond the Geneva school, are reviewed in the study, and various problem areas are discussed. One of Lunzer's principal contentions is that problems of logical inference constitute a special task and should not be considered a major factor in the quality of thinking in general. He suggests that ALC plays a prominent role in both everyday thinking and logical thought development. Finally, he discusses the acquisition of grammar as a key concern of formal thought development and general competence. He concludes by casting doubt on both the logical processes and generative grammar as the road to formal thought. He calls for further research, particularly in studies of analogy and rule-bound problem-solving.

Gallagher proposes further and new research on the development of formal operations in Piaget's theory. Two ideas are stressed as the main focus of this research. First, the adolescent's understanding of metaphor and analogy should be examined within the context of Piaget's system of correspondences. Second, the emphasis on metaphor and analogy research should be evaluated in terms of the possibility of forging a rapprochement between science and the arts. Gallagher reviews some of the latest developments in Piagetian theory within an analysis of the main concepts of genetic epistemology. The importance of transformations and the system of correspondences is carefully outlined, particularly in the development of formal thought. Formal thought research is reviewed historically, including Lunzer's testing methodology and the significance of the propositional system of the INRC group. Gallagher shows how the use of analogies and metaphors in arguments carries people beyond ordinary discourse and propositional reasoning. She likens this phenomenon to the key hypothesis of Piagetian theory on the active invention or construction of knowledge itself. Metaphors as complex comparisons become a key element in the adolescent's development of formal thought. The use of metaphors is shown to be as productive in the arts as in Piaget's more traditional disciplines of mathematics and science. Several further research areas in formal operations are suggested by Gallagher, and the possibility is raised of yet another stage of cognitive development in middle and old age.

J. A. Easley, Jr. approaches the epistemological problem of the certainty of man's knowledge. His philosophical discussion centers on problems arising in attempts to compare two fundamentally different ways of conceptualizing phenomena. From one point of view, that of the logical or linguistically oriented empiricists, language provides a solution through the testing of knowledge claims at several different levels of abstraction. Another point of view, that of Piaget, accepts the knowledge man has developed as an expression of biological structures and processes. In contrasting these two points of view, Easley reminds the reader of the dynamic process of Piaget's operations. Easley presents several examples of research on formal operations, showing the differences that exist between Piaget's point of view and that of the current dominant scientific approach. He suggests that a scientific paradigm can evolve in the field of human cognition through the recognition of the positive accomplishments of both the evolutionary and the mechanical epistemological views.

The rapidly growing concern with social cognition is highlighted by the three papers in the next section. The development of moral judgment and self-other differentiation is described within the context of the development of operational thought, a perspective that has led to numerous fresh insights into these age-old topics.

Burton first outlines the behavioral approach to research in morality. He stresses the contributions of Hartshorn and May and the emphasis on the significance of overt behavior in their studies. He notes the importance of the doctrine of specificity in the behaviorists' work and suggests that new multivariate methods of analysis should now be applied to the earlier body of information. In his review of the cognitive-developmental approach, Burton finds a significant overlap between Piaget and the behaviorists. The importance of the rules of the game and their relationship to actual deeds is stressed as something separate from verbal descriptions. The increased importance of cognitive structures of both approaches is underlined, and the followers of Piaget's cognitive-developmental school are characterized as having been unfortunately sidetracked on moral judgment as an end in itself. Further research on the relationship between moral development and other factors influencing actual conduct is encouraged.

Gilligan and Kohlberg focus on the adolescent's transition from childhood to adulthood in the realm of moral reasoning. Questioning and the resolution of moral dilemmas are the major vehicles used in their study to examine the adolescent's development through various states of moral judgment. They discuss research on the significance of formal operational thinking in the sequence of moral stages. They further consider the problem of moral relativism and the nature of postconventional moral development, and they discuss the relationship of moral and ego development in the later years of adolescence. Piaget's logical structures are seen as providing limits to the adolescent's moral development and the gradual reconciliation of idealism and reality. Formal cognitive processes are hypothesized as the logical prerequisites of advanced moral reasoning. Gilligan and Kohlberg document their findings with interview responses of subjects to particular dilemmas. The capacity for abstraction made possible by formal operational thought stands out as an important factor in resolving the adolescent's conflict between reason and experience. The authors discuss some implications of their research for educational programs fostering moral development. However, they stress the need for long-range observation of their subjects. They cite related studies in the United States and England on similar problems of moral development.

Michael Chandler centers his discussion on some of the complexities of the more usual forms of adolescent development, and in particular on the process of self–other differentiation. This process is reviewed by Chandler in a series of developmental milestones, beginning in infancy and continuing through adolescence. Failure to differentiate between self and other is described as egocentrism, whereas successful differentiation leads to what Chandler terms *epistemological loneliness*. Chandler describes a number of ways in which the adolescent attempts to cope with this potential loneliness, such as negotiated consensus with peers, prejudice and stereotypy, ideological companionship, and abstraction.

The applications of Piagetian research and theory to education are growing rapidly. The two papers in the last section focus on areas of concern to most educators—reading and science education—and highlight the role of these areas in the development and assessment of operational thought.

A review of a research project and the presentation of a program for non-readers are the emphases in Hildred Rawson's paper. Rawson's research considers the relationship between cognitive operations in concrete and reading situations and the relationship between cognitive operations and learning to read. She suggests that a program oriented toward developing the cognitive operations characteristic of the concrete period concurrent with a reading program would be of assistance to nonreaders. Rawson goes on to describe an attempt to develop and evaluate such a program, entitled "Reading Instruction and the Development of Cognitive Operations: A Program for Nonreaders."

Robert Karplus examines science activities at various levels and in various scientific fields in order to identify the type of reasoning that may occur. Karplus describes a number of activities and the criteria used to determine the reasoning patterns required by each activity. If the subject, in carrying out the experiment, uses seriation, one-to-one correspondence, conservation, transitivity, or class inclusion, he is said to be using concrete reasoning patterns. If the subject formulates and tests hypotheses, uses functional relationships quantitatively, plans a series of interdependent steps that account for available alternatives, etc., then this subject is said to be using formal reasoning patterns. Karplus shows in his discussion that concrete and formal thought may be revealed by the method that an individual uses to solve a problem. An answer to a problem, in and of itself, rarely indicates the level of reasoning. He concludes that it would be very worthwhile for teachers to use only a few questions on a test and to require explanations.

PART I

LANGUAGE DEVELOPMENT

CHAPTER 1

Thought and Language

Bärbel Inhelder and Annette Karmiloff-Smith

University of Geneva
Geneva, Switzerland

This paper, written on the half-century anniversary of Jean Piaget's first book, *The Language and Thought of the Child* (French ed., 1923), does not claim to be an original contribution to this problem. Rather, our aim is to review some of the essential aspects of Piaget's position with regard to language and cognition.

When one browses through this early book and some of the even earlier articles written by the then young zoologist, Piaget, still in his twenties, one is constantly struck not only by the precocity and depth of his thoughts but by the way in which Piaget intuitively anticipated so many of the later developments in psychology and even in psycholinguistics. Indeed, these early writings already included the embryos of Piaget's theory of equilibration, which he first presented in 1971 (Piaget, 1977). We believe that the reasons that Piaget was so far ahead of his time reside in his much broader approach to the human mind, from both a biological and an epistemological viewpoint. The fact that Piaget was inclined to take a stand against extreme empiricism and nativism and approached human psychology from a relativistic position led him to envisage cognition as merely one special case of the biological continuum. Piaget has always maintained a constructivistic and interactionist approach, and he sought an explanation of cognitive evolution through very general regulatory and self-regulatory mechanisms, which he also studied at the biological level. This early vision of the self-regulatory systems led our cybernetician colleague Guy Cellérier recently to call Piaget "the cybernetician before cybernetics even existed"—and this means some twenty years before Chomsky joined the MIT research laboratory and the extraordinary revolution in psycholinguistics took place.

It may seem paradoxical that having gained the reputation of rejecting language as a constructive factor in cognitive development, we now witness that psycholinguists no longer can allow themselves to ignore Piagetian theory. Roger Brown's recent book (1973) not only makes numerous references to Piaget's theory but actually devotes several pages to stressing the relevance of the sensorimotor, preverbal period to the development of language.

In some respects, the title of Piaget's first book, *The Language and Thought of the Child,* was a misnomer, for indeed its main emphasis was on thought through language. This is why it was decided to change the order of the words and to call this introductory paper "Thought and Language." As you know, numerous were the books and articles that ensued, none of which dealt specifically with the structure of language as an isolated phenomenon; Piaget has always looked upon language as merely one aspect of the overall semiotic function, which is referred to in more detail later.

However, to return to Piaget's first book, it can be seen that he already stressed the functional role of verbal behavior; the book already contained some insights into child logic and child explanations of physical phenomena and of moral judgment, which Piaget was to develop in far more detail in his later writings. The first book also placed emphasis on the concept that language first accompanies action as if it were a very part of it, whereas with the gradual process of decentration, language can replace effective action.

While we are on the subject of decentration processes, brief reference should be made to Piaget's concept of the "egocentric speech" of the young child as opposed to the "socialized speech" of the more advanced child. As is well known, the very notion of egocentricity sparked off a lengthy retort by Vygotsky (1967). Although Piaget frequently reinterpreted this notion for those who had misunderstood it, it is nonetheless striking to see that still in the 1970s Arthur Blumenthal (1970) wrote: "egocentric speech . . . is the notion that a child first talks only for himself and for his own pleasure." For Piaget, egocentric speech does not imply *ipso facto* a lack of desire to communicate; what Piaget wanted to convey was something far more profound about the psychological function of language: that the young child, although often attempting to communicate, cannot yet differentiate between his own point of view and that of others. It is just as if the child assumes that everything that he can see or that he knows is seen or known identically by his listener. How often a child has merely covered his eyes to hide from another person (because the *child* can no longer see the person). The problem of the acquisition processes of the verb *to see* have since been analyzed by Cambon and Sinclair (1974). In his first book, Piaget demonstrated the frequent use of exophoric pronouns and deletions in child speech to relate happenings not experienced by the listener. Thus, to overcome egocentricity in action and in language, the child needs to decenter from his own single perspective, to take into account another's perspective, which he must coordinate with his own.

In the second chapter of *Language and Thought,* Piaget undertook an acute analysis of the positive role of genuine argument that develops slowly out of children's clash of ideas. Indeed, just as the child needs to accommodate to the particularities of an object that he tries to assimilate into his ongoing schemes, so the listener resists, by his opinions, the ongoing opinions of the child, who will gradually have to accommodate to them. The child's attempt to convince others of his own arguments and the clash with their different views is a dialectic process that gradually induces internalized argumentation. Indeed, the conflict generated by becoming aware of contradictions is a very necessary step toward cognitive growth. Fifty years after Piaget's first book, cognitive conflict has become the direct focus of two recent books: Piaget *et al.*'s *Recherches sur la contradiction* (1974), dealing with the epistemological problem of the role of conflict in development, and a book analyzing the essential role of cognitive conflict in the learning process (Inhelder, Sinclair, & Bovet, 1974).

This admittedly brief discussion of the relevance of Piaget's early work to later developments seems to demonstrate that it would be an oversimplification to assume, as do many of Piaget's critics, that he neglected the role of language in cognitive development while simultaneously using language to study child thought. Although it is true that much of the experimental work did include verbal exchange as one of the indispensable tools for attaining child concepts of space, causality, time, and so forth, we rapidly introduced new experimental designs with material that can be manipulated. Furthermore, more recent experimental work on imagery (Piaget & Inhelder, 1966), on memory (Piaget & Inhelder, 1968), and on cognitive strategies (Karmiloff-Smith & Inhelder, 1975, Inhelder, Ackermann-Valladao, Blanchet, Karmiloff-Smith, Kilcher, Montangero, & Robert, 1976) has been almost nonverbal in approach and has confirmed indirectly the basic tenets of Piagetian theory, while breaking new grounds in symbolic representation.

Piaget did not neglect language. What he did reject, however, was a long-established view that knowledge of the human mind would necessarily stem from knowledge of the human language. He also questioned that it was language that structured thought. The first journal of *Psychology and Linguistics* in 1860 defended the latter concept, and it is striking that, over one hundred years later, numerous psychologists and psycholinguistics still uphold the theory that thought results from a combination of linguistic signifiers alone. We have already mentioned in what respect Piaget has stressed the positive role of language, but an important distinction should be made with regard to the place language has in cognitive development.

It was in *Play, Dreams and Imitation in Childhood* (1951), a rather unfortunate translation of the original French title (1946), which actually meant *The Formation of the Symbolic Function,* that Piaget attached great importance to the developmental interdependence of symbolic play, deferred imitation, mental images, and the first verbal utterances. Thus, not language alone but all of the aspects of the semiotic function are symptoms of the gradual process of decentration from the immediate spatiotemporal restrictions of the sensorimotor action schemes. In essence, the semiotic function is the capacity to represent sensorimotor actions through signifiers that are differentiated from their significates. Piaget's work has also demonstrated conclusively that this capacity to represent reality develops very gradually out of the evolution of imitation throughout the prerepresentational period.

In the tradition of the great Genevese linguist de Saussure, Piaget laid stress on the important distinction between two types of signifiers: on the one hand, the symbol, which remains subjective and personal (as in symbolic play, deferred imitation, and mental images), and, on the other hand, the "sign" (as in verbal utterances), which is conventional and communicable. All such behavioral manifestations are signifiers of reality. Although Piaget has in his writings tended to underline the common relationship between the various aspects of the semiotic function, one obviously cannot ignore the fact that, whereas symbolic play, deferred imitation, and mental images remain loosely related symbols, language, on the other hand, evolves slowly from an early stage of "semisymbol/ semisign" to a highly structured system of "signs." The structures governing overall cognitive development cannot then solely be invoked to explain the intricacies of the linguistic system. With hindsight it seems astonishing that a school well known for its seemingly nonlinguistic studies should now be harboring a flourishing, dynamic Piagetian-inspired psycholinguistics unit, led by Professor Hermine Sinclair.

There are at least two essential *direct* contributions of Piaget to the theory of verbal signifiers: first, he has not only talked of action in terms of structured schemes but has also interpreted verbal utterances in terms of *verbal schemes,* which not only mark the continuity between sensorimotor actions and language but also clarify the place of language within the semiotic function in general. Second, Piaget's psychological interpretation of holophrases has added significantly to our understanding of the structures and functions of early child language. At the turn of the century, William and Clara Stern (1907) no longer considered one-word utterances as isolated words but rather as one-word "sentences," whose function it was to enable the child to "take a position" about external events. However, the latter concept already tends to imply predication. Piaget made a more subtle analysis of the psychological function of the holophrase and early two-word utterances. First appears what Piaget called "action judgments." These are not mere denominations but the direct verbal manifestation of a potential action scheme in which the subject pole and the object pole remain undissociated. Piaget cited (1951) the example of his child, who first uses "wow-wow" for a dog passing beneath the balcony, then "wow-wow" for a man passing beneath the same balcony, then for a train, etc. In other words, the same signifier is used to represent the same action scheme *of the child,* a "me-looking-from-the-balcony" scheme, rather than the same objective external event. It is only at a second level that we witness the beginnings of predication, when topic and comment become dissociated psychologically. A decentering process takes place by which the child is able to make "observation judgments" about external reality, for instance, "allgone milk," "cup broken."

The most essential contribution of Piaget to a theoretical interpretation of the origins of language lies perhaps in his extraordinarily comprehensive study of the sensorimotor origins of the basic categories of knowledge: object, space, time, and causality. The recent revival of nativistic interpretations of the creative aspect of language has paved the way for the study of linguistic universals. Piagetian theory has pinpointed the universality of the basic categories of knowledge, not only in their highly structured final forms of thought but at every stage of the construction process. Thus, there seems to be a universality in the common structures that the human child gradually builds during the sensorimotor period. Contrary to Chomsky's position, Piaget has posited continuity between the sensorimotor action patterns and the semiotic function. If there are "cognitive universals," is it really so surprising that there exist "linguistic universals"? Is it really necessary to invoke innate linguistic structures, or can we not rather look upon the gradual construction of the early cognitive universals as preparing the ground for the later linguistic ones (Sinclair 1971, 1973, 1974)?

Much Piagetian-inspired cross-cultural research (e.g., Bovet, Dasen, & Inhelder, 1974) has essentially confirmed the universality of cognitive structures and processes. Despite enormous differences in culture, child-rearing practices, and physical environment, identical modes of behavioral patterns and coordinations were found in the formation of preverbal intelligence, even if the rate and the interconnections between the developing categories may differ very slightly.

To gain greater insight into the transitional processes between the sensorimotor action schemes and the semiotic function, Genevan researchers joined forces with two Parisian specialists in early child development, Irene Lezine and Mira Stambak, to undertake a systematic observational experiment on the sensorimotor activities of babies between the ages of 12 and 36 months, some of whom were also studied longitudinally. Without our going into the details of the experimental results here (Inhelder, 1971: Inhelder, Lezine, Sinclair, & Stambark, 1972), suffice it to state that, at this very early age, it is already possible to detect the beginnings of the bipolarization between the physical and logicomathematical aspects of the construction of knowledge. Two distinct behavioral patterns were observed. First, "physical actions" on objects: the baby sucks objects, shakes them, bangs them, and drops them, as if he were trying to discover the relevant properties of each specific object. The constant interaction between the child's action schemes and the particular features of each object refines the development of the system of action schemes. The second type of activity is what might be termed "prelogical actions": for instance, the baby places one object inside another, on top of another, next to another. It is as if he were endeavoring to introduce into reality an organization between himself and objects and between objects themselves. Such organizational actions are not limited to a specific object but rapidly become generalized to all available ones. Both of these types of activity precede and seem to prepare for a third type, which we termed *make-believe* behavior. The baby uses objects as symbols for others, as in symbolic play: the baby uses a doll and a teddy bear as partners in a nonverbal symbolic game, then holds a mirror in front of the doll's face, inclining it so that it can see itself, etc.

It is heuristically useful to consider the evolution toward the semiotic function in terms of generations of schemes. The baby's innate tendency to function will lead gradually to a generalization of its schemes and thus to their coordination. Moreover, at some point, the child must necessarily go beyond the here and now, which is only possible through representation—in other words, through development of the semiotic function. Not only must the child have attained object permanency, but the functional relations that he introduces between objects must be stable. It thus seems plausible that the close relationship between physical activities and organizational activities in the infant can be considered not only as analogous to the relationship that later develops between the lexicon and syntax but also as a preparation for it. Just as organizational activities introduce meaningful relations between objects, so syntax organizes the lexicon into meaningful relations. It is to be hoped that such a hypothesis regarding child language development will provoke more new experimental approaches in psycholinguistics.

Outside Piaget's school of thought, there has frequently been a tendency to explain cognitive development either by isolated factors or by combinations of factors. For years, philosophers, linguists, and psychologists posited a causal relationship between language and thought. More recently, we have witnessed the dethroning of language in favor of mental imagery (Segal, 1971; Inhelder & Karmiloff-Smith, 1974) as explicative of the development of thought. Piaget has always avoided such a stand: factors of development cannot be considered in isolation or in causal combinations. Piaget views cognitive growth as an increasingly integrated network of interacting systems, and he has sought an explanation of growth in the very basic self-regulatory mechanisms underlying the developmental changes both of language and of thought.

In concluding this opening paper, in which the importance of sensorimotor actions has been frequently stressed, we should like to quote a simple, yet most telling statement of Piaget's: "Nommer, c'est agir sur les objets," in other words, by naming an object the child already acts on it.

References

Blumenthal, A. L. *Language and psychology: Historical aspects of psycholinguistics*. New York: Wiley, 1970.

Bovet, M. C., Dasen, P. R., & Inhelder, B. Etages de l'intelligence sensori-motrice chez l'enfant Baoulé: Etude préliminaire. *Archives de Psychologie*, 1974, *41*, 164.

Brown, R. *A first language: The early stages*. Cambridge, Mass.: Harvard University Press, 1973.

Cambon, J., & Sinclair, H. Relations between syntax and semantics: Are they easy to see? *British Journal of Psychology*, 1974, *65*, 133–140.

Inhelder, B. The sensory-motor origins of knowledge. In D. Walcher & D. Peters (Eds.), *The development of self-regulatory mechanisms*. New York: Academic Press, 1971.

Inhelder, B., Ackermann-Valladao, E., Blanchet, A., Karmiloff-Smith, A., Kilcher, H., Montangero, J., & Robert, M. Des structures cognitives aux procédures de découverte. *Archives de Psychologie*, 1976, *54*(171) 57–72.

Inhelder, B., & Karmiloff-Smith, A. Elementary, my dear Watson, the clue is in the image: Review of S. J. Segal (Ed.), in Imagery: Current cognitive approaches. *Contemporary Psychology*, 1974 *19*(7), 532–533.

Inhelder, B., Lézine, I., Sinclair, H., & Stamback, M. Les débuts de la fonction symbolique. *Archives de Psychologie*, 1972, *41*, 187–243.

Inhelder, B., Sinclair, H., & Bovet, M. *Learning and the development of cognition*. Cambridge, Mass.: Harvard University Press, 1974.

Karmiloff-Smith, A., & Inhelder, B. If you want to get ahead, get a theory. *Cognition*, 1975, *3*(3), 195–212.

Piaget, J. *Play, dreams and imitation in childhood*. London: Heineman, 1951. (Originally published, 1946.)

Piaget, J. *The language and thought of the child*. London: Routledge, 1959. (Originally published, 1923.)

Piaget, J. L'équilibration des structures cognitives: Problème central du développement, EEG XXXIII, Paris: Presses Universitaires de France, 1975.

Piaget, J. Problems of equilibration. In Marilyn H. Appel and Lois S. Goldberg (Eds.), *Topics in cognitive development, I: Equilibration: Theory, research, and application*. New York: Plenum, 1977.

Piaget, J., & Inhelder, B. *Mental imagery in the child*. New York: Basic Books, 1971.

Piaget, J., & Inhelder, B. *Memory and intelligence*. New York: Basic Books, 1973.

Piaget, J., *et al*. Recherches sur la contradiction, I EEG XXXI, Différentes formes de la contradiction, II Relation entre affirmations et négations XXXII. Paris: Presses Universitaires de France, 1974.

Segal, S. J. (Ed.), *Imagery: Current cognitive approaches*. New York: Academic Press, 1971.

Sinclair, H. Sensorimotor action patterns as a condition for the acquisition of syntax. In R. Huxley & E. Ingram (Eds.), *Language acquisition: Models and methods*. New York: Academic Press, 1971.

Sinclair, H. Language acquisition and cognitive development. In T. E. Moore (Ed.), *Cognitive development and the acquisition of language*. New York: Academic Press, 1973.

Sinclair, H. Le développement des structures sensori-motrices en tant que modèle heuristique pour l'élaboration des premières structures linguistiques. *Bulletin d'Audiophonologie,* 1974, *4*(6), 355–366.

Stern, C., & Stern, W. *Die Kindersprache.* Leipzig: Johann Ambrosius Barth, 1907.

Vygotsky, L. *Thought and language,* Cambridge, Mass.: MIT Press, 1967. (Originally published, 1934.)

CHAPTER 2

The Relevance of Piaget's Early Work for a Semantic Approach to Language Acquisition

H. J. Sinclair

University of Geneva
Geneva, Switzerland

More than 50 years after its first publication, Piaget's *Le language et la pensée chez l'enfant* (1923) remains a very exciting work. Although Piaget was not interested in language *per se* but only in children's utterances inasmuch as they reveal something about their way of thinking, it contains a very rich material for psycholinguists and prefigures some of the issues we have been struggling with recently. The chapter that was chosen for a closer look was the one on questions. The material for this chapter consists of 1,125 questions asked by one child over a period of 10 months in spontaneous conversation with an adult, which was noted for two hours each day. Observation started when the child was aged 6 years and 3 months and ended when he reached 7 years and 1 month. For developmental comparisons, three sets of 250 questions each were taken from the total: 250 questions asked between September 1 and November 3, 250 between March 3 and March 24, and 250 between June 3 and June 23. The questions formed part of a dialogue during which the adult remained fairly neutral, that is to say, often gave evasive answers. The exhaustive notation of all that happened during the observation period allowed for the elimination of pseudo-questions (such as polite refusals, as in "It's time for dinner"—"Why?" and of polite commands, such as "Will you come and help me?").

These 750 questions were analyzed in detail and classified according to the type of answer the child expected to his question and the content of the question itself. Taking into account some data from Stern and Stern (1907) and Descoedres,

Piaget also briefly referred to the type of question asked before the age of 6 and gave us some of his ideas about the meaning of questions asked at ages 1½–2½ and 3–5. From this analysis, he sketched the development of thought in a way that anticipated the much deeper analysis of the growth of cognitive structures that is to be found in his later work.

Why did Piaget start with the analysis of questions? Would not an analysis of assertions have given us a much more direct view of what children think? Piaget referred to his mentor and predecessor Claparède and asserted that the basic concepts that preside over the progress of human knowledge preexist neither in the objects of the physical world nor in the human mind: they are slowly built up during the course of development. As he was to argue in his later work, they are built up from sensorimotor beginnings through biological mechanisms of self-regulation. During the first two years of life, children deal directly with their environment through immediate action. When man became aware of the inadequacy of his actions, said Claparède, he came to think in terms of causality, necessity, time, etc. Piaget, similarly, saw such a nascent awareness in the questions asked by children. The establishment of this link between questions and basic concepts reminds us of Aristotle's categories, several of which are labeled with question words: where, when, of what kind, of what quantity, etc.

Below the age of 2½ or 3, said Piaget, the child deals with the immediate here and now in his utterances as he deals with it in his actions. During this period, his questions are either yes or no questions ("Daddy coming?" "That my cup?") or what and where questions. At that age, the child is mainly concerned with things and events as they are apprehended in the light of his own actions and desires. His questions concern the names of things and the places they may have disappeared to. But toward the beginning of the third year, a fundamental awareness appears: the child begins to distinguish immediate reality from something that precedes and underlies this reality. At first, this "something" is mainly seen in terms of "intentions," and "intentions" are attributed to objects as well as to people. At this point appear the first genuine "why?" questions (the "why" questions that are polite refusals should be excluded, as, for example, "It's time to go to bed"—"Why?").

These first types of questions—"What is . . . ?" "Where is . . . ?" "Why . . . ?"—already indicate the two complementary ways that the child's thinking will develop: on the one hand, there is a search for *explanation,* which will later provide knowledge about the physical world; on the other hand, there is a feeling for *implication,* which will later develop into logical thinking. Explanation reaches outward, toward the link between events and between cause and effect in the outer world; implication reaches inward, toward the links between one judgment and another.

Looking at recent studies of children's questions (Klima & Bellugi, 1966; Ervin-Tripp, 1970), we find a very different approach. The form of children's questions is analyzed in their spontaneous utterances or their comprehension of adult's questions, and the authors trace the slow development toward the adult interrogative system. In a Genevan study, it was found that children aged 8 still may have difficulties with the syntactical form of certain questions: "Which bear did the monkey push?" is often understood as referring to a situation in which a bear pushed a monkey (Stewart & Sinclair, 1975). Though Klima and Bellugi's interest was in the syntactic form of questions rather than in their content, they did note that in the earliest records of their subjects' yes/no questions, "what" and "where" questions appeared. The yes/no questions consist of a nucleus with rising intonation, such as "Ball go?" "Sit chair?" Adults respond to these questions as if they were yes/no questions, and children appear to be satisfied with such answers. "What" questions have the form "What's that?" or "What NP doing?" (e.g., "What cowboy doing?"), and "where" questions have the form "Where NP?" or "Where NP go?" Klima and Bellugi suggest the following paraphrases for these types of questions: "I want to know the name of that thing; I want to know what you call that action; I want to know the location of that object." In a second period, Klima and Bellugi noted the appearance of "why" and "why not" questions, and only later of "how" questions. Their observations and interpretations correspond to those of Piaget. Their main interest, however, was in syntactic development.

Klima and Bellugi studied questions as part of language as an object to be known, an object with which the child comes into contact and whose properties and rules he infers from what he hears around him. Piaget looked at questions as one of the ways in which children communicate what they think about reality and what they would like to know about it. It is the dual aspect of language, both as an object to be known and as a means for expressing knowledge, that makes this double approach both necessary and possible.

Recently, semantics has come in for a certain amount of attention from linguists and psycholinguists. It is interesting to find in their studies the use of the term *presuppostion*. In *Language and Thought* Piaget made several remarks about the presuppositions or assumptions that underlie the child's questions. The analysis of the different types of precausal explanations and prelogical implications of the child's questions is partly based on an analysis of their semantic aspect. In many cases, the fact that the child has ideas about reality that are different from those of the adult results in questions that are semantically anomalous. Some examples, all taken from the same work (Piaget, 1923), are the following:

> The teacher and the child are looking at a pigeon.
> Child: "If you kill him at that bit of his wing, does he die?"

The verb *to kill* has come in for quite some attention from semanticists recently. The child's question violates a number of constraints that adults attach to this verb. In the first place, you cannot kill somebody at the tip of his wing: you kill a whole living being and not a little part of it. Furthermore, once you kill him, this is equivalent to making him die. So one cannot really ask, "If one kills him, does he die?" This is against adult assumptions about the semantics of the verb *to kill*. But the fact that such a question is formulated in this way by the child indicates something about *his* suppositions, not only about the verb *to kill* but also about a whole part of the very mysterious qualities of the real world he has to deal with. Another example is when the child and the teacher are playing marbles and there is a slight slope on the floor that makes one of the marbles roll toward the teacher. The child asks, "How does the marble know you are down there?" Now once again, there are semantic restraints on the word *to know* that make us say that *to know* needs as a subject an animate person—even an animal will not always do. Certainly a marble, in our present ideas about *to know,* cannot be the subject of this verb phrase. In the child's system of presupposition, it can be and it is. Many other examples evidence the confusion between animate and inanimate: "Who makes the river flow?"—once again the child is violating part of the semantic constraints and thereby indicating different presuppositions.

It seems almost surprising that this type of analysis has not been used more often by psycholinguists, except perhaps for the earliest period of language acquisition. Combined with certain findings of the more recent semantic theories, such an approach might well yield highly interesting findings.

In one experiment done in Geneva (Cambon & Sinclair, 1974), an interesting difference between children's presumptions and adults' ideas about the semantic content of a verb was discovered. Cambon replicated in French a study originally carried out in English by C. Chomsky (1969). This study concerned sentences such as "The doll is easy to see." Such sentences can be paraphrased as "It is easy to see the doll"—they do not mean that the doll can see easily, in contrast with "The doll is ready to see (or happy to see)." C. Chomsky set up an ingenious situation—blindfolding the doll—that enabled her to ask several questions to find out the meaning young children gave to this sentence. The same type of sentences exists in French, and when the experiment was repeated, similar results were found: around the age of 6, the sentence is understood as "The doll can see easily," whereas by the age of 8, most children give it the same meaning as adults do. However, some subjects aged 5 and some younger ones gave an apparently correct solution: when the doll was blindfolded, they answered, "Of course I can see the doll, I have good eyes." These young children seemed, unlike the slightly older subjects, to get the meaning right, but it soon became clear that this was not because of a deeper understanding of the syntactic structure but because of an incapacity on their part to imagine that when we were talking about "seeing easily" we could think of the doll—of course, they themselves were the ones that were supposed to do the seeing. This behavior already raised some questions about the possible meanings attached to the verb *to see,* and some 7- or 8-year-olds who did not evidence any particular difficulty with these sentences in most situations sometimes answered in an intriguing way. When the face of the doll was covered, they answered "no" to the question "Is the doll easy to see?", apparently regressing to a lower level. However, when they were asked why, they explained, "Like that you can't really recognize her," thereby indicating their correct understanding of the syntactic structure but an unusual interpretation of the word *to see.* A further study of the semantic aspect pointed out some interesting differences between the 4- to 5-year-olds and the 7- to 8-year-olds. Asked what things they could see easily, the youngest subjects seemed to try to think of properties of the objects: big things or red things. The oldest children, by contrast, thought of several criteria and were capable of combining them. At this age, not only properties of the observed objects but also properties of the observer and of the environment are mentioned, and a positive property of the one can compensate for a negative property of the others. These subjects gave answers such as, "A small red ball in the grass you can see easily, but a green ball in the grass, well, then you need good eyes." In a further study (Barblan, 1977), other interpretations of *to see* were discovered and contrasted with the children's apprehension of *to hear, touch, smell,* etc. It looks as if the verb *to see* is in many ways an exception and as if our adult impression of the semantic simplicity of this verb does not correspond to the children's assumptions.

These rather unexpected findings raise a number of questions. What is the relationship between semantic and syntactic development? How do possible differences in semantic interpretation influence children's understanding of syntactic patterns and vice versa?

We are still very far from having unraveled the intricacies of language acquisition and its link with thought development in general. Though Piaget's book on *Language and Thought* has more to say about thought than about language *per se,* it contains observations that are astonishingly relevant to issues raised by semanticists today, more than 50 years later.

References

Barblan, L. *Developmental problems concerning sentences with "easy to see."* Salzburg: International Symposium for Psycholinguistics, 1977.

Cambon, J., & Sinclair, H. Relations between syntax and semantics, are they easy to see? *British Journal of Psychology,* 1974, *65,* 133–140.

Chomsky, C. *The acquisition of syntax in children from 5 to 10.* Cambridge, Mass.: MIT Press, 1969.

Ervin-Tripp, S. Discourse agreement: How children answer questions. In J. R. Hayes (Ed.), *Cognition and the development of language*. New York: Wiley, 1970.

Klima, E. S., & Bellugi, U. Syntactic regularities in the speech of children. In J. Lyons & R. J. Wales, (Eds.), *Psycholinguistic papers*. Edinburgh: Edinburgh University Press, 1966.

Piaget, J. *Le langage et la pensée chez l'enfant*. Neuchâtel–Paris: Delachaux et Niestlé, 1923.

Piaget, J. *The language and thought of the child*. London: Routledge, 1959.

Stern, C., & Stern, W. *Die Kindersprache*. Leipzig: Johann Ambrosius Barth, 1907.

Stewart, J., & Sinclair, H. Comprehension of questions by children between 5 and 9. *Linguistics*, 1975, *151*, 17–26.

CHAPTER 3

What the Child Brings to Language

William Kessen and Katherine Nelson

Yale University
New Haven, Connecticut

To the question "What does the child bring to language?" the best answer in our time is "The developmental theories of Jean Piaget." Piaget has so restructured the way that psychologists think about children and so dominated theoretical discourse in the United States over the last 15 years that when we come together to talk about children, we find ourselves inevitably and appropriately talking about them in his language. Even when there are mild demurrers or reservations about the Geneva canon, they sound a bit like the English philosopher's comment on the Gospels: "Jesus was somewhat muddled on this point." We will not, therefore, pause to list and to praise the Genevan transformations of developmental psychology; rather, we will attempt to build out a short way from the platform of observation and speculation that Piaget has provided for us all.* In so doing, we will inevitably call attention to the changes in theoretical attitude that have been wrought in the fields of language development and early concept formation by the pressure of the Genevan critique. Of course, it would be a moment of memorial grandeur to assert as well that Piaget's critique had at last and forever chased abstraction theory—in its classical and in its modern modes—off the psychological field, but the dragon still limps around, still breathing out obfuscating smoke. We hope to honor Piaget by striking another

---

*Provocation to think about children's language and its origins can be found in several parts of Piaget's work, from *The Language and Thought of the Child* (1959) to *Sagesse et illusions de la philosophie* (1965). The books most influential in the formation of the present paper were the three volumes on infancy, particularly *Origins of Intelligence in Children* (1952).

17

blow or two at that monster that has misled and stupified us for almost three centuries.

The first strand of our argument has to do with the child's congenital competence, the second with the importance of context, and the third with the peculiar role of the particular, the specific concept, in the life of infants. We were led to consider these issues by two apparent antinomies in early development. The contradictions can be put crudely in the following way. (1) The infant seems at once finely tuned to certain presentations,* and yet he seems insensitive to many aspects of his surroundings, apparently more moved by context and setting than by specific events. (2) Throughout these first months—and in our view, critically for language development—the child is creating particulars (specific concepts, if you will), and at the same time, he is creating general categories or concepts.

We cannot hope, in the course of these pages, to resolve or reconstitute these antinomies. Rather, we would like to use them as the grounds on which we can provoke a renewed consideration of the confusions of early cognitive development. Piaget has been guided in all of his work by a commitment to regularity, simplicity, and the finished forms of human thought. We argue here for irregularity, complexity, and, most strongly, for the significance of the unfinished forms of infantile thought. In turn, we discuss fine tuning and the inherited categories, the construction of figure, the move from schememes to schemes, the categorization of particulars, and, finally, the importance of unfinished forms.

Fine Tuning and the Inherited Categories

Fortunately, the baby does not start the road toward language empty. Over the last 10 years, we have become newly sensitive to the remarkable congenital capacities of the human being. He possesses the reflex structures that Piaget has put to extensive theoretical use; he is tuned to particular aspects of his surroundings—consider for a moment the implication of the baby's differential sensitivity to sounds in the usual range of human speech—and, further, he can at birth or shortly thereafter divide parts of the world categorically, that is, in aggregates of elements defined physicalistically. Let us give only three demonstrated examples. Nowlis and Kessen (1976), in our laboratories, have recently shown that the newly born infant makes a differentiated response to sweet tastes and, further, that he can differentiate both different kinds of sugars and concentration levels of a single sugar. Bornstein (1975), also in the Yale laboratories, has begun to amass evidence that the child, before language, organizes the visual spectrum into the adult categories of red, yellow, blue, and green. Aside from

*We use the word *presentation* to avoid the unfortunate implications of *stimulus*.

putting in jeopardy a long history of speculation about cultural variation in color perception, the studies assure us of the child's ability to structure environmental presentations in a categorical way long before language (or, for that matter, any tuition) has an impact. Finally, the work of Eimas and his colleagues (Eimas, Siqueland, Jusczyk, & Vigorito, 1971) has shown that on the most critical issue of the child's sensitivity to certain speech sounds, there is categorical perception like that of the adult. Now, findings like these still leave unanswered many important questions about the character of early perception, and they do not necessarily call into question Piaget's observations about the early history of objects. What they do is to enlarge our sense of how orderly, in its way, is the life of the child in the first months of life and how sensitively he can behave in an unnamed—even an unnameable—world. As Piaget has taught us, we will not escape the paradoxes of the infantile mind by ascribing a Jamesian confusion to the baby.

In trying to understand the baby at the start of his 18-month-long march toward language, we must be aware not only of his perceptual sensitivity but also of what can be called strategies of the middle range, the mind-building functions that are, on one hand, more limited in scope or range than assimilation and accommodation and, on the other, more inclusive and general than specific reflex activity. Again, the field is barely begun, but two examples can be cited. First, there is the tendency of the infant to seek out and investigate contour in presentation (Kessen, Salapatek, & Haith, 1972). We have only part of the evidence in hand, but it is reasonable to believe that such a tendency can form the basis for the construction of form, much in the way that Hebb (1949) hypothesized so long ago. Second, and perhaps closely related, is the young infant's working relation with movement. Systematic laboratory studies have begun, and much common and some organized observation (Bower, 1974) suggests that attention to movement may be a critical strategy in early cognition. In any case, one cannot help but be struck by the importance of moving presentations in Piaget's work with his children; the trilogy on infancy, particularly when it is concerned with the first parts of the construction of reality, is filled with reports of the largely immobile child's behavior in the presence of something moving—watches, crib fringes, faces.

Strategies like those that underlie the baby's use of contour and movement are productive in at least two ways: they are relevant to the child's management of attention and they play a part in the separation of figure from ground, an issue to which we will turn shortly. It may be assumed that continued close study of infant behavior will reveal other strategies or, as Bower (1974) calls them, rules that govern the child's use of presented events.

Thus, one arm of our first antinomy is revealed; the young child is finely tuned to certain aspects of his surroundings, he is able to make categorical differentiations, and he possesses procedures or strategies for increasing his understanding of the world.

The Construction of Figure

But what of the other side of the argument? The infant seems, at least at first, so often indifferent to minor perturbations in his environment: any human face will do for a smile; any room is suitable for feeding if food is available there. Often is seems that all that matters is the tone of the setting, the climate. Where is our well-tuned strategist now? Frankly, we are as puzzled by this mystery as anyone else but we would like to suggest some lines of development that may reduce the mystery somewhat.

First, much of the intellectual work of the first six months of life can be seen as the construction of figure—the organization of the environment so that particular aspects will stand out and apart from the general ground. This process is not the same as assuming congenital *Gestalten* although there is no reason to dismiss the phenomenon; rather, the construction of figure is an active and interactive process whereby the adult and the child together break up the world and differentially evaluate the resulting pieces.

Second, as we shall maintain shortly, the first constructions of figure are, by adult standards, small in scale—in our most important example of the mother, they are not necessarily whole continuing objects. Palpable discrete reality is so sure for adults that we need all of Piaget's data and many of his arguments to persuade us that the baby seizes the world in pieces different from ours, so different on occasion that he sees many where we see one and one where we see many. In brief, the permanent substantial *thing* is no more an element of the child's life than is the physicalistically defined stimulus.

Third, and crucial, we have vastly underestimated the importance of context and background even in the first months of life. One may suspect that we have all been led to a biased attitude because of our constrained settings for observation, our greater interest in foreground events, and the absence of any customary research tactics for the study of context.* However, it is a truism that the child's behavior is always in a particular setting, and we have not done well in our investigation of the dimensions of settings. To cite only one important case in point, the dynamic events represented by the gross-motor behavior of the child himself, as well as that of other people, must be at least as important to the child as the objects he meets. In spite of Piaget's insistence upon the importance of the child's own actions in structuring thought, he, in common with most modern American psychologists, usually observed his children in settings where the child was confined to crib or chair and was reacting to a manipulation of the investigator. However, it is important that from about the age of 6 or 7 months, most

---

*The tricky issue of what constitutes foreground and what constitutes background can be dealt with, initially at any rate, by a definition of foreground either as the circumstances of the psychologist's chief interest or, better, as the circumstances on which the child's attention is focused.

infants in our society are highly mobile—creeping, standing, walking, climbing—investigating the far as well as near spaces of the world, the distant and large as well as the close and small objects. This new mobility surely influences the kind of information that the child obtains and the concepts that he constructs.

But the issue of context becomes pivotal when we move to an understanding of the nameable. Names can be used only when the named is, in some degree, disconnected from context. Let us hurry to forecast a conclusion that we will defend when we talk about the importance of unfinished forms of thought: the nameable does not have to be context-independent or context-indifferent; rather it need only be defined over several different contexts.

The point is worth pausing over. The desire for simplicity and elegance, which Piaget shares, moves toward a view of *object,* and ultimately *nameable,* that is free of all contextual constraints. We separate ourselves from such a position. The baby can make sense of and, perhaps, even aggregate presentations that appear in only a few contexts; thus, it is not necessary for a potential nameable to be disconnected from all its backgrounds. More to the research point, degree of disconnection or decontextualization may be a complexly determined and critical part of the child's construction of reality. As usual, dimensions are better than dichotomies.

So we see that, in the first year of life, the child is constructing figure from his experience and he is simultaneously and necessarily elaborating a theory of ground. Psychologists have made interesting and productive observations about foreground activities—what the child writes on his cognitive blackboard, if you will—but we are far less knowing about the contexts of his activity, or the characteristics and influence of the varying blackboards on which he writes. We have hinted that our first antinomy will be resolved, at least for the case of language development, when we recognize that the nameable must be disconnected from context, though it need not be context-free.

The Move from Schememes to Schemes

Let us gather these scattered comments of ours together in an examination of the notion of object; perhaps we can thereby illustrate why we believe we are only at the beginning of understanding the child's first speech.

Objects and categories of objects are of special importance in the child's development of both concepts and language. This is an ancient and well-established observation, and Piaget's emphasis on the child's developing knowledge of objects and object relations during the sensorimotor period makes his work uniquely pertinent. In particular, the notion that objects are first defined in terms of the sensorimotor schemes that can be applied to them is of great importance to an understanding of how the child begins to categorize the world of things. In the beginning, as Piaget has demonstrated so convincingly, the child's schemes are not coordinated or systematized, and they may be very generally applied. Sucking, grasping, and pulling, for example, may each be applied to many different objects that have nothing more in common than that they produce a common action. At the same time, however, some parts of the world have been defined by the child in considerable detail, for example, the mother's face and the taste of strained apricots. It would appear that the child has two strategies available at once: one that deals with important particulars through representations already finely tuned to the details of presentation and reaction, and another that provides general action schemes with which to investigate figures that are not yet important.

We would like to propose, however, that the child is also accumulating other kinds of specific knowledge, relating even to these still-unimportant objects, that will turn out to be critical to him later in forming nameable concepts. Two kinds of events stand out as important to the infant.

Of first importance (and underestimated by our current models, which have rightly tried to see the infant as initiating and influential in his encounters with adults) are the defining acts of adults. Without at all denying the importance of the insight that the infant is the prisoner of his egocentrism and can only (at first) know his own actions, it is at the same time vital to recognize that he must very early come to know and to predict the action of others. The ways in which the infant's world is at the disposal of adults are no less important because he cannot at first reliably predict them. They are a large part of the base of presentations on which he must build; adults pick him up, put him down, carry him from place to place, and determine to a large extent what he will see and hear and when the important events of his life such as eating and sleeping will take place. His obviously increasing ability to predict the event structure provided by the actions of adults during the first year has important implications in regard to what we can observe about his understanding of relations between people and things. For example, we have seen evidence of primitive notions of causality in recent experiments involving object hiding. Some infants of 8 months who do not yet lift a cloth to find the toy that has been hidden beneath it will search the experimenter's face and hands with their eyes instead. Although they do not know where to find the toy, they appear to know that the adult can make it reappear. Similarly, in the more familiar setting of his home, the child predicts with great accuracy, not to say rigidity, the events that the adults have provided (for example, bedtime) to such an extent that any disruption is met with violent protest.

The actions of other people may lead the child to notions of causality and event structure, and his own actions and interactions with stable objects in the world may lead him to correct conceptions of stability and permanence and relations of space and time. In addition, there is a class of dynamic social and biological phenomena heretofore neglected in our theories that may be of central importance to the kinds of categories that the child develops. We refer to those open systems in which change is often irreversible and objects are of transitory, not permanent, existence. The most immediate for the child, of course, are events such as eating and eliminating, but there are innumerable common changes with which the child must deal: cooking food, melting ice, burning cigarettes, rain, and snow. There is as well for the child the phenomenological irreversibility of many object experiences, for example, the disappearance of objects under the control of adults (even, we should note, in psychological experiments) before the child has time to note and process the events. All of these—and many more such unstable phenomena—must be entered into our models of what the child brings to language. His categories of understanding of the dynamic characteristics of the social, biological, and impermanent world may prove to be more relevant to his ability to learn language than we have imagined, and they may give us some insight into the kind of knowledge that he is acquiring. What such observations have demonstrated to us is that we need, but do not yet have, an ecological taxonomy of the infant's world.

With these points in mind, let us return to the central importance of the object in the child's increasing understanding of the world and its relations, because while we agree that it is truly central, we also believe that it is central only within the *context* of these other actions and relations. How then can concepts of particular people, objects, and events be formed and generalized into nameable general categories on the basis of the information and structure available to the infant? We would like to propose a model for dealing with this question that depends upon the child's gradually increasing ability to represent more and more parts of his world and to integrate those representations first into wholes and then into categories of wholes.

The first sensorimotor schemes of the child appear not to be systematically organized, so that, for example, some children as old as 8 months appear to be undisturbed by the apparent discrepancy of the mother's speaking in a stranger's voice; and, as Gratch (1972) has noted, it is not until 7½ months that a child will remove an opaque cover from his own hand while he is grasping a toy, although he will remove a similar transparent cover a month and a half earlier. Apparently only gradually does the motor scheme (grasp) come to imply the visual (toy), which in turn directs the action (uncover) that reveals the toy. We would like to suggest that there are specific figurative components to the child's cognitions at this point, each of which represents a fragment—in the best example, his mother's face. We want to call these fragments or components *schememes* to indicate their elementary quality and to suggest that in the first half of the first year they include separate and specific "cues" for specific actions and expected consequences. Now we postulate that sometime at around 6 months the child integrates two or more of these previously separate schememes, such as his mother's face and his mother's voice, in regard to a particular familiar person or object and thus forms a representation of a *valued particular whole*. Prior to this integration, representation has been finely tuned to the details of the presentation but has been fragmented and context-defined. We see the child moving then from a point where his predictive information is highly reliable for familiar presentations, such as his mother's footsteps or her voice or face, and, in another case, for presented indications of an approaching feeding or bath to the point where he has organized these specific components into an expectation about an entire enduring single person or object. It is interesting to note in this connection that the child does not give early names to the presentations that were categorized early—*red* and *sweet* and *labial consonant*. Names rather are first given to particular valued ensembles of presentations. Let us emphasize again that the earlier components are finely tuned to context; for example, if the infant has just awakened, hearing his mother's footsteps may have a very different implication from the implication they have if he has been left to sleep when he is still ready for company. When these various schememes that represent parts of a particular valued whole person or object are integrated into a *schema* uniting the components, the contextual schememic relations are not lost but remain as expectations about the possible relations of the *whole* to other objects, people, and events. In addition, moreover, at this time, one *part* of the whole begins to imply the entire; for example, the mother's voice comes necessarily to imply the mother's face and other aspects of the mother. It is at this point, as many have observed, that stranger anxiety appears. When a part of the presentation of the stranger (voice, face, or movement) seems to imply the mother schema but the implication is not borne out, anxiety results.

The integration of schemas representing familiar particular objects, people, and events, incorporating all of the rich specific contextual information previously associated with fragmented components—the schememes—is a vitally important task that must occupy the child in the last half of the first year. At the same time, however, it must be remembered that the child lacks general operative knowledge that would enable him to predict the actions of unfamiliar objects and events. As Piaget has so convincingly demonstrated and as others have verified with controlled large-group studies, the child's cognitive reach does not extend beyond familiar things in familiar spaces. We would argue that such general knowledge is not necessary to the child's adequate formation of concepts and the learning of names for them. The knowledge of whole particulars and the subsequent generalization to categories of particulars is sufficient.

There is a further important advance that must take place, however, for true language to begin, and it is again one that Piaget has emphasized. The child must possess the ability to evoke the representative schema of the organized particular in the absence of its external presentation. We suggest that this important advance takes place during the last six months of the first year and that it is exactly the organized contextual knowledge within which the schema is represented that makes it possible. That is, we hypothesize that at some point the information about familiar figures against familiar grounds has become so well organized that the child notices when a context or setting that should imply a familiar person, object, or event fails to do so; the structure of the familiar context leads the child to note the *absence* of a familiar person or object. Here we see the theoretical importance of the detailed specific knowledge that we have suggested is incorporated into the components of the integrated schematic whole. For example, when the suppertime and bedtime context usually contains his father's homecoming, then his father's approaching footsteps or his father's arriving car imply to the child the appearance of his father at this time. But if his father does not appear as usual, the child's contextual structure may lead him to notice the absence of the expected familiar person in the familiar context and to indicate this by looking out the window, fussing, or even saying "Dada." This reaction requires, of course, considerable specification of the details of the context—the figurization of the ground, if you like. We would expect, then, to find the first evidence of the child's representations or re-presentation in the absence of the external presentation when a familiar valued particular is absent from the familiar relational context. We plan to explore this hypothesis experimentally over the next few years. Such exploration demands, of course, that we observe the child in his familiar surroundings over a sufficiently long period of time to know what the relevant contexts and the probable organized schemas are. We can state, on the basis of our recent observations of the comprehension of speech forms at around 1 year, that it is clearly the case that many if not most children have achieved the representation of some familiar objects by the end of the first year in that they are able to "go get" certain familiar absent objects when requested to do so by the mother. But this requires a still further integration—namely, a response to an appropriate speech form. It suggests that the ability to re-present to consciousness a schema of the most valued and most familiar objects—for example, mother and father—in their absence probably occurs early in the second half of the first year.

The Particular Becomes Concept

And now, the most magical development of all: the child's move from particulars to categories of particulars, from specific to general, from thing to concept. There can be no doubt about the data; the child who learns to say *ball*, for example, talks about more than a single ball; *car* is not just his special favorite. And, in a larger sense, the child's inclusion of objects and events that can be discriminated from one another in a single concept is the hallmark of human thought.

In our more radically simplifying moods, we like to believe that all early concepts start with particulars, that there is a prototypic dog around which all the other dogs gather and that the concepts that start in language (*quadrupled,* for example) are consequentially different from the concepts of the child new to language. The radical form of the argument, which we cannot spell out in detail here, is tested by a recognition of three variations on the importance of the particular. We have already talked about one sort, the valued particular: sun and moon and self and mother—particulars that are irreducible and probably ungeneralizable except through language-based analogy.

A second case in point is the child's handling of the situation in which there are a large number of instances simultaneously present. He may not be able to discriminate between members, but he can determine in some curious way that the concept applies to more than one. But again, the recognition of the numerosity of identical things is not the same as the categorization of recognizably different things. It is interesting to note the number of things in the child's world that are reduplicated, for example, diapers, bottles, crib bars, and pacifiers, not to mention many toys, such as nesting cups and rings. Harris (no date) has reported an interesting phenomenon that occurs with children at around 9 months in the standard object-hiding situation. When the object is hidden at Place A and is subsequently hidden at Place B, the child goes back to search at Place A even when the object remains visible at B! Harris has suggested that the child is operating on the theory that things come in multiple copies. Perhaps when the child is just beginning to integrate schemas, he distinguishes things on the basis of one versus many, that is, whether there is a unique thing or many different appearances of the same things, such as diapers, bottles, and crib bars. Perhaps his looking toward A checks the hypothesis that the object comes in many copies. Incidentally, we must wonder here about the connection between the multiple-copy theory and the child's theory of adult efficacy and power. Would the baby search at A so regularly if the hidden object were of great value to him?

But the most important case for understanding the shift from particular to general is the one that requires recognition of both particularity and group membership. In this case, the child must assign to a single concept (or name) objects that are distinguishable from each other on the basis of some other property or characteristic. Thus, a single schema must assimilate new members that have and retain their own identity. This is a different move from that of the incorporation of new members, which thereby take on the identity of a preexisting schema. We return to our guesses about how the move takes place shortly.

Our studies have shown that the three critical prerequisites to language develop in the second half of the first year and are therefore available to the child who begins to respond to and utter some speech forms at about 1 year of age. That is, the child (1) integrates previously fragmented information into schemas that represent particular whole objects and people in contextual relationships; (2) is able to represent these particular wholes to himself in their absence; and (3) extends his particular schemas to bring new members into a common category. These cognitive capacities are exhibited in the child's first word-learning and response to speech and routinely thereafter.

The child's ability, particularly in the second year of life, to build out new concepts, to name them, and to develop a hierarchical structure of concepts that includes notions of agent, action, and object implies a particular type of internal structure. To understand this line of development, let us consider first two possible alternative forms of concept structure and ask what they would imply about the acquisition of words and sentences.

First, consider the concept as a linear combination of attributes relating to the internal structure of an object—for example, its form, color, and size—and other stable invariant perceptual features. If words refer to concepts defined in this traditional way, we would expect the generalization of labels to new instances of the concept to proceed in line with such features, but they seldom do. Color and size, for example, are rarely used by young children as dimensions along which the referent class is extended. Further, we would expect to find word classes built up along these dimensions so that the child's first hypotheses about the language might involve the restricted use of a class of words referring to all big things or all things with particular features, such as two legs. Now, in the absence of evidence to the contrary, one could argue that this is what the child does and that his first word classes are based, for example, on the features of humans—say, two leggedness and uprightness. Perhaps, but the hypothesis is hardly compelling, and it says nothing about how such word classes would be related to each other so as to form sentences. Again, it is instructive to note that the child's ability to make differentiated responses to certain particular presentations ("dimensions of stimuli") does not necessarily or even usually entail his naming along the dimension.

Second, consider the concept as a complex of relations of the object to the child himself, for example, as a throwable, graspable, wearable, or eatable object. This is a plausible possible structure and it fits nicely with the particularization of Piaget's schemes. But we would argue that it does not go far enough. Although it may account for many of the extensions of early concepts (which, incidentally, are extraordinarily hard to trace in the speech of most children), it does not account for apparent word classes and relations between classes as expressed in early sentences. For example, early sentences more frequently comment on the actions, locations, possessions, and so on of others than on similar relations to the child himself. Think only of the innumerable cases of "Daddy car" or "Mommy sock" in the literature.

Rather, drawing on the dynamic relations that we noted earlier in regard to the child's world, we hypothesize that early concepts of objects consist of the various kinds of relations into which the object can enter—with others as well as self—through time and space. This proposal assumes that the contextual information about objects, people, and events that was integrated into a schema representing the whole particular is the basis for the later development of concepts representing categories of objects, people, and events (Nelson, 1974). The broader, more general concept retains the functional and relational context while it ignores the specific identifying features of particulars. But much of the functional and relational information reflects the experience of the child with the actions of others, with irreversible events (for example, the child's preoccupation with relations such as "all gone," "broken," "hurt"), and with his own movements through space ("up," "down," "out").

To put the argument in vividly abbreviated form, early general concepts are *collections of maintained particulars successively defined by function and by context*. The fixed and finished form of the "object" and its aggregations—context-indifferent and disrespectful of the particular so dear to Piaget's sense of the oncoming adult—is a rare, perhaps nonexistent, entity for the young child and perhaps even for many children in school.

Concepts that incorporate the kind of functional context-relational information that we have suggested here also afford a basis from which the child can form generalized word classes that express the semantic relations found in early sentences, for example, classes of animate agents, of actions, of inanimate objects, of locations, and of possessions. Thus, our proposal about the internal structure of early concepts predicts the kind of sentences produced, the word classes that can be formed, and the dimensions along which the concept can be extended.

We have been concerned here with the development of natural language concepts from the earliest fragmented and highly specific schematic components to the formation of general semantic word classes. The process of categorization—discrimination, classification, and generalization—underlies the entire sequence. Categorization is the general cognitive skill that enables the child to learn language as well as to organize thought. It cannot be itself language-dependent, although language may come later to dictate to a large extent the categories that can be formed. We believe—and we think we are in accord with Piaget's formulation, as well as Cassirer's—that the first concepts are based on action, movement, and other dynamic relations and that it is the categorization of this information that leads easily and naturally to language. Our emphasis on the valued particular, on the early importance of representation in the absence of external presentation, and on the actions of others in the child's world are to some extent additions to Piaget's account of the sensorimotor period. But as we are concerned with the basis for the figurative symbolic component, not of the logical, operative component, they loom as necessary to the account and help us to see how the semantic is related to the syntactic aspect of language. As Sinclair has noted (1973), semantics and syntactics must be related in much the same way that the physical is related to the logical, and the two must interact and influence each other in development. In identifying those components of the child's experience that enable him to form particular schemas and to apply names to them, we think that we may be able to understand more about the development of general concepts and their relation.

The Importance of Unfinished Forms

Let us, in closing, make explicit a point that has run through our remarks. Piaget, in his lifelong search for regularities in human thought, has kept our attention on origins, and at the same time, he has organized and simplified the developmental lines that lead to the finished forms of adult human thought. His ascription of equilibrated logical operations to us hapless, inefficient grownups has often been characterized as too optimistic, too logical, and too little psychological. A parallel and even more forceful statement can be made about Piaget's ascriptions to the infant. To be sure, the child's thought is unfinished and unfixed, but we want to emphasize that even in the first year of life—long before the child meets the strong requirements of object permanence—the child has a mind well-enough organized for him to understand significant parts of human language and to begin to speak it. The dating is, of course, not important. What matters is our recognition that objects do not have to be context-independent and memorable in their absence to be nameable. The baby will speak, though his thought—even his sensorimotor thought—is incomplete.

ACKNOWLEDGMENT

The preparation of this paper was supported by a grant to the authors from the Carnegie Corporation of New York.

References

Bornstein, M. H. Qualities of color vision in infancy. *Journal of Experimental Child Psychology,* 1975, *19,* 401–419.
Bower, T. G. R. *Development in infancy.* San Francisco: Freeman, 1974.
Eimas, P. D., Siqueland, E. R., Jusczyk, P., & Vigorito, J. Speech perception in infants. *Science,* 1971, *171,* 303–306.
Gratch, G. A study of the relative dominance of vision and touch in six-month-old infants. *Child Development,* 1972, *43,* 615–623.

Harris, P. L. Search strategies and object permanence. Unpublished paper, no date.

Hebb, D. O. *The organization of behavior*. New York: Wiley, 1949.

Kessen, W., Salapatek, P., & Haith, M. The visual response of the human newborn to linear contour. *Journal of Experimental Child Psychology*, 1972, *13*, 9–20.

Nelson, K. Concept, word and sentence: Interrelations in acquisition and development. *Psychological Review*, 1974, *81*, 267–285.

Nowlis, G. H., & Kessen, W. Human newborns differentiate differing concentrations of sucrose and glucose. *Science*, 1976, *191*, 865–866.

Piaget, J. *The language and thought of the child*. London: Routledge, 1959. (Originally published, 1923.)

Piaget, J. *Play, dreams and imitation in childhood*. New York: Norton, 1951.

Piaget, J. *The origins of intelligence in children*. New York: International Universities Press, 1952.

Piaget, J. *The construction of reality in the child*. New York: Basic Books, 1954.

Piaget, J. *Sagesse et illusions de la philosophie*. Paris: Presses Universitaires de France, 1965.

Sinclair, H. Language acquisition and cognitive development. In T. E. Moore (Ed.), *Cognitive development and the acquisition of language*. New York: Academic Press, 1973.

CHAPTER 4

Some New Prospects for Neurophysiological Research on Disorders of Perception and Language

Eric H. Lenneberg
Late of Cornell University
Ithaca, New York

Linda Chapanis Fox
Department of Health, State of Hawaii
Honolulu, Hawaii

In a recently created section of neuropsychology at the New York Hospital–Cornell Medical Center (Departments of Neurology and Psychiatry), we have begun to investigate certain pathological interactions between different sensory modalities as well as between sensory and motor activities. Although we have so far worked only with adult patients with acquired neurological disease, our preliminary findings suggest that similar research on children with given congenital abnormalities may provide insight into learning difficulties, particularly in the area of reading. We have just begun these investigations. We allude to them here because they have provided the motivation for the speculations that form the basis for this contribution and because they readily lead to further thoughts à la Piaget about the nature of space and time concepts and symbolization.

Earlier Work: Our First Encounter with Cross-Modal Extinction

In connection with work on her doctoral dissertation, Chapanis (1974) discovered in one of her stroke patients with left hemiplegia a curious phenomenon. When the patient was stimulated simultaneously by a flashing light bulb in front of him and a beep tone presented through earphones binaurally, the sound became entirely inaudible, even though he had no trouble detecting either the sound or the light when they were presented to him singly. Further experimentation revealed (1) that a mild prick delivered mechanically to the volar aspect of the right index finger was also capable of extinguishing the sound; (2) that when the visual stimulus was paired with the touch stimulus, the former could extinguish the latter; (3) that the effect could be obtained even when the stimuli were presumably directed to the intact hemisphere (i.e., right hand paired with right monaural stimulation, while the left ear heard continuous narrow-band noise centered around 350 Hz); (4) that the effect was not dependent on simultaneous stimulation but could still be obtained reliably when the stimuli were separated by up to 250 milliseconds; (5) that varying the relative intensity of the two stimuli did not block or reverse the extinction; and (6) that the effect was independent of the patient's state of attention: he was unable to hear even if warned of the impending sound immediately preceding stimulation; and it was possible to make him suddenly sentient of the sound by increasing the interstimulus interval to 750 milliseconds. When the interval was decreased again to 250 milliseconds or less, the sound would disappear (an interstimulus interval between 250 and 750 milliseconds caused the patient to fluctuate in his report).

This phenomenon could be repeated indefinitely, and the patient was unable to "learn" to hear the sound in the presence of (or when preceded by) the light, even after he had been fully informed about the situation. Observations on this patient were extended and repeated over a period of three weeks without any change in the extinction.

Once alerted to this effect, we looked for it in other left-hemiplegic stroke patients and found cross-modal extinction phenomena to be present in 9 (one of whom had a left-sided lesion and mild aphasia and one who had amyotrophic lateral sclerosis in addition to a possible cerebral infarct) out of 17 patients. In some of these patients, the cross-modal extinction was enhanced when the patient either exerted pressure downward with his functional foot or tapped rhythmically with foot or hand; counting to himself aloud also increased the extinction. We have reasons to believe that attention cannot satisfactorily acount for all of the manifestations of extinction, although further work will still be needed to settle this point.

History of the Discovery of Extinction

The extinction phenomenon has been known for almost 100 years (Loeb, 1884; Oppenheim, 1885; Bruns, 1886) and has been the subject of extensive research in recent years (Teuber, Battersby, & Bender, 1960; Schwartz & Eidelberg, 1968; Bender, 1970); the literature has been reviewed by Bender (1952), who is also responsible for introducing the term *extinction*. Extinction has been demonstrated for most sense modalities, and although it is most frequently referred to as an intrasensory phenomenon, in which a point on one side of the body is pitted against a homologous one on the other by double simultaneous stimulation (tactual or visual extinction being interpreted as a sign of a lesion in the contralateral hemisphere), cross-modal extinction has also been observed by clinicians in the past (Bender, 1970). Most of the earlier work has been confined to relatively gross bedside testing. Since it is our opinion that extinction and related phenomena may contribute heavily toward our understanding of certain difficulties experienced by brain-lesioned patients and, perhaps, even explain certain behavioral disorders, we are carrying out a detailed laboratory investigation of extinction and other untoward interaction. We wish to study their physiological dimensions and certain stimulus and response characteristics and to explore further the relationship between extinction and associated symptomatology. We are also planning to do some clinical-pathological correlations.

Incidence of Extinction

Bender (1970) has reported that extinction on double simultaneous tactual stimulation is frequently observed even within the same side of the body, where a fairly constant dominance hierarchy exists: the hand extinguishes most easily when touched at the same time as some other part on the same side; next is the lower trunk; then the upper trunk; then the genital region; and lastly the face, which is the most persistently recognized stimulated zone. Tactual extinction is normally observed in small children, the incidence decreasing to a very small percentage among subjects between the ages of 11 and about 60 years. The incidence increases again with advancing age. In the late 80s, it is as common as in the 3-year-old child (about 85%). Extinction to tactual double stimulation is very rare (less than 5%) during that period of life when the human brain is fully mature and before the onset of senescent changes.

It is noteworthy that this hierarchy is reminiscent of the natural history of cutaneous sensitivity and of local responsiveness in the human fetus noted first by Minkowski (1921) and later confirmed by Hooker (1952) and Humphrey (1969). Consider also the finding so common throughout the embryology of behavior (Gottlieb, 1973) that the first responses to stimulation are not confined to those muscles that move the stimulated part but frequently involve much larger portions of the motor system. When these different sets of data are seen together, one gathers that the nervous system is not wired together by means of mutually isolated connections but that there is interaction between systems from the beginning and that the differentiation of behavior that takes place during development is, to a large extent, a history of developing inhibitions that allow some systems to function more and more independently from others.

It appears that the incidence of abnormal sensory interactions increases dramatically in the presence of any kind of structural brain disease. In patients with hemiplegia, Bender found, either some type of extinction, obscuration, displacement, or mislocalization occurred in 50 of 50 consecutively tested patients. Further, cross-modal extinction has never been described for normal subjects of any age (though peculiar types of synesthesia are occasionally encountered—production of an acoustic sensation caused by an optic stimulus, for example—that may be indirectly related to the pathological finding of extinction). From our preliminary observations, we are under the impression that any cortical or subcortical lesion is likely to cause a certain constellation of abnormal interactions between normally autonomously functioning systems of the brain.

Clinical Symptoms Related to Extinction

In the past, extinction has been regarded as a strictly sensory phenomenon. The common denominator is some sort of "imbalance" (Denny-Brown's, 1958, amorphosynthesis) in the processing of two simultaneously presented stimuli. Apparently, one stimulus "overshadows" or outweighs the other, or perhaps even interferes physiologically with the other. We should like to argue that extinction may be merely one manisfestation of a closely interrelated family of symptoms. The argument is based on the fact that any one of these symptoms is behaviorally, clinically, and pathologically intimately associated with several others (McFie, Piercy, & Zangwill, 1950). One may discern one cluster of symptoms in the realm of spatial organization, another in the realm of temporal organization.

Spatial Organization

Extinction to double simultaneous tactual stimulation has certain aspects in common with impairment of so-called two-point discrimination. In the latter case, each stimulus (a pin prick) is recognized and localized correctly when presented independently, but the double stimulation (two pin pricks applied to one finger tip) is not appreciated as such. The general assumption is that a parietal lobe lesion is capable of producing both types of impairment (two-point discrimination and double stimultaneous stimulation of both sides of the body).

Bender (1970) rightly points out some important clinical differences between these two types of tests, although we still have no data on the incidence of co-occurrence of the two symptoms nor of the anatomical and physiological correlates of either.

Whatever may eventually be revealed along these lines, it is conceivable that both impaired two-point discrimination and extinction may be associated with an alteration of the patient's own body schema; the geometry of his body is

subject to "warping." Bender's (1952) finding of the common association between extinction and mislocalization or sensory displacement would bear out this
claim. Kolb (1950) has made the connection between extinction phenomena and
alteration in the body schema quite explicit. The easiest way to think about this
connection is that the patient with a cerebral lesion causing hemiparesis and/or
hemisensory defect undergoes an alteration in the integration of his afferent
input. Normally, this afferentation would constitute the necessary information
for the cognitive construction of personal space—the source of his knowledge
about his own body and its topography. Somatic sensation and proprioception on
the affected side are extinguished by the relatively "overacting activities" on the
intact side (cf. also Roth, 1949).

As in so many other acquired behavioral disturbances, the healthy person
may at times undergo transient alterations in his proper functions that are, in fact,
mild replications of pathological symptoms. For example, most aphasic symptoms may also be observed in nonlesioned individuals but in much attenuated
form, aphasia probably being a vast exaggeration of a normally occurring transient "misfiring" of the system. Distortions of body image or changes in personal
space are also not totally unknown to most of us. The best example is provided by
the odd sensations produced during local anesthesia for dental work. Here the subjective sense of facial and oral topography undergoes pronounced changes, including a feeling of bulging or of shrinking and an incapacity for bringing the tongue
into the correct position for articulation. If we remember that patients with parietal-
lobe syndromes frequently also have impairment of primary somatosensory sensations (often a complete hemisensory defect), the affinity to the common
"dentist's chair phenomenon" may not seem so farfetched.

The proposal that primary and secondary sensory defects due to parietal-
lobe disease interfere with the cognitive construction of personal space or body
image is strengthened by the fairly common finding (Hécaen, 1969) that such a
patient also suffers from varying degrees of asomatagnosia. He cannot find his
affected limbs, or he fails to realize that part of his body belongs to him (Frederiks, 1969; Hécaen & de Ajuriaguerra, 1952; Denny-Brown, Meyer, &
Horenstein, 1952; Denny-Brown, 1958). The disturbance in afferentation may
not be confined to a diminished sense of touch; Chapanis's recent discovery of
cross-modal extinction and the extinctionlike interaction between sensory and
motor activities suggests that the afferent inflow associated with motor events,
muscular tonus, and maintenance of posture may also play upon those higher
integrative functions that have to do with the construction of personal and extrapersonal space. In this connection, it is interesting that we were able to induce
auditory extinction or obscuration by asking patients to press a foot against the
floor. (The role of attention is currently being explored in follow-up investigations.) Similarly, we have some preliminary indications that the propensity for
extinctions of auditory stimulation varies even with a patient's posture.

In the light of these findings, one is tempted to relate certain types of apraxia to the same complex of symptoms, most obviously dressing apraxia. If the body schema is altered, it seems to follow logically that a patient should have difficulty in relating garments spread out before him to his own body. What seems to be involved here are the types of mental operations that have to do with topological transformations, as pointed out and experimented with by Piaget and his students.

As already mentioned, posture may have various effects on sensory processing. This is true for the healthy individual (Lackner, 1974) and takes on special significance in the presence of disease. Bender (1970) found that the localization of a tactual stimulus applied to the dorsum of the hand was disturbed when the hand was in a certain position; apparently, the patient was unable to judge even where the agent that stimulated his hand was located in extrapersonal space. Chapanis noticed that one of her patients referred a binaurally delivered stimulus to his hand, which was lying on a cushion at shoulder height. In retrospect, it would have been interesting to see whether the imagined locus of the sound source would have changed systematically with alteration in position of the hand (an experiment we are planning to do in the near future). Another patient even experienced an increase in auditory extinction as he went from a sitting position into a supine position. If it could be shown experimentally that a patient's central impairment of gross position sense and knowledge of posture can interfere with his spatial localization of stimulus sources, we would have an empirical basis for relating knowledge of personal space to knowledge of extrapersonal space. The importance of sensory and motor integration in the construction of spatial concepts has been stressed by many psychologists, most forcefully by Piaget. It is possible that systematic observations on the disintegration of spatial organization in the presence of brain disease would contribute the most powerful evidence in support of this view. The idea is not new. Benton (1969) found that many right-hemisphere patients found it difficult to locate objects in space and to estimate distances or relative sizes; they also had an impaired memory for location of objects and experienced difficulty in tracing a path, following a route, or relating spatially separate objects; they were also found to have a visuoconstructive disability. It is well known that patients with right-hemisphere lesions have marked difficulty in learning a spatial layout and in orienting themselves in new (and often even in familiar) surroundings. While these difficulties are more commonly described for patients with right-sided lesions (Hécaen, 1969), a visuoconstructive disorder may also be seen in conjunction with left lesions (McFie, Piercy, & Zangwill, 1950). Lastly, we should mention visual neglect of a hemifield or hemispace (Welman, 1969). It is possible, though it has not yet been shown, that this symptom, too, may be related to extinction, especially in the domain of vision. This matter, too, is currently being investigated by A. Menyhert in our laboratory.

Temporal Organization

There is much less information on disorders of temporal organization. However, we have found that some of our patients have difficulty in remembering what time of day it is, even though they can tell the date correctly. They may also have difficulty in recognizing rhythmic patterns and time sequences. It would be worthwhile investigating to what extent these unstructured observations could be correlated to abnormalities in time perception that have been observed in connection with extinction. Chapanis has been able to demonstrate that the extinction phenomenon does not require perfect synchrony of the two stimuli; they may be temporally separated by as much as a quarter of a second, and extinction is still observed. One is reminded of the lowering of the flicker-fusion threshold observed by Teuber, Battersby, and Bender (1960) in patients with traumatic lesions to the visual cortex and alteration in auditory-fusion threshold observed by Lackner and Teuber (1973) in patients with other cerebral injuries. The normal subject recognizes a larger number of flicks per second as isolated flashes than the injured patient, for whom even a few flashes per second fuse into a continuously experienced light. Presumably, the interstimulus interval for the metacontrast effect might also be found to be increased with central lesions in the visual system or perhaps even elsewhere in the brain (Donchin & Lindsley, 1965; Bartlett & White, 1965; Ciganek, 1964). This question deserves to be investigated further. One may conceptualize the patient's difficulty in resolving temporal sequences as being due to physiological activity that persists abnormally long or fails to be damped rapidly enough, perhaps because the recovery period for physiological states of cells is lengthened (Floris, Morocutti, Amabile, Bernardi, Rizzo, & Vasconetto, 1969). In other words, the temporal aspects of extinction and extinction-related phenomena may disturb the "microstructure" of a sense of time lapse and of the perception of time patterns and rhythms; this disturbance may translate itself, for example, into a confusion about time of day or a difficulty in recogniton of melodies.

In summary, we are proposing, as a working hypothesis, that symptoms such as impairment of two-point discrimination, distortions in the subjective sense of the body's geometry, lack of awareness of body parts and their location relative to one another, mislocalization of stimuli in extrapersonal space, and misapprehension of spatial nexus may all have an inner relationship. Upon further examination, one may find that these disturbances are intercorrelated to a greater degree than has been appreciated so far, and it may be possible to begin to understand certain causal connections in these interrelationships by systematic study of pathological interactions and the phenomenon of extinction. The basic idea here is that lesions throw a formerly equilibrated system into disarray, causing some parts to play a disproportionately greater role in integration than others. Whether or not the organization of space is also related to the organization of time remains to be ascertained, but there are some indications that these two realms, also, are not totally independent.

Implications for Theories on Brain Function

In brain research, one frequently finds that excitatory events here have inhibitory effects there, suggesting that the brain is a dynamic system in which excitation and inhibition are in a state of tonic balance. Relationships between excitation and (lateral) inhibition have been demonstrated in sensory functions in the realm of vision, audition, and somesthesis. When the physiological function of a particular system becomes compromised by trauma or other illness, the effects are not merely deletion of one skill out of a fixed repertoire of otherwise undisturbed capacities; instead, one encounters again and again release phenomena together with impairment. This phenomenon is particulaɪ obvious in the realm of motor function. Most alterations caused by lesions above the foramen magnum produce losses together with overreactions; it is the resulting imbalance that constitutes the clinical disability. Examples of this are spasticity, rigidity, and involuntary movements; the pathological reappearance of certain reflexes, such as the grasp, avoidance, or rooting reflexes, has been interpreted as release phenomena by Denny-Brown and his students. (Even hallucinations have been interpreted as manifestations of disinhibition.) Sensory extinction as discussed above may be seen as imbalances in the mode of interaction of anatomically and physiologically related systems. If a faint light is capable of obscuring or extinguishing even a loud, simultaneously presented sound, one may postulate either that the visual system is overreacting (released) or that the auditory system is being unduly checked (inhibited) by the event. However this may be, extinction and related phenomena seem to indicate that the brain's integrative activity is based on the continuous interaction of specific physiological processes in many different neuroanatomical structures and systems. Pathology deforms the interaction pattern in ways that should be amenable to empirical investigation. If the details of the extinction phenomena strike us at present as a crazy quilt of accidental disturbances, it is probably because of our failure in the past to investigate the problem systematically and thoroughly.

At this point, we must clarify a common confusion with respect to the notions of *brain localization* and *dynamic system*. These are not opposites but parallel and independent issues. "Localization" versus "nonlocalization" has become a slogan or even a fighting matter, especially for the uninitiated. The controversy is more apparent than real. All experts agree that every differentiated structure of the central nervous system contributes in its own specific way to the neurophysiology of the brain; its presence or absence (well- or malfunction) does make a difference to the integrity of the brain to an either more or less noticeable degree. However, the contribution is of a *physiological* nature. If the destruction is significant enough, some aspects of motor, perceptual, cognitive, or visceral function are certain to be affected. All of these facts are beyond dispute. The question is whether *different aspects of behavior* are the exclusive province of specific brain structures (the "localizationist" point of view) or whether the behavior that we observe is the integral output of many different, interacting structures and their physiological functions (the "nonlocalizationist" point of view). Although the authors are of the latter persuasion, it should be evident that this particular controversy is actually quite irrelevant to our interpretation of data or, indeed, to our research as a whole.

More interesting is the notion of a dynamic, active system, which is best contrasted with a conception of the nervous system as a static, passive system. We are personally motivated in our work because it seems to us to give weight to the former point of view. It is based on a fundamental approach to behavior and the behaving organism that constitutes a departure from the more common psychologist's approach to behavior (except for that of Piaget and his school). In the first place, it necessarily implies an erosion of the distinction between behavior on the one hand and the biological processes on the other. The embryogenic activities of a system and the formation of patterns, as well as their physiological functions, are regarded by us as objectively and methodologically indistinguishable from the system's "behavior." The watertight distinction between what the psychologist calls behavior and what the psychologist relegates to the biologist's domain is taken by us to be untenable—an artifact. Behavior in the common sense of the word is the necessary by-product of proliferation, differentiation, and growth of structure as well as function. This notion differs from the more traditional one, in which behavior is attributed only to systems of a given biological maturity—psychologists treat it as if it were analogous to the use a machine is put to by extraneous agents. The constructional history of the machine that is said to behave is regarded in traditional psychology as irrelevant.

This brings us to the second distinguishing feature of the notion of dynamic systems. A dynamic system is considered to be inherently active in the following sense. It owes its maintenance of highly specific structures, functions, and potentialities to the constant absorption and dissipation of energy, that is, its metabolic processes in the widest sense of the term; it is inherently active (Katchalsky, Rowland, & Blumenthal, 1974). The peculiarities of its behavior, including the special irritabilities it develops and the morphology of its motor output, are a consequence of its own history of formation and the instabilities of its internal structure. In this view, certain behavioral acts may well be regarded as the consequence of given environmental situations, but stimulus and response need not stand in a direct cause-and-effect relationship—behavior is not a transform of its input in a mechanical sense. Whether a potential stimulus is effective or not depends on the nature and state of the system; therefore, no stimulus has an absolute stimulation potential. There is an *active* process within the system that determines the effectiveness of the stimulus; which explains why the amount of energy in a potential stimulus correlates very poorly with its actual effectiveness in any given instance. It is the energy available within the system that is of paramount importance.

The third distinguishing feature of dynamic systems is the familiar notion of structure (or *Gestalt*). When this notion is applied to the brain, one emphasizes the interlocking dependencies of all brain structures and their functions and the importance of these interrelationships in the elaboration of behavior. Local brain destruction of a given magnitude has widespread consequences; it does not affect only one single aspect of behavior but several all at once. Conversely, a particular aspect of behavior may be disturbed by lesions in many different parts of the brain—not just in one locus.

The concept of interacting neurophysiological processes is too obvious to need elaboration here. (Especially relevant is the old work by Dusser de Barenne, 1936, and Dusser de Barenne and McCulloch, 1939, 1941; and more recent work by Grüsser and Grüsser-Coenehls, 1960; Morrell, 1972; and Taylor, 1974). On the behavioral side, too, we find that interaction of systems is probably the rule, while totally independently functioning sensory systems are the exception—if they exist at all. The sensory quality of visual, auditory, tactual, and even olfactory stimuli is heavily influenced by the stimulus field or space as a whole, always having relative rather than absolute threshold values. Recent work by Lackner (1973a) is particularly relevant to this discussion. He has shown that posture plays a decided role in a normal subject's adaptation to an experimentally disarranged visual input. In another study (Lackner, 1973b), he has shown that visual arrangements may also affect auditory localization in space. Taylor (1974) offers a theoretical model for interaction between auditory and visual interaction. In general, then, extinction phenomena and our theoretical framework for their explanation may easily be fitted into current physiological and behavioral conceptualizations of brain function.

Present Research

From our pilot work so far, we feel confident that we may rule out spurious or strictly psychological attitudes as the causative factor. Extinction does not seem to be due to lack of attention, motivation, or concentration. Since we have already demonstrated that extinction varies reliably with physiological conditions under the control of the experimenter, we assume that it is caused by pathophysiology that may be explored by objective means.

In our present research, we are studying by precise and objective means the temporal dimensions of extinction across sensory modalities, particularly the critical interstimulus interval and the dimensions of the proactive and retroactive inhibition already alluded to. It is also possible to study electrophysiological correlates of this phenomenon and thus to come closer to an understanding of the nature of the response in the course of extinction. Our plan is first to obtain evoked potentials from the isolated visual, auditory, and tactual stimuli and then to study these potentials when the stimuli are presented with an interval between them that is short enough to elicit cross-modal extinction. For every patient on whom these studies are carried out, we are also obtaining other behavioral data, including various aspects of space and time perception and other cognitive functions. The hope of these empirical investigations is to discover whether there are fixed hierarchies of interactions or merely loose clusters of associations between symptoms.

Practical Implications of the Proposed Research

Quite apart from the theoretical interest of this research, there are important practical consequences that may be of immediate benefit to the patients being studied in this investigation, as the following example illustrates. After our first discovery of auditory extinction in patient *CAr* through either visual or tactual simultaneous stimulation, we were curious to know whether this effect played any role in his daily activities. We watched him during a physical-therapy session and observed that the therapist would tap his thigh above the knee vigorously, while saying loudly to him: "Lift your leg! Lift your leg!" This seemed to confuse the patient, and he looked incomprehendingly at the therapist. However, when he was asked to lift his leg without the tactual stimulation, he at once responded appropriately, which our extinction data might have predicted. By bringing about a sudden change in his tactual experience, the therapist was actually interfering with the patient's auditory perception. Instead of helping him by means of multiple simultaneous stimulation (a general practice throughout rehabilitation medicine), the therapist was reducing her efficiency and undermining her own treatment. If, on the other hand, there had been information available to her in the patient's chart warning her of the propensity for auditory extinction, treatment might have been streamlined from the beginning.

The extensive tests that we are planning for our subjects in this investigation will enable us to prepare a list of the most sensitive types of interferences and extinction that characterize every patient's illness. These data may then provide a rational basis for the planning of rehabilitation, giving the therapist an idea of how to approach the patient and what types of tasks should be easy, difficult, or impossible for him.

Relevance to Congenital Reading Disability

Since it is known that extinction is much more pronounced in children than in adults (Bender, 1970), it may be worthwhile to extend the study of extinction to the so-called dyslexic child. At present, it is common practice to increase stimulation in these children and to make them (painfully?) aware of the correlation between sound and visual patterns; all of their drills consist of simultaneous cross-modal sensory bombardment. It is possible that these children have preserved an extinction pattern that might be normal for a younger child but that should have disappeared by school age. If cross-modal extinction could be demonstrated on the dyslexic child, multiple stimulation during reading instruction would be the very thing that is keeping him from learning to read. Once we are set up for the testing of extinction in adult patients, it is our plan to obtain normative data on children and adults and then to proceed with testing children with special language disabilities, particularly in the realm of reading.

References

Bartlett, N. R., & White, C. T. Evoked potentials and correlated judgments of brightness as functions of interflash intervals. *Science*, 1965, *148*, 980–981.

Bender, M. B. *Disorders in perception*. Springfield, Ill.: Thomas, 1952.

Bender, M. B. Perceptual interaction. In D. Williams (Ed.), *Modern trends in neurology*. London: Butterworth, 1970.

Bender, M. B., & Wortis , S. B. Patterns of perceptual, motor, and intellectual functions in organic brain disease. *Transcripts of the American Neurological Association*, 1947, *72*, 31–38.

Benton, A. L. Disorders of spatial orientation. In P. J. Vinken & G. W. Bruyn (Eds.), *Disorders of higher nervous activity, III: Handbook of clinical neurology*. Amsterdam: North Holland, 1969.

Brain, R. Visual disorientation with special reference to the lesions of the right cerebral hemisphere. *Brain*, 1941, *64*, 244–272.

Bruns, L. Ein Beitrag zur einseitigen Wahrnehmung doppelseitiger Reize bei Herden einer Grosshirnhemisphaere. *Neurologia Centralblatt* (Leipzig), 1886, *5*, 198–199.

Chapanis, L. Intramodal and cross-modal pattern perception in stroke patients. Doctoral dissertation, Cornell University, 1974.

Ciganek, L. Excitability cycle of the visual cortex in man. *Annals of the New York Academy of Science*, 1964, *112*, 241–253.

Denny-Brown, D. The nature of apraxia. *Journal of Nervous and Mental Disorders*, 1958, *126*, 9–32.

Denny-Brown, D., Meyer, J. S., & Horenstein, S. The significance of perceptual rivalry resulting from parietal lesions. *Brain*, 1952, *75*, 433–471.

Diamond, S. P., & Bender, M. B. On auditory extinction and alloacusis. *Transcripts of the American Neurological Association*, 1965, *90*, 154–157.

Donchin, E., & Lindsley, D. B. Visually evoked response correlates of perceptual masking and enhancement. *Journal of Electroencephalography and Clinical Neurophysiology*, 1965, *19*, 325–335.

Dusser de Barenne, J. G. Simultaneous facilitation and extinction of motor responses to stimulation of a single cortical focus. *American Journal of Physiology*, 1936, *116*, 39–40.

Dusser de Barenne, J. G., & McCulloch, W. S. Factors for facilitation and extinction in the central nervous system. *Journal of Neurophysiology*, 1939, *2*, 319–355.

Dusser de Barenne, J. G., & McCulloch, W. S. Suppression of motor response obtained from Area 4 by stimulation of Area 4S. *Journal of Neurophysiology*, 1941, *4*, 311–323.

Floris, V., Morocutti, C., Amabile, G., Bernardi, G., Rizzo, P. A., & Vasconetto, C. Recovery cycle of visual evoked potentials in normal and schizophrenic subjects. *Journal of Electroencephalography and Clinical Neurophysiology Supplement*, 1967, *26*, 74–81.

Frederiks, J. A. M. Disorders of the body schema. In P. J. Vinken & G. W. Bruyn (Eds.), *Disorders of speech, perception, and symbolic behavior*, IV: *Handbook of clinical neurology*. Amsterdam: North Holland, 1969.

Gottlieb, G. (Ed.). *Behavioral embryology*. New York: Academic Press, 1973.

Grüsser, O. J., and Grüsser-Coenehls, U. Mikroelektrodenuntersuchungen zur Konvergenz vestibulärer und retinaler Afferenzen an einzelnen Neuronen des optischen Cortex der Katze. *Pflügers Archiv für die gesamte Physiologie des Menschen und der Tiere*, 1960, *270*, 227–238.

Hécaen, H. Cerebral localization of mental functions and their disorders. In P. J. Vinken and G. W. Bruyn (Eds.), *Handbook of Clinical Neurology*. Amsterdam: North Holland, 1969.

Hécaen, H., & de Ajuriaguerra, J. *Méconnaissances et hallucinations corporelles*. Paris: Masson, 1952.

Hécaen, H., Penfield, W., Bertrand, C., & Malmo, R. The syndrome of apractognosia due to lesions of the minor cerebral hemisphere. *Archives of Neurological Psychiatry*, 1956, *75*, 400–434.

Hooker, D. *The prenatal origin of behavior*. Lawrence: University of Kansas Press, 1952.

Humphrey, T. Postnatal repetition of human prenatal activity sequences with some suggestions of their neuroanatomical basis. In R. J. Robinson (Ed.), *Brain and early behavior: Development in the fetus and infant*. New York: Academic Press, 1969.

Jaffe, J., & Bender, M. B. The factor of symmetry in the perception of two simultaneous cutaneous stimuli. *Brain*, 1952, *75*, 167–176.

Katchalsky, A. K., Rowland, V., & Blumenthal, R. *Dynamic patterns of brain cell assemblies*. Neurosciences Research Program Bulletin, Vol. 2, No. 1, 1974.

Kolb, L. Observations on the somatic sensory extinction phenomenon and the body schema after unilateral resection of the posterior central gyrus. *Transcripts of the American Neurological Association*, 1950, *75*, 138–141.

Lackner, J. R. The role of posture in adaptation to visual rearrangement. *Neuropsychologia*, 1973, *11*, 33–44. (a)

Lackner, J. R. Visual rearrangement affects auditory localization. *Neuropsychologia*, 1973, *11*, 29–32. (b)

Lackner, J. R. The role of posture in sound localization. *Quarterly Journal of Experimental Psychology*, 1974, *26*(2), 235–251.

Lackner, J. R., & Teuber, H. L. Alterations in auditory fusion thresholds after cerebral injury in man. *Neuropsychologia*, 1973, *11*, 409–415.

Loeb, J. Die Sehstörungen nach Verletzung der Grosshirnrinde. *Pflügers Archiv für die gesamte Physiologie des Menschen und der Tiere*, 1884, *34*, 67–172.

McFie, J., Piercy, M. F., & Zangwill, O. L. Visual spatial agnosia associated with lesions of the right cerebral hemisphere. *Brain*, 1950, *73*, 167–190.

Minkowski, M. Über Bewegungen und Reflexe des menschlichen Foetus während der ersten Hälfte seiner Entwicklung. *Schweizer Archiv für Neurologie, Neurochirurgie und Psychiatrie*, 1921, *8*, 148–151.

Morrell, F. Integrative properties of parastriate neurones. In A. G. Karczmar & J. C. Eccles (Eds.), *Brain and human behavior*. Berlin-Heidelberg-New York: Springer, 1972.

Oppenheim, H. Über eine durch eine klinisch bisher nicht verwerthete Untersuchungsmethode ermittelte Form der Sensibilitätsstoerung bei einseitigen Erkrankungen des Grosshirns. *Neurologia Centralblatt* (Leipzig), 1885, *4*, 529–533.

Paterson, A., & Zangwill, O. L. Disorders of visual space perception associated with lesions of the right cerebral hemisphere. *Brain*, 1944, *67*, 331–358.

Roth, M. Disorders of the body image caused by lesions of the right parietal lobe. *Brain*, 1949, *72*, 89–111.

Schwartz, A. S., & Eidelberg, E. "Extinction" to bilateral simultaneous stimulation in the monkey. *Neurology*, 1968, *18*, 61–68.

Semmes, J., Weinstein, S., Ghent, L., & Teuber, H. L. Spatial orientation in man after cerebral injury, I: Analyses by locus of lesion. *Journal of Psychology*, 1955, *39*, 227–244.

Taylor, R. L. An analysis of sensory interaction. *Neuropsychologia*, 1974, *12*, 65–71.

Teuber, H. L., Battersby, W. S., & Bender, M. B. *Visual field defects after penetrating missile wounds of the brain*. Cambridge, Mass.: Harvard University Press, 1960.

Welman, A. J. Right-sided unilateral visual spatial agnosia, asomatognosia, and anosognosia with left hemisphere lesions. *Brain*, 1969, *92*, 571–580.

PART II

FORMAL REASONING

CHAPTER 5

Formal Reasoning: A Reappraisal

E. A. Lunzer

University of Nottingham
Nottingham, England

A Backward Look

In a paper that appeared over 10 years ago (Lunzer, 1965), this author spoke of a

> desire to arrive at a clearer understanding of the kinds of advances in reasoning that appear as the child approaches adolescence. Are these advances sufficiently homogeneous and distinctive to warrant the use of the general term *"formal reasoning"* in opposition to the term *"concrete reasoning"* to characterize the achievements belonging to the years between six and nine? (p. 19)

The problems to be discussed today are exactly the same. To anticipate a conclusion right away, it is tentative, but it is opposite to the one reached in 1965. For then, the answer to the question about the unity of formal reasoning was affirmative. Today, it is probably more correct, and almost certainly more productive, to answer it in the negative.

Concrete Reasoning

Before venturing into the treacherous seas of so-called formal reasoning, perhaps we should take one brief cruise on the well-charted waters of concrete reasoning. After all, we can at least try to locate our point of departure as accurately as is possible. Let us refer once more to the 1965 paper; the argument was made then that the essential achievement of concrete operativity lay in the definability of its concepts: *operational = operationally definable,* where *preop-*

erational = *fluid* or *situationally variable*. This equation is quite near the truth. Its appropriateness is well brought out by the conservation experiments. In each of these, the child is first presented with two objects or two arrangements that are clearly and perceptibly equal in some respect. This step is followed by a transformation, which alters the perceptual appearance of the things but does not affect the equivalence just established. Now if we pause to consider what we are doing when we are establishing that initial equivalence, it is clear that we are defining the concept with which we are concerned. To define weight, we put objects on a balance; to define number, we place them in one-to-one correspondence (either with other objects or with the ordered set of positive integers); to define length, we put things end to end. True, in many cases these definitions can be further refined by appropriate advances in scientific and mathematical thinking. But these are the definitions that serve us well enough in the transactions of everyday living, and they are the ones with which the child must start.

Although this characterization of concrete reasoning as reasoning in terms of precise, definable criteria is correct, it is not explanatory. On reflection, it seems that we can go further in the direction of explanation, at least to the extent of bringing out what is an important intermediate stage. Consider a well-known experiment in which the child is shown an array of objects varying in more than one dimension and is asked to sort them into two groups. The objects could be red and blue circles and squares. We know that the typical 4-year-old uses shifting criteria, which result in complete failure. Using shifting criteria leads him to *alignments* (Inhelder & Piaget, 1964), for example, red square–red circle–blue circle. But this error is gradually overcome between the ages of 5 and 6 (Campbell & Young, 1968; Calvert, 1971), that is, well before what Piaget and others would take to be the level of concrete operations. Moreover, there is a further development long since recognized as crucial by such writers as Reichard, Schneider, and Rappaport (1944), which is the ability to *shift* deliberately from one completed classification to another, for example, from color to form. It is this second development that is crucial to what Piaget terms *concrete operativity*. It is very close to cross-classification, the only difference being that the two classifications are successive instead of simultaneous. Likewise, it is close to class inclusion, since the child must be aware of two criteria and not just one.

These considerations would lead to a revision of the earlier formulation by asserting that the hallmark of concrete operativity consists in the child's awareness of the criteria of his own actions in relation to alternative opposing criteria. The child of 5 or 6 who can sort by color *or* by shape without involuntary shifts of criteria is using a criterion correctly. At least at the level of action, his concept is precise. But his consistency is achieved by the inhibition of the alternative criteria. Conversely, the child of 7 is aware of the alternative criteria, and it is precisely this awareness that enables him to shift (deliberately) or to cross-classify.

This formulation (Lunzer, 1970) is more powerful than the analysis offered in 1965, for two reasons. One is that instead of several characteristics' being offered (e.g., perceptual prepotence), a single model is suggested, one that is adequate to cover nearly all the acquisitions characteristic of this phase of development (cf. White, 1965; Lunzer, 1970). The other reason is that it is now apparent that for a criterion to become an object of reflection, it must exist. In other words, the use of stable criteria precedes their recognition.

Formal Reasoning

Turning to the concept of *formal reasoning,* which is our chief concern in this paper, in 1965 one might quarrel with Piaget's emphasis on the INRC* group as a unifying structure underlying both the understanding of proportionality and the use of hypothesis in experimentation. If one selects one out of several characteristics provided by Piaget and gives it a personal twist that may or may not make it simpler to apprehend, the argument could be made that the distinctive characteristic of formal operations was the recognition of second-order relations, as in the relation of equivalence of relations between two pairs of terms linked by an analogy, or as in the equality or inequality of two ratios.

As this author looks back on that discussion in the light of more recent evidence, as well as maturer reflection, the definition in terms of second-order relations seems woefully inadequate. At the same time, the critique of the INRC group as a unifying structure did not go far enough. Both these comments should become clearer in the analysis that follows.

The following section introduces a feature that appears to be a necessary but not a sufficient condition for most forms of advanced reasoning: *acceptance of lack of closure* or ALC. The next section introduces a second feature of advanced thinking—*multiple interacting systems* or MIS—and consists mainly in an overview, representative but not exhaustive, indicating six rather disparate areas of more advanced reasoning. At least one of these does not even feature ALC. The fourth section focuses on development in logical thinking as such. The evidence appears to indicate that this is a relatively specialized skill, and one in which a high degree of efficiency is rare in the absence of specific training. Finally, the fifth section attempts to pull together some of the threads. In this section a formulation is suggested of the relation between thinking and logic that is very different from that of Piaget. This last section concludes with a consideration of the educational implications of the present survey.

*Identity, Negation, Reciprocal, Correlative; see p. 57.

Acceptance of Lack of Closure (ALC)

In a recent paper (Lunzer, 1973), the distinction is made between two categories of inference: simple and complex. Simple inference is said to occur whenever the information that is provided or that the subject obtains enables him to make an unambiguous inference with respect to the state of any variable about which he is concerned. Complex inference is the complementary case, in which such initial information does not permit an unambiguous inference about a relevant variable but instead permits a reduction of alternatives so that the final determination can only be made at a subsequent stage, when more information has been obtained.

The evidence for this distinction rose primarily out of an investigation carried out by Ann Pocklington, which will be described, and, secondly, out of a reconsideration of certain other evidence and especially of a seminal paper by A. Matalon (1962). However, shortly after this author completed the paper referred to, the important thesis by K. Collis (1972) appeared. Collis also drew on Halford's (1968) previous work and found that this author had come to a precisely similar conclusion in relation to the solution of mathematical problems. Collis defined the distinction in terms of tolerance for unclosed operations. Consider the following tasks:

$$(1)\ 3\ +\ 4\ =\ ?$$
$$(2)\ 3\ +\ ?\ =\ 7$$
$$(3)\ 3\ +\ 4\ +\ 2\ =\ ?$$
$$(4)\ 3\ +\ 4\ +\ ?\ =\ 9$$
$$(5)\ 3\ +\ ?\ =\ 7\ +\ 2$$
$$(6)\ ?\ -\ 7\ =\ 7\ -\ 3$$
$$(7)\ ?\ -\ 7\ =\ 4$$

It is clear that (1) and (2) require only one operation. (3) and (4) each require two operations, but the first operation to be effected is clearly indicated and the result of that operation sufficiently pinpoints the second. Thus, if the task is taken as a whole, the sequence of operations is defined (for the average schoolchild) from the outset, and each step is that sequence is closed before the solver is required to proceed to the next. By contrast, (6) suggests an unclosed operation:

$? - 7$ is some number and that number equals $7 - 3$.

Even if $7 - 3$ is executed, it may not be immediately apparent whether the 4 is to be inserted as it stands, is to be added to the 7, or is to be subtracted from it. (5) and (7) may be thought of as intermediate. Collis's own results will be discussed more fully below.

Acceptance of lack of closure coincides exactly with the notion of complex inference described above. Because Collis's formulation is neater and more descriptive, it is preferred to my own. In the rest of this paper, it will be shortened to *ALC*. The clearest and simplest illustration of the significance of ALC is the work of Pocklington referred to earlier.

The apparatus consisted of a box with a single light and up to four buttons to press. More complex problems used all four buttons, and in this case, the subject was told that one was a *switch,* which would cause the light to come on if it was off and vice versa; one was neutral and would have no effect; one was an *on* button and would cause the light to come on if it was off but would have no effect if it was off already; and the last was an *off* button, its action being the exact opposite of the *on* button. Simpler problems involved only two or three of these buttons. The task for the child was always to establish in as few moves as possible which button was which. Briefly, it was found that most children managed to solve all but the most difficult problems at all ages between 5 and 18. But there was evidence of cognitive growth both in the progressive elimination of errors and, to a lesser extent, in the kind of error that predominated.

However, the single most important observation concerned the use of alternative labels. To help them keep track of events, the children were offered a selection of eight labels for some of the problems. These could be used to tag any buttons that they had identified. The labels were *on, off, change, neutral, on or change, on or neutral, off or change,* and *off or neutral.* It will be seen that the last four were deliberately provided to enable the child to handle the ambiguous situations that arose when one of the buttons was pressed for the first time. At 11 years old, these were used freely whenever they were appropriate. At 9 years old, only half the children examined used them at all, and then only once on the average over all the problems. At 7 years old, none of the children ever used the alternative labels. The improvement in the use of the alternative labels between 9 and 11 was dramatic. It is difficult to resist the conclusion that younger children fail to see the need for the alternative labels because of *premature closure;* that is, they cannot accept, say, that a button that they have pressed could be *off or change* since it must be either one or the other. Conversely, the older children use these labels freely because of their ALC.

Perhaps one of the earliest demonstrations of the relatively late emergence of ALC is that offered by Matalon in a study of implication. He used a box with two compartments, each of which could be inspected separately. One concealed a red light, the other a green light. The subjects were told, ''Whenever the red light is on, the green light is on.'' The problem was to decide what could be said about the state of the other light after the state of one had been seen. *Red on* implies *green on* is given. *Green off* implies *red off* is correct, but it is also uninformative as a response, because it can be arrived at on the basis of incorrect as well as correct reasoning. The critical problems consist in showing red off and green on. In both these cases, the state of the hidden light is ambiguous. Matalon found that until the age of 11 or 12, children insist on making the inference one way or the other, usually in the direction of symmetry, as if the implication were an equivalence.

Matalon's findings have been verified and extended in a paper by Peel (1967), who investigated the understanding of implication, incompatibility, and disjunction using a game technique. The experimenter and the subject have four boxes, each containing counters of different colors. In each pair of moves, the first player selects a particular color; the second must play a counter in turn, but in doing so, he must observe whatever rule has been laid down for the game in question. For instance, the implication rule is *If and whenever I draw a red, you must draw a red.* Although there was a persistent tendency for children to match the experimenter's color when playing II, even when it was not red, it was found that children of 5 and 8, but not of 11 faulted the experimenter whenever he failed to match under the same condition. In other words, the spontaneous behavior was to economize on cognitive strain by adhering to a universal matching rule. But from the age of 11 on, this did not preclude a recognition of the distinction between implication and equivalence.

In the following section, a variety of tasks will be reviewed, each of which may be taken as instances of more advanced thinking, and in each case the role of ALC will be considered. Anticipating a little, it may be noted that whereas ALC is a feature of most of them, it is certainly not the sole feature. Its role may be thought of as an enabling one. Moreover, whereas ALC in the relatively simple tests used by Pocklington and Matalon is well-nigh universal, even at the age of 11, success in the problems that follow is by no means universal, and usually if success does become the rule, rather than the exception, this happens a good deal beyond the age of 11.

Varieties of Task

While Inhelder and Piaget's celebrated work on the growth of logical thinking (1958) is still the most fruitful source of ideas and of evidence compiled by a single group, it is no longer the sole source of evidence with regard to the development of more advanced thinking, as it was when it first appeared. Nor can the complex of interpretations that it contains be assimilated as an adequate theory, for it is neither sufficiently precise to function as a model nor consistent with all the facts. However, it is not proposed in what follows to set up an alternative and better model. I am content with the much more pedestrian task of putting together a number of task varieties, each of which appears to involve a more advanced type of thinking than that which is entailed in the development of operativity between the ages of 5 and 8.

This exercise would nevertheless be relatively unproductive if it did not include some attempt to bring out what appear to be the key features of each such variety. It is proposed in what follows to concentrate on two such features. One is the relevance of ALC. The other is the presence of multiple interacting systems, or MIS. These are defined as follows:

> If a task is such that its solution can be effected by assimilation to one system of co-variations, it is defined as *simple*. It is also simple if it permits of several independent objectives, provided that each of these involves an independent system of variation. However, if more than one system of covariation is involved in the solution strategy, and successful solution depends on the interaction of the two systems, the task is *complex*. For the remainder of this paper, this interaction will be abbreviated to *MIS*.

By way of example, consider the action of an Etchasketch. This is a toy that allows a child to produce a drawing by manipulating two knobs, one of which causes the sketching point to move up and down, while the other makes it go from side to side. In either case, the direction of movement is reversed when the relevant knob is turned backward instead of forward. As long as it is used for rectangular drawings, Etchasketch involves two noninteracting systems. But if an oblique line is required, the two systems must be brought into action simultaneously, and the task becomes complex. It should be added that because the toy itself is a concrete realization of the combined systems designed to provide constant feedback, its manipulation may not involve the user in any advanced thinking. However, advanced thinking is demanded when the subject is required to analyze oblique motion as the resultant of two orthogonal forces or motions, as illustrated in several of the Geneva experiments, for example, the movement of a snail (Piaget, 1946) and the location of a point in a rectangle (Piaget, Inhelder, & Szeminska, 1960).

More generally, the author hopes to bring out the relevance of MIS along with that of ALC in the following paragraphs. But he does not propose to end such an argument by seeking to impose an overall interpretive model designed to account for all the tasks concerned. Not only is the undertaking too difficult; in the present state of knowledge, it is speculative and counterproductive. In particular, we know far too little about the relative effectiveness of specific training or of general *education* with respect to each group of tasks. In the main, therefore, the present section takes the form of an annotated list.

Experimental Control of Variables

This heading is intended to subsume several of the key studies described in the first part of Inhelder and Piaget's (1958) volume, notably those that require explanations of the motion of a pendulum, the bending of rods, movement on an inclined plane, the role of an invisible magnet, and the combination of liquids. These studies are too well known to warrant description in any detail. In each case, the subject must first discover an explanation by experimenting with the material provided. But the true test of the adequacy of the subject's reasoning lies in his or her ability to prove that his or her explanation is the only one that is consistent with all the facts. For instance, the subject has to show that the oscillation of the pendulum varies with its length and is independent of other factors, such as weight. The successful subject does this by the method of *other things equal,* that is, by varying one factor at a time and holding the remainder constant.

It is clear that these behaviors feature both ALC and MIS. To take an example, when in the pendulum experiment the subject varies length and weight simultaneously, the effect that is observed may be due to either factor taken separately, or it might be contingent on their interaction. In order to select among these possibilities, the subject needs to carry out further controls. So far, the situation is parallel to the one obtained in the simpler Pocklington experiment. If, moreover, the subject avoids the ambiguity by controlling variables from the outset, it is reasonable to infer that he is aware of the ambiguity that would arise if he failed to do so. In other words, the subject has anticipated the possibility of lack of closure and has circumvented it. The authors argued that the anticipation marks a further substage in these experiments, IIIB, whereas a correct reading of the alternatives by itself is characteristic of the earlier IIIA. The relevance of MIS is even more obvious, since the action of any one factor is, in accordance with our definition, a system, and the task of the subject is precisely to disentangle the actions of the several systems concerned.

However, even in these experiments, it is almost certainly incorrect to deduce that the subject who possesses ALC and MIS is thereby a *formal reasoner* and that his success is guaranteed. Inquiries such as those of Lovell (1961) and Jackson (1965) reveal considerable intraindividual as well as interindividual variability. It is wholly probable that familiarity with scientific experimentation in general is an exceedingly relevant factor. So too is the plausibility, and hence the availability, of the correct interpretation. The evidence for the latter is at present indirect, being obtained principally from studies in logical thinking as such (e.g., Roberge & Paulus, 1971).

Yet another factor to be considered is the role of abstraction. This is often closely bound up with MIS. When only a single factor is involved, as in the spring-balance experiment described by Inhelder and Piaget (1964), its correct elucidation is mainly a matter of categorizing objects: heavier boxes depress the scale and cause the lever to project beyond the apparatus. When more than one system is involved, the variables do not correspond directly with objects as given or with ready-made events. If one hypothesis is to be tested against alternatives, the desired events and/or objects need to be constructed or reconstructed. It is the laws governing the systems that specify the mode of construction. Elements such as weight, length, etc., are to that extent abstract. They are no longer thought of simply as properties of given objects (or events) but rather as variables that can be manipulated to construct the properties to any specification. The role of abstraction is clearer in the next group of behaviors.

False Conservation

The false-conservation tasks are fairly fully described elsewhere (Lunzer, 1968). Two situations were selected and these are further illustrated (see Figure 1). The essence of the problem is similar in the two setups. If one starts with a square, it is possible to elongate the shape while preserving a constant perimeter. In this case, the area of the figure is progressively reduced. The apparatus consists of a board with nails appropriately placed to enable the same closed length of string to describe a square or a more- or less-elongated rectangle. Alternatively, one can extend the perimeter while preserving a constant area by simply cutting off a larger or smaller portion and transposing it. In both experiments, the critical behavior consists in recognizing and explaining the nonconservation of one of the variables while allowing the conservation of the other. Characteristically, the *concrete* reasoner insists that either both perimeter and

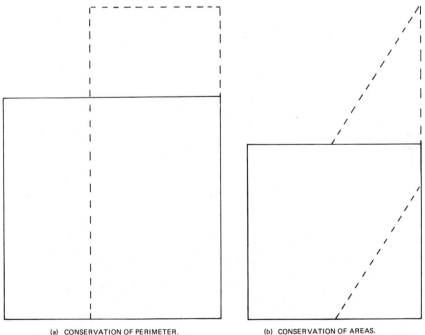

(a) CONSERVATION OF PERIMETER.
NONCONSERVATION OF AREA.

(b) CONSERVATION OF AREAS.
NONCONSERVATION OF PERIMETER.

FIGURE 1. False-conservation problems (from Lunzer, 1968).

area are conserved, and this is the modal response at age 9, or if he or she is persuaded by the experimenter that one variable is not conserved, he or she argues that neither is the other.

It goes without saying that there is an earlier phase (Level I) at which there is no conservation of either variable. Level II is transitional. The false-conservation response is therefore characterized as Level III. It is also possible to distinguish two levels within the next phase, which marks the abandonment of false conservations. At Level IV, the recognition of nonconservation (especially of area) is reluctant, and the subject often retains the false conservation when the deformation of the original square is minimal, even after he or she has allowed that conservation does not obtain when the change is large. By contrast, at Level V, although his or her discovery of nonconservation may be gradual, once it is attained the subject immediately generalizes to the whole set of transformations (elongations or transpositions). At the same time, he or she can give a correct account of the reason that only one of the variables is conserved.

The two problems offer a clear illustration of the role of MIS, since the effects of the transformation on area and on perimeter are distinct, and the difficulty is essentially one of reconciling the two *systems*. ALC is less obvious, although it can be argued that the insistence on false conservation—that is, that area and perimeter must vary together—is an instance of *premature closure*. However, what the inquiry illustrates most sharply is the role of abstraction. The insistence on false conservation derives from failure to consider area and perimeter in abstraction from the figures from which they are derived. The square is seen as an object that is the same under transformation, in which case both perimeter and area are conserved, or else the object is, as it were, transmuted, in which case both the essential properties must alter. The role of abstraction is well brought out by the difference in the difficulty of the two problems. Nonconservation of perimeter is accepted more readily than nonconservation of area because the former notion is much less closely linked to the concept of a figure as object. It is interesting to note that despite the demand for abstraction in the analysis of area and perimeter as independent of the object from which they are derived, success in these tasks is more general at age 14–15 than it is in most of the problems used by Inhelder and Piaget.

Compensation and Proportionality

In the experiments just described, there are two systems involved: change in area and change in perimeter. However, the situations are so devised that the only operations allowed are those that result in an identity transformation with respect to one of these interacting systems. A number of the experiments described by Inhelder and Piaget are similar, except for the fact that the two systems can be varied independently by means of distinct operations. The

TABLE 1
Incidence of False Conservation
(from Lunzer, 1968)

	Constant area					Constant perimeter				
Age	I	II	III	IV	V	I	II	III	IV	V
9	1	—	6	—	—	—	—	5	1	—
10	—	1	4	1	—	—	—	4	2	—
11	—	—	3	4	—	—	—	—	—	—
12	—	—	—	5	—	—	—	—	1	1
13	—	—	—	5	1	—	—	—	2	4
14	—	—	—	4	10	—	—	—	2	10
15	—	—	—	3	5	—	—	—	1	7

communicating-vessels problem and the hydraulic press are relatively pure examples. In both cases, one may alter the dependent variable—the height of a column of liquid in one arm of the apparatus—by raising or lowering the arm itself or by altering the position of the other arm of the U. In the second case, further variables are introduced: the density of the liquid and the weight of the piston. If we concentrate on what is common to the two problems, we note that both are clear instances of MIS. Moreover, Piaget correctly diagnosed the source of their difficulty with reference to the INRC group. Raising one arm of the U has the effect of lowering the height of the column. If this is taken as the reference operation I, its effect may be negated by lowering the same arm, this being the opposite operation which may be designated as N. However, the same nullifying effect can be achieved by a compensatory operation: raising the opposite arm, this being a reciprocal to the first, R. Finally, the other arm can be lowered, negating the reciprocal action, with an effect correlative to the first: C. The four actions, each of which can be performed quite readily and independently by the subject, are related as a group in which $N^2 = R^2 = C^2 = I$, $NR = C$, $NC = R$, $RC = N$, and $NCR = I$. Moreover, all operations are commutative. The structure, well described by Piaget, is that of a group.

However, Piaget goes further in arguing that the INRC group is *the* underlying structure that plays a crucial role in all formal thinking. It seems that MIS is far more general, although one would not argue that even this is a universal feature of problems requiring advanced thinking strategies for their solution. The false-conservation experiments involve MIS but do not feature the INRC group. Neither do most of the Piagetian experiments on the experimental control of variables. Piaget has argued that they do, maintaining that they imply the transformation of logical propositions. However, the role of logical transformation is speculative in all of these examples of reasoning. Logical reasoning as such presents problems of its own, and these will be considered separately in the next section. Meanwhile, there is little warrant for an *a priori* assertion that advances in thinking are a function of advances in logic.

For the most part, the problems contained in the second part of Inhelder and Piaget's work present a compound difficulty. In addition to the compensatory structure of the several factors involved, there is a requirement of quantification that takes the form of an inverse proportionality. The problems concerned are those of equilibrium in the balance (law of moments), projection of shadows, and motion on an inclined plane. However, unlike the problems discussed in the first paragraph of this subsection, the direction of compensations as such generally presents little problem. This fact is not without interest, for it strongly supports the conclusion that complexity of structure taken by itself is an insufficient index of task difficulty. But there is abundant evidence that an understanding of proportionality comes hard.

To begin with, a distinction should be made between direct and inverse proportionality. Not surprisingly, the former is easier. Nevertheless, several investigations have shown that even problems that involve only direct proportionality are rarely solved before the age of 11. Published studies include Lunzer (1965), Lunzer and Pumfrey (1966), and an earlier study by F. Orsini, M. Meylan-Backs and H. Sinclair which has since appeared as Chapter 3 in Piaget *et al.* (1968). It appears that children prefer addition to multiplication when the latter is the correct strategy, as in reproduction to scale. The reason is not clear and may be at least in part a result of bad teaching. Multiplication is usually taught as a shortcut for cumulative equal addition. Although a valid interpretation, this is not the only one. An alternative and equally valid interpretation sees multiplication as a function, or a one–many relation. It is the latter that is relevant to direct proportionality. Moreover, it is this aspect that is essential to a correct understanding of inverse proportionality, since the mathematical inverse here takes the form of a many–one relation. Unlike direct proportionality, realizations of inverse proportionality invariably involve MIS. A simple but very clear illustration of the difficulty of these problems is provided by the large-scale inquiries of Karplus (Karplus & Peterson, 1970). The problem consists simply in predicting how many large paper clips are needed to make a mannikin who will be the same shape and size as one made of small clips, given the ratio of the two sizes of clips. The percentage of subjects who gave a correct solution together with an adequate explanation rose from 6 at grade 6 to 80 at grades 11–12.

MIS may be said to feature in these problems in the sense that the relation between the size and the number of clips in each instance forms a simple system. The problem is to establish a relation between the two. However, before leaving the topic of proportionality, let us note that while an adequate mastery of the topic certainly entails an understanding of the whole set of relations, together with their inverses, it has not been shown that this realization comes about spontaneously as a result of a maturing logic (Inhelder & Piaget, 1958, pp. 176 ff).

$$\frac{a}{b} = \frac{c}{d} \rightarrow ad = bc \rightarrow \frac{a}{c} = \frac{b}{d}$$

It is more probable that these relations need to be taught. But the evidence suggests that even given good teaching, they will not be applied spontaneously to new problems until the subject's powers of reasoning have reached an advanced level of development.

Problem Solving in Mathematics

We now pass from proportionality as a special case to mathematical reasoning in general, referring once more to the work of Collis (1972). Collis incorporates two dimensions within a single model of development. One dimension relates to the form of a problem, the other to its content. When the content is both specific and intuitable, it is classed as *concrete*. In the context of mathematics, this dimension reduces to a condition that the problem must be confined to the manipulation of small integers. When the numbers are large, or when they are replaced by algebraic variables, the content is *formal*. As to the operational structure of a problem, this is concrete when it takes the form of a series of closed operations; that is, even if the solver is required to execute more than one operation, he or she is always able to complete the one he or she is executing before proceeding to the next, and the sequence is clear from the outset. When these conditions do not obtain, the structure is formal. This twofold classification leads to a two-by-two matrix. $8 \times 3 = 3 \times ?$ and $8 \times 4 - 4 = ?$ are examples of concrete form and concrete content. $a \times b = b \times ?$ and $428 + 517 = 517 + ?$ are examples of formal content in a concrete-operational structure. $7 - 4 = ? - 7$ is an instance of concrete content in the context of a formal structure. Finally, $576 + 495 = (576 + 382) + (495 - ?)$ and $a/b = 2a/?$ are (relatively simple) instances of formal content in a formal structure. It should, of course, be stressed that the problems can have a formal structure for the solver only if he or she has not been taught an algorithm for their solution. If the solver has learned the proper algorithm, then he or she knows just what sequence of operations should be performed, and so, by definition, the problem ceases to be formal.

Collis predicted that the structural dimension ought, on the basis of Piagetian theory, to be more critical than content. So, indeed, it appeared. Thus concrete-content–concrete-structure problems are solved by most 9-year-olds most of the time. Formal content–concrete structure adds to the difficulty of the problem, but an acceptable criterion of success is achieved at about the age of 10.

For concrete-content–formal-structure problems, a similar criterion is not reached until nearer 15, while the formal–formal problem is solved only at 16–18.

This analysis seems to be essentially correct, and it is certainly productive. The difficulty of a problem is found to depend on the manipulability of the elements and on the complexity of structure. The latter is even more critical than the former.

It need hardly be added that the inquiries referred to constitute no more than a beginning in relation to what must be involved in the study of development in mathematical thinking. Even if we confine ourselves to the topic of equation solving alone, at least two sets of problems require exploration.

The first is the business of writing equations. It would seem that inventing an equation to describe a state of affairs involves three sets of abstraction. One is the selection of the mathematically significant content from the circumstantial. Another is the abstraction that is entailed in the selection or acceptance of a mathematical symbolism to describe the elements involved. At an elementary level, this abstraction entails no more than the acceptance of algebraic symbols to describe unknown quantities, and there is evidence that this presents little problem even at the ages of 7–9 (Hill, Kapadia, Dadds, Lunzer, & Armitage, 1973). However, it is likely that the distinction between algebraic constants and variables is far more difficult to accept. More difficult, too, is the abstraction involved in the generalization of operations, closely bound up with the idea of function.

A second problem concerns the use of equations. Equations are useful in that they engender complete or partial solutions. The solution of equations is rarely possible without a set of transformation rules. In practice, there are two ways of using such rules. The first consists in acquiring a limited number of fixed algorithms embodying a determinate sequence of transformations. Pupils who learn mathematics in this way (perhaps the majority) can pass examinations, but their mathematical understanding remains low. The alternative involves two sorts of ability: the ability to generate sequences of transformations and the ability to select those that are useful for any given problem. Even the business of generating sequences of transformations is more complex than it sounds. Certainly, it includes an understanding that transformations express equivalences. But if the sequence is more than a few steps in length, there is always the possibility of error, and therefore there is a need to check. An unpublished study by one of our students shows that few pupils below the age of 15 understand the need to carry out such checks. But it is reasonable to presume that the ability to select fruitful paths is a far more subtle process, involving a mathematical intuition based on adequate learning experiences.

On a still more general plane, Dienes (1972) has described what he sees as six steps in the process of learning mathematics. The first is a stage of free play in which the learner is confronted with a suitably structured mathematical environment and is free to discover what can be done with the material. The second consists in the introduction of constraints or rules. In effect, these will usually correspond to manipulative sequences that correspond to practical equivalences. The third stage introduces a variety of isomorphic materials designed to facilitate the abstraction of mathematical structures. A fourth stage provides a kind of mathematical image for the abstraction in the form of graphs, Venn diagrams, etc. The fifth stage introduces a symbolism that will enable the learner to represent sequences of transformations. The sixth and final stage consists in devising a suitable set of axioms and theorems to provide a complete description of the system under consideration.

The above stages are clearly designed as a prescription for optimizing the teaching of any given mathematical topic. Two questions would seem to warrant further research. One is the degree to which it is desirable to introduce several embodiments of the same structure to facilitate abstraction. The experience of the team at Newcastle, New South Wales (reported in Collis, 1972), would seem to indicate that such a procedure is more often confusing. A second question concerns the separation of visual and symbolic representation (Dienes's stages five and six). One wonders (1) whether these should indeed be held separate and (2) whether all systems lend themselves equally to such visual representation and, if so, whether such a procedure is equally suitable for all learners. It appears that mathematicians themselves include in their ranks some who are visualizers and others who are not.

Finally, it should be said that one can regard logical and mathematical proof as an activity *sui generis,* fairly removed from the business of everyday reasoning, and even from most scientific reasoning. The demand for proof arises even, and especially, when the adequacy of a sequence of operations for the solution of applied problems is already known. Its aim is to test the limits of what has been obtained and to establish a system of interrelations with existing conceptualizations. It is for the second reason that not all proofs are equally illuminating, and the mathematician will generally not rest content with a clumsy proof if he suspects that a more elegant proof is possible.

Most of the activities described involve ALC, since they require choices in sequences of transformations. Once again, however, the role of MIS is less obvious, although it is likely to be a factor in the devising and selection of suitable sequences for the solution of equations or for establishing proofs. However, the one characteristic of reasoning that figures most prominently is that of abstraction. More specifically, it is an abstraction based on operations carried out by the subject in relation to the material, that is, what Piaget (1970) calls *reflective abstraction.*

Explanatory Behavior in Verbal Contexts

Let us turn now to a very different area, consisting of the now quite extensive group of studies carried out by Peel and his collaborators, the majority of which are reported in his most recent book (1971). These workers have been concerned with the description and measurement of development in the quality of children's explanations in such fields as history, geography, and economics. The technique adopted is beautifully simple and consists in presenting the child with a passage followed by a question. The passage contains information relevant to the question. However, there are usually irrelevancies in addition, and the evidence is always ambiguous or inadequate, so that a good answer demands evaluation and judgment. The following is an example, first reported in Peel (1966):

> Only brave pilots are allowed to fly over high mountains. This summer a fighter pilot flying over the Alps collided with an aerial cable railway, and cut a main cable, causing some cars to fall to the glacier below. Several people were killed and many others had to spend the night suspended above the glacier.
>
> 1. Was the pilot a careful airman?
> 2. Why do you think so?

The types of response made to the two questions generally fall into one of three categories, such as:

1. *Restricted.* Irrelevancy, tautology ·and inconsistency may dominate. Often the child focuses on a trivial point, or he may fabricate, for example, *Yes, he was brave. Yes, the cable shouldn't have been there. No, he was a show-off.*
2. *Circumstantial.* The content as given is taken to be decisive, for example, *No, because he hit the cable. No, because if he was careful, he would not have cut the cable.*

Peel has argued that the second of these represents a higher substage. If two of the facts given in a passage point to opposite conclusions, as is true of most of the examples, the subject simply seizes on one and ignores the other.

3. *Imaginative.* Extenuating circumstances are invoked, for example, *You can't tell, it depends on the weather/state of the plane.* More generally, the subject takes account of all the evidence as given, and in the event that this is insufficient to settle the problem, he adduces further evidence from his store of general knowledge or points to the need for such evidence.

It is easy to see that the chief characteristic of the second or circumstantial level is a sort of *premature closure* due to a failure of ALC. Similarly, the presence of ALC at the third level enables the subject to begin to reconcile a variety of factors and this process in turn entails MIS.

Some of the investigations reported by Peel permit four response categories, a distinction being made between those that merely take account of all the material given, which can be called *minimal MIS,* and those that offer a more thorough examination, showing a genuine grasp of the ramifications of the topic at issue. These enquiries offer clear evidence of development in the quality of children's explanations throughout the adolescent years. An example is the results obtained by Rhys (1964) in a study of the quality of thinking in the area of geography (see Table 2). The passage presented to the students dealt with the problems of farming in the Andes and was concerned with soil erosion produced by the cutting down of trees and the subsequent excessive cropping. The question asked was *Why did the deep fertile soil cover disappear and make farming impossible?* Typical responses at each level were:

1. *Restricted. Because there were less trees growing on the good soil.*
2. *Circumstantial. The soil was washed away by flooding.*
3. *Comprehensive. When the trees were taken away, the rain fell direct onto the soil, washing it away down the hillside.*
4. *Imaginative. Through getting rid of the trees, they make it possible for the rain to wash the good soil away. This is because the roots of the trees hold the good soil in place. The fact that he always planted maize would not have helped. When farming the crops should be changed to replace what the other crops take out.*

In the same volume, Peel defined judgment as:

> a form of thinking invoked whenever we are in a situation for which we have no ready made answer learned off pat. But in addition, judgment refers to a situation for which there is no single final correct response to be discovered, but rather a spectrum of responses satisfying different numbers of different criteria. Some decisions, therefore, may be better than others on certain grounds. But in extreme conditions, none is outstanding and the decision turns on what the judge wants to fulfil. (p. 19)

Peel suggested that there are five stages in the process of arriving at a judgment: (1) an arousal of interest; (2) the recognition of conflict, for example,

TABLE 2
Quality of Explanation in a Geographical Context (Ages in Months)[a]

Response category	N	CA(mean)	CA(SD)	MA(mean)[b]	MA(SD)
Restricted	21	135.6	10.5	138.1	17.7
Circumstantial	26	141.5	12.6	147.1	15.3
Comprehensive	33	160.3	14.4	166.9	17.9
Imaginative	40	180.4	10.2	195.4	19.0

[a]From Peel (1971). Data based on an enquiry by Rhys (1964).
[b]MA calculations based on Raven's Progressive Matrices.

between the new facts presented and what is already known to the subject; (3) generation of hypotheses or explanations; (4) rejection of inadequate hypotheses; and finally, (5) controlled testing of the hypotheses that are retained. He went on to argue that while the generation of hypotheses as such rarely presents much difficulty, the fourth and fifth steps offer a far more searching test of cognitive functioning. It may be, however, that Peel underestimated the importance of his Step 3. While it may be easy enough to suggest trivial explanations, it is by no means always easy to invent fruitful hypotheses. The latter depends on recognizing the constraints of the situation, that is, on the ability to assimilate what is presented to one or more adequately structured frames of reference.

Network Problems

The topic of constraints leads to the consideration of a further class of problems, perhaps limited in scope, but interesting precisely because it is very different from all those considered so far. These are problems that are essentially sequential, and the job is to find the right sequence of moves from a beginning state to an end state, within a given set of constraints. The moves themselves may be quite simple and easy to envisage. Moreover, if a position can be reached in several ways, it does not matter which path has been taken to reach it. The problem is to find an appropriate sequence of moves to reach the objective without breaking the rules. The particular examples we have studied are all river-crossing problems. There were four of these:

Problem 1. Two soldiers are marching through the jungle. They come to a crocodile-infested river that they must cross. There is only one small boat, which belongs to two small boys. The boat is big enough to carry the two boys alone or one soldier by himself. How do the two soldiers get across the river if the two boys are willing to help but want their boat back again?

In order to obtain a correct solution to this problem, one must be willing to allow the two boys to go across and one to return before a soldier can cross, two apparently pointless moves. One must watch the condition of the boat, either two boys or one soldier. One must ensure that the boys get the boat back; one of them must be on the far bank when the second soldier arrives.

Problem 2. A man is traveling with a wolf, a goat, and a basket of cabbages. They come to a crocodile-infested river over which they have to cross. There is only one small boat, which will carry the man and one other thing, either the wolf, the goat, or the basket of cabbages. If the goat and the cabbages are left alone together, then the goat eats the cabbages. If the wolf and the goat are left alone together, then the wolf eats the goat. How does he get across the river safely without losing any of them?

In order to obtain a correct solution to this problem, one must be willing to take across the goat, go back for either the wolf or the cabbages; but on arriving on the far bank with either of these two things one must take back the goat; a backward move. The condition in the boat presents little problem, the man plus one other thing; but one needs to watch both banks carefully throughout the problem to ensure that one does not bring about the wolf-and-goat or the goat-and-cabbage condition.

Problem 3. Three beautiful native girls are traveling through the jungle with their husbands, who are young, handsome, and jealous. They come to a crocodile-infested river over which they must cross. There is only one small boat, which can hold no more than two people. How do they cross the river if only the men can row and no girl is ever left in the company of a man unless her husband is present?

In order to obtain a correct solution, one must again be prepared to take someone across the river but later take him or her back again. The condition in the boat plus the fact that only men can row means that either two men or one man and his wife can be in the boat. One must also watch the condition on both banks: a wife must never be left in the company of a man unless her husband is present.

Problem 4. Three cannibals and three missionaries want to cross a river. There is only one small boat available, which can carry two people at a time. If at any time there are more cannibals than missionaries at any place, then the cannibals eat the missionaries. How do all six of them get safely across the river?

In order to obtain a correct solution, one must be prepared to incorporate a backward move at some stage in the solution. The condition in the boat is straightforward, two people. One also has to watch both banks in order to ensure that while two people are in the boat there are never more cannibals than missionaries. Another difficulty, however, presents itself; in this case, one must also consider the period of change from boat to bank: when the boat leaves one bank it is necessary to add together the cannibals in the boat and on the opposite bank and check that they do not outnumber the missionaries in the boat and on the opposite bank.

The four problems were set as a written test for four groups of subjects, three composed of schoolchildren and the fourth of college students. The order of the problems was varied but was not found to be a significant factor. The percentage of success achieved by each group is shown in Table 3.

One can only speculate as to the reason that the college students' performance was inferior to that of the 14- to 15-year-olds. Presumably, however, a more highly selected group of young adults would have a higher percentage of success. It is clear that the more demanding the constraints and the larger the sequence of moves required for solution (8 crossings in Problem 1, 7 in Problem 2, and 11 in Problems 3 and 4), the greater the difficulty of the problem. But it is no less clear that problems of this kind do not entail either ALC or MIS in the

TABLE 3
Success in River-Crossing Problems (%)

| Age | N | Problem | | | |
		1	2	3	4
10–11	32	62	6	0	0
12–13	32	72	62	12	0
14–15	32	94	92	33	19
19+	40	87	65	17	10

strict sense. Nor can even the more difficult problems be described as abstract, although they are certainly artificial! These considerations lead to the possibility that the identification of ALC and MIS as constituents of most of the problems that require advanced thinking is by no means definitive. Perhaps, in spite of their generality as noted in earlier paragraphs, ALC and MIS are too content-loaded to constitute specifications for thinking as such.

In order to arrive at a more embracing psychological account of thinking, we may need to consider only the type of *program* required by the thinking subject, that is, the number of elements to be processed and the number and structure of the rules needed for the processing.

Let us now consider the nature of the difficulties involved in logical problems as a separate class. It should be emphasized that the problems reviewed in this section are representative but not exhaustive. For instance, analogies have not been mentioned, although they have been drawn on rather heavily in earlier studies. References to the understanding of proverbs, as in the familiar Terman–Mezzill test, have also not been made. However, such tests are fairly obvious instances of ALC, MIS, and, perhaps, abstraction, in varying combinations of difficulty.

Logical Problems

One of the principal contentions of this paper is that problems of logical inference constitute a special class and should not be taken as a touchstone for the quality of thinking in general. There are two reasons for taking this stand. From the theoretical point of view, logical inference differs from most instances of reasoning because of the key importance attached to material implication. From an empirical standpoint, we note an ever-increasing body of evidence attesting to the fact that students who are otherwise effective (though perhaps not outstanding) thinkers may nevertheless perform very poorly in tests of logical inference. A third reason is that in the present state of our knowledge, a sort of null hypothesis is a safer assumption, if only because it leaves more roads open for enquiry.

At the very least, we have to recognize that the principle of material implication plays only a very limited part either in everyday thinking or in scientific thinking. It is still crucial to most logics, and certainly to the kinds of logical problems that have been designed as tests of formal reasoning. A logic is an axiomatization of the principles of valid inference. Within the axiomatic system, the propositional calculus holds a prior position—and with it a prior importance—since the principles that are first established within the propositional calculus are carried over into the remainder of logic. The propositional calculus is a set of rules that enables one to deduce the truth or falsehood of any compound proposition, given the truth value of all the simple propositions that enter into it. A logical truth table provides a simple algorithmic device for the making of such decisions. Logical, or material, implication is meaningful because it corresponds to a precise specification of entries in such a table (see Table 4).

The compound proposition *P implies Q (P → Q)* is equivalent to *Q or not-P*, and hence to *not-Q implies not-P*. It is asymmetrical, since the truth table for *P → Q* differs from that for *Q → P*. The validity of these relations is in no way dependent on the content or meaning of the simple *P* and *Q*. If *P* stands for the true sentence *Piaget is a psychologist* and *Q* stands for the true sentence *Piaget is a human being,* then *P implies Q* yields the true and plausible sentence *Piaget is a psychologist implies that Piaget is a human being.* But the logic is unchanged when the second sentence becomes *Piaget is Swiss* or *wine is intoxicating.* Moreover, if we substitute the false sentence *Piaget is French* for *P,* we note that *P → Q* is true whatever the truth value of *Q* (and of course whatever its content). Thus *Piaget is French* implies *Piaget is a psychologist* or *2 + 2 = 4* or *2 + 2 = 5* or any proposition whatever. Within logic, though not outside it, a proposition is meaningful if it is either true or false. In conformity with this requirement, any true proposition is held to imply every other true proposition, and any false proposition implies any proposition whatever, be it true or false.

The assertion that *Piaget is a psychologist implies that wine is intoxicating* is true makes the logician look silly. But looking silly is a small price to pay for a watertight set of rules of inference. In practice, such sentences do not occur, but the theory is adequate for all contingencies. Alternatives are less adequate for any purpose whatever.

Taken by itself, the propositional calculus is insufficient to enable the logician to provide a logical representation of the structure of reasoning as embodied in ordinary language. In order to do this, he requires a set of procedures for representing the internal structure of simple sentences, that is, the elements, predicates, and relations that figure in them. Through the introduction of two sorts of quantifiers, the universal and the existential, together with rules for their use, such a representation becomes possible, yielding first-order (and higher-

TABLE 4
Material Implication

P	Q	P → Q	Q → P
T	T	T	T
T	F	F	T
F	T	T	F
F	F	T	T

order) predicate logic. However, while new rules are necessary within this richer system (and a universal algorithmic procedure is lost), the rules of the propositional calculus continue to apply, including, of course, the principle of material implication.

The kind of logic under discussion is concerned solely with deduction or inference. It deals with the reduction of compound propositions to simple propositions but is not at all concerned with the origin of the simple propositions themselves. In conformity with this there is a total abstraction from content, and only the formal relations between elements are considered. The irreversibility of implications is central to formal logic, just as is the abstraction and the lack of concern for causal relations. By contrast, in most cases of scientific and everyday thinking, causal relations are of paramount importance. The problem is rarely one of deducing whether one compound proposition does or does not imply another by reducing both to simples. Much more often, it is one of establishing a frame of reference that will permit the formulation of fruitful hypotheses. Thus, outside the field of pure logic, there is a close relation between deduction and induction.

It follows that even the irreversibility of implication plays an inconspicuous part outside logic itself. Generally speaking, a causal hypotheses asserts the dependence of a comparatively rare phenomenon, q, on a set of comparatively rare antecedents, p. For instance, the presence of a disease or an abnormality is attributed to a metabolic disturbance (e.g., phenylketonuria) or a chromosomal abnormality (e.g., Down's syndrome), which is itself rare. It is interesting to note that in the two cases noted, which are quite typical, the relation between the syndrome and the cause is assumed to be symmetrical: where there is a specified chromosomal abnormality, the child exhibits the symptoms of mongolism and vice versa. Moreover, it makes sense to test the validity of the thesis by examining either chromosomal abnormalities or mongoloid children. It is much less sensible to examine all children, not-q for chromosomal abnormality, p, simply because this would falsify the implication in a logical sense. In practice, such a procedure would be very wasteful.

Such considerations (Chapman & Chapman, 1959) lead one to question the role of logical inference in thinking on theoretical grounds. As to the actual levels of success attained by children of various ages on tasks of this kind, there are seemingly four general conclusions:

1. Error rates are high in logical problems and tend to remain high at all ages. Some problems, the difficulty of which may not be obvious to the problem setter, lead to a preponderance of error even in otherwise intelligent adults.
2. The difficulty of these problems is greatly increased when the content is either abstract or obviously false (e.g., reasoning involving the premise *Elephants are smaller than mice*).

3. Despite what has been said, there is an improvement in the solution of logical problems over the age range with which we are concerned. However, IQ is generally a more important feature than chronological age.
4. The superiority of older and more intelligent subjects is often most apparent in their ability to overcome initial error.

Much of the evidence for these conclusions has been reviewed in a recent paper (Lunzer, 1973). The first part, the unsuspected difficulty of problems of pure logic, is well attested to by such studies as those of Sells (1936) and Chapman and Chapman (1959), in which university students obtained well under 50% of correct solutions in syllogistic problems. In both experiments, the content was abstract, premises being given in the form *All K are M,* etc. However, in a more recent series of studies, O'Brien has shown that throughout high-school age, children arrive at false conclusions when faced with problems of the form, "If the car is shiny, it is fast; the car is fast; therefore . . ." Moreover, at all ages from 9 to 17, about a third of the subjects consistently tackled these problems as if implication were reversible (O'Brien, Shapiro, & Reali, 1971). There was little improvement even when medical students were chosen as subjects (Shapiro & O'Brien, 1973), and there was no apparent improvement in college students who had followed a year's course in logic (O'Brien, 1973).

In a similar vein, Karplus and Karplus (1970) presented the following problem to groups of children at ages ranging from 11 to 18 and also to two groups of teachers:

> There are four islands (in the Pacific): Bird, Snail, Fish, and Bean. You can go by plane between Bean and Fish, but you can't go between Bird and Snail. . . . You can also go between Bean and Bird. Can you go (a) between Fish and Bird? or (b) between Bird and Snail?

While there was a distinct improvement with age in the ability to reply correctly *Yes* to (a) (via Bean), there was only moderate improvement in the percent of correct *No* responses to (b), only one group of teachers producing 13% (*sic*) such responses.

An even more striking rate of failure among intelligent adults was found by Wason in his four-card problem: Subjects are shown four cards, showing, respectively, a five, a two, a *B,* and a *U.* They are informed that all the cards bear a letter on one side and a number on the other. The question is to decide which of the four cards needs to be turned over to decide whether the statement *Every card with a vowel on one side has an even number on the other* is true.

The correct solution, the *U* and the five, was given by only 5% of these subjects, the majority replying either the *U* and the two or the *U* alone. The problem is fully discussed by Wason and Johnson-Laird (1972). A somewhat different interpretation can be made (Lunzer, 1973). Whichever the interpretation, the experiment will illustrate the deceptiveness of apparently simple problems of inference.

Turning to the second point, there are still three pieces of evidence to discuss. The first is the study of Roberge (Roberge & Paulus, 1971). These authors found constant and highly significant differences as between conditionals or syllogisms having an abstract content, those having a suggestive content (*If mice are larger than elephants*), and those having a plausible content (*If it is raining, Jane carries an umbrella*). The last category seems very much easier. In the area of mathematics, reference has already been made to Collis's demonstration of the greater difficulty of problems involving large numbers or algebraic symbols, and a similar conclusion was reached by Keats as early as 1955. Finally, in the four-card problem referred to in Wason and Shapiro (1971), it was found that the use of thematic material (*train, car, Leeds, and Manchester*, with the sentence *Whenever I go to Leeds, I go by train*) greatly reduced the difficulty. A similar result was found by Lunzer, Harrison, and Davey (1972), using a concrete content (*full lorry, empty lorry, red, and yellow*, with the sentence *Every red lorry is full of coal*). In both experiments, the problem is facilitated because the association between the terms involved—that is, destination and mode of transport or color of vehicle and load—is plausible and even imageable and not arbitrary, as in the original form used by Wason. In the face of this kind of evidence, one is led to deny Piaget's assertion: "In contrast with the preceding (concrete) level, the operational form is entirely dissassociated from thought content" (Inhelder & Piaget, 1958, p. 265).

As to the third point, despite the fact that many logical problems produce unexpected difficulties at all ages and at most levels of intelligence, there is evidence of age-linked improvement in most cases (e.g., Roberge & Paulus, 1971). Another inquiry by Lewis is described fully in Lunzer (1973). Subjects were required to make inferences about the tribe of a *native* encountered on *an island* on the basis of two pieces of written information and a picture, for example, *All the AMLAGS have long hair. None of the BRIDS have green eyes.* A picture shows a short-haired man with his back to the viewer, and the conclusion is that he cannot be an AMLAG, but he may or may not be a BRID. Mean scores at successive ages from 11 to 15 were 13.5, 14.7, 16.4, and 21.4. At 18, the mean was to 24.9, and university students achieved a mean of 34.5, the maximum score being 47. Since many of the less able children leave school before they reach the age of 18, while the university population in Britain is even more selective, one can safely conclude that over and above the age-related improvement, there is an IQ effect, the variance of which is possibly greater, at least over the ages with which we are concerned.

In the same paper (Lunzer, 1973), another study by Lewis is reported in which we were able to show a sequence of difficulty in logical problems, beginning with classifications and approaching implication. The material here consisted of an array of geometrical figures (squares, circles, triangles), some of which were striped or dotted, while others were plain. The first and easiest question was to decide whether *All the squares are striped,* etc. Such questions elicited a high rate of success even in 9-year-olds. The second type of question required the child to fill in gaps in the two sentence frames. *All the ——— are ——— and None of the ——— are ———.* The percentage of success at successive ages from 9 to 12 now fell to 61, 74, 86, and 75. The third question, which proved the most difficult in the series, required the child to draw in an extra figure that would falsify a true sentence. For instance, assuming that *All the squares are striped* is true, the student was required to draw a plain or dotted square. The corresponding percentage fell yet further, to 39, 58, 73, and 76. It should be noted that a 75% success rate at 12 is rare in true problems of inference. Thus, taken as a whole, this series of studies shows a gradation in problem difficulty as well as an age improvement.

Finally, at least three studies can be quoted that give substance to the fourth point. Two of them are extensions of the Wason four-card problem. In an earlier study (Lunzer, Harrison, & Davey, 1972), we had found that a single explanation of the problem did not in general suffice to enable sixth-formers and university students to solve analogous problems. Generally speaking, what they did was to extract an algorithm that was applicable only when the transfer situation was maximally similar to the original problem. But a more extensive study by Abbott yielded a very different picture. Abbott gave instructions in no less than seven variants of the four-card problem, and his posttest included a new problem based on the same principle, but very much more complex. At ages 7–8, the lengthy teaching program failed to produce an algorithm for even the simpler problems used in the pretest. At 10–11, there was considerable success with these problems but little with the new problem based on the supposedly well-established principle. However, at 13–14, there was evidence of considerable learning, even to the extent of good attempts at the new problem. Another study, again by Lewis, showed that sixth-formers (aged 16–18) could be led to a greater success level in the four-card problem (albeit only 37%) by means of a series of simpler problems designed to alert them to the solution strategy. Younger subjects were generally unsuccessful with some of the simpler problems themselves. Finally, a preliminary study by Lake used a conditional reasoning test based on those of O'Brien. Lake had two groups of subjects, one aged 15 and the other aged 19. The experiment was in three stages. First, the subjects were given the test of conditional reasoning. Next, they were shown a worked test by an imaginary student called A. Dunce, who had made the most common error in answer to each and every question, and they were asked to discover where he had gone wrong. Finally, they were given a retest with an alternative format. It turned out that the 19-year-olds were very much better than the 15-year-olds, especially in explaining Dunce's errors and in improving their scores on retest.

Concluding Comments

We have just seen that problems of logical inference are solved with increasing efficiency as the adolescent grows in cognitive competence. Moreover, even when initial performance remains at a relatively low level, there is an improvement in responsiveness to teaching and experience. Yet, even intelligent adults often appear strikingly inept when asked to tackle formal problems, that is, problems that require the use of inferential procedures on the basis of arbitrary associations between elements that carry no meaning for the subject. One is left to conclude that whatever it is that produces gains in scientific and everyday thinking also plays a major role in such gains as do appear in logical thinking as such. Nor will it have escaped the reader's attention that ALC (but not MIS) figures as prominently in the latter as it does in the former. But one is bound to question whether competence in logic can itself be the principal determinant in effective thinking.

It is instructive to look at the acquisition of grammatical competence, since the problems that it raises closely parallel our own. There are those researchers, such as B. F. Skinner, who maintain that the acquisition of grammar is simply a matter of generalization. One formulates new sentences, previously unheard, by substituting elements in old sentences that have been heard. But how does the child know what elements can be substituted where and with what effect? At the opposite extreme, there are those who maintain that the child is born with a language-analyzing device (LAD), which is a set of rules for making up a variety of grammars that he or she can then try out on the speech that he or she hears. The grammar that the child ends up with is simply what is left after he or she has discarded the rules that do not fit the speech heard. Since a grammar is itself a set of rules, it follows that an LAD is a set of rules for constructing other rules. Nevertheless, such a view is less implausible than it sounds, provided that one retains a number of provisos.

First, one should not assume that LAD is necessarily rich in elements or complex in structure. The system might work perfectly well if it consisted in the recognition that categories of lexical symbols correspond to categories of experience (things, actions, descriptions) and that it may be necessary to shift around not only individual elements but also chunks or strings of such elements in order to achieve an acceptable communication.

Second, the categories themselves (universals of language) are not necessarily restricted to language but are simply reflections of the categories of experience, that is, of the construction that makes up the sensorimotor world of the child.

Third, it should not be assumed that all new sentences are necessarily constructed on the basis of generative rules. It is altogether more probable that the sentence-frame system and the trial-rule system exist side by side. Once categories are recognized and legitimate sentence frames have become familiar, substitution is by far the most economical way of making up speech. This could be as true of transformationally complex frames (passives, conditionals, relative clauses, etc.) as of simple frames. Even the convoluted sentences so beloved of Piaget and of Piagetians can, if desired, be arrived at quite easily by the simple process of substituting whole strings instead of single words within quite simple frames.

Fourth, it follows that the generative mechanism plays a far more important role in the early formative period than it does in later life. There is indeed much evidence for the trial-and-error exploration of rules in young children, as in the acquisition of negation, or of tag questions, noted by Brown (1970). By contrast, the importance of transformational rules in adult language is questionable (Herriot, 1970).

Fifth, it should not be assumed that the rules for making rules are themselves available to consciousness. The child may use them, but he or she cannot reflect on them. Nor is there any evidence that the adult ever engages in such reflection, if the adult is no more than a competent speaker. The grammarian and the psychologist clearly do, but that is their trade.

Finally, we cannot take it for granted that reflection on the rules of grammar always results in more elegant or even more grammatical speech. Indeed, it has been repeatedly shown that time spent on teaching formal grammar of the classical style is time wasted (Thouless, 1969). It remains to be proved that the same is not true of grammar based on modern linguistics.

What of the role of logic in thinking? The case for the relevance of a protologic based on classification and seriation is very similar to the case for an LAD. Unlike LAD itself, there is evidence that at least the criteria of classifications do become accessible to reflection and it is this accessibility that underlies the development of concrete operativity. But are we to assume, with Piaget, that a later development enables the adolescent to reflect on the system as a whole and that it is such reflection that facilitates effective thinking?

It is at least equally possible that productive thinking is primarily analogic, that it is based, like language, on substitution within familiar frames, but that the frames as such are rarely, if ever, available in pure form. Thinking is a matter of anticipating moves to enable the thinker to arrive at a desired end, setting out from a starting point that is in some way unsatisfactory, within the constraints that are imposed by nature, by society, or simply by the rules of the game. To be successful, the thinker must be efficient and competent in surveying the field that is his or her starting point and in assessing the gap that he or she needs to fill to arrive at the end. The thinker must also be aware of the constraints that are operative as well as the constraints that are not. He or she must, too, have a stock of analogies from which to select trial strategies. There are also effective heuristics of some generality based on a combination of forward and backward thinking. Thus, one can make an imaginative anticipatory leap: if such and such were the case, would the problem be solved? Nor is it irrelevant to observe that all the procedures just outlined are especially relevant to structured problems, in which at least the goal is formulated for the subject. Much thinking has been described by Bartlett (1958) as thinking within closed systems, and he has stressed the importance of the further dimension entailed in what he has called *adventurous thinking*, in which the goal—and often the constraints—is largely unknown and must be clarified as the work progresses. It is this adventurous endeavor that others call *creative thinking*.

But all of this is part of the forward-looking, inductive aspect of thinking. If throughout this paper special attention has been paid to ALC and MIS, it is because both belong at least as much to the inductive process as they do to the deductive process.

If there is a moral to be drawn from what has been said, it is simply that it would be inadvisable to concentrate our energies either on the study of logical process or on the teaching of logic as an aid to effective thought. Much more research is needed to clarify the role of analogy: of the origin and availability of trial rules and of trial procedures in problem solving. Why is it that some children and some adults are more effective thinkers than others? It is certainly possible, as argued by McLaughlin (1963) and Halford (1968), that the capacity of the short-term memory store imposes a limit on the complexity of problems that a person can tackle. It is possible, too, that sheer speed of information processing constitutes an important component of intelligence (Jensen, 1970). But it is highly possible that over and above the constraints that are imposed by the limitations of brain power, the ineffective thinker, like the ineffective operator or the ineffective athlete, makes poor use of the equipment that he or she has. There is considerable evidence of the effectiveness of limited *thinking programs* in a laboratory context (Covington, 1970; Peel, 1971). But there is also scope for developing such programs on a wider scale, for experimenting with alternatives, and for implementing them within the educational system.

References

Bartlett, F. C. *Thinking: An experimental and social study.* London: Allen and Unwin, 1958.

Brown, R. *Psycholinguistics: Selected papers.* New York: Free Press, 1970.

Calvert, W. M. A short-term longitudinal study: The development of classificatory behaviour in children at the pre-operational and concrete operational stages. M.Ed. thesis, University of Birmingham, 1971.

Campbell, R. N., & Young, B. M. Some aspects of classificatory behaviour in pre-school children. Paper read to the Annual Congress of the British Psychological Society, Education Section, September 1968.

Chapman, L. J., & Chapman, J. P. Atmosphere effect re-examined. *Journal of Experimental Psychology,* 1959, *58,* 220–226.

Collis, K. A study of concrete and formal operations in school mathematics. Ph.D. thesis, University of Newcastle, New South Wales, 1972.

Covington, M. V. The cognitive curriculum: A process-oriented approach to education. In J. Hellmuth (Ed.), *Cognitive studies,* Vol. 1. New York: Brunner/Mazel, 1970, 491–502.

Dienes, Z. P. Six stages in the process of learning mathematics. Unpublished monograph, 1972.

Halford, G. S. An investigation of concept learning. Ph.D. thesis, University of Newcastle, New South Wales, 1968.

Herriot, P. *An introduction to the psychology of language.* London: Methuen, 1970.

Hill, R., Kapadia, R., Dadds, M., Lunzer, E. A., & Armitage, V. The child's conception of the structure of numbers. Interim report to the Social Sciences Research Council (unpublished manuscript), 1973.

Inhelder, B., & Piaget, J. *The growth of logical thinking.* New York: Basic Books, 1958.

Inhelder, B., & Piaget, J. *The early growth of logic in the child.* London: Routledge, 1964.

Jackson, S. The growth of logical thinking in normal and subnormal children. *British Journal of Educational Psychology,* 1965, *35,* 255–258.

Jensen, A. R. Hierarchical theories of mental ability. In W. B. Dockrell (Ed.), *On intelligence.* London: Methuen, 1970.

Karplus, E. F., & Karplus, R. Intellectual development beyond elementary school, I: Deductive logic. *School Science and Mathematics,* 1970, *70,* 398–406.

Karplus, R., & Peterson, R. W. Intellectual development beyond elementary school, II: Ratio, a survey. *School Science and Mathematics,* 1970, *70,* 813–820.

Keats, J. A. Formal and concrete thought processes. *Educational Testing Service Research Bull. No. 17,* Princeton, 1955.

Lovell, K. A follow-up study of Inhelder and Piaget's *The growth of logical thinking. British Journal of Psychology,* 1961, *52,* 143–153.

Lunzer, E. A. Problems of formal reasoning in test situations. In P. H. Mussen (Ed.), European research in cognitive development. *Monographs of the Society for Research in Child Development,* 1965, 30 (2, Whole No. 100), 19–46.

Lunzer, E. A. Formal reasoning. In E. A. Lunzer and J. F. Morris (Eds.), *Development in human learning.* New York: American Elsevier, 1968.

Lunzer, E. A. *On children's thinking* (University of Nottingham, Inaugural lecture). London: National Foundation for Educational Research, 1970.

Lunzer, E. A. The development of formal reasoning: Some recent experiments and their implications. In K. Frey and M. Lang (Eds.), *Cognitive processes and science instruction.* Baltimore: Williams and Wilkins, 1973.

Lunzer, E. A., Harrison, C., & Davey, M. The four-card problem and the generality of formal reasoning. *Quarterly Journal of Experimental Psychology,* 1972, *24,* 326–339.

Lunzer, E. A., & Pumfrey, P. D. Understanding proportionality. *Mathematics Teaching,* 1966, *34,* 7–12.

Matalon, A. Etude génétique de l'implication. In E. W. Beth, J. B. Grize, R. Martin, B. Matalon, A. Naess, and J. Piaget (Eds.), Implication, formalisation et logique naturelle. *Etudes d'épistémologie génétique,* 1962, *16,* 69–93. Paris: Presses Universitaires de France.

McLaughlin, G. H. Psycho-logic: A possible alternative to Piaget's formulation. *British Journal of Educational Psychology,* 1963, *33,* 61–67.

O'Brien, T. C. Logical thinking in college students. *Educational Studies in Mathematics,* 1973, *5,* 71–79.

O'Brien, T. C., Shapiro, B. J., & Reali, N. C. Logical thinking: Language and context. *Educational Studies in Mathematics,* 1971, *4,* 201–209.

Peel, E. A. A study of differences in the judgments of adolescent pupils. *British Journal of Educational Psychology,* 1966, *36,* 77–86.

Peel, E. A. A method for investigating children's understanding of certain logical connectives used in binary propositional thinking. *British Journal of Mathematical and Statistical Psychology*, 1967, *20*, 81–92.

Peel, E. A. *The nature of adolescent judgment*. London: Staples, 1971.

Piaget, J. *Les notions de mouvement et de vitesse chez l'enfant*. Paris: Presses Universitaires de France, 1946.

Piaget, J. Piaget's theory. In P. H. Mussen (Ed.), *Carmichael's manual of child psychology*, Vol. 1. New York: Wiley, 1970. Pp. 703–732.

Piaget, J., Inhelder, B., & Szeminska, A. *The child's conception of geometry*. London: Routledge, 1960.

Piaget, J., Grize, J. B., Szeminska, A., & Vinh Bang. Epistémologie et psychologie de la fonction. *Etudes d'épistémologie génétique*, 1968, *23*. Paris: Presses Universitaires de France.

Reichard, S., Schneider, M., & Rappaport, D. The development of concept formation in children. *American Journal of Orthopsychiatry*, 1944, *14*, 156–162.

Rhys, W. T. The development of logical thought in the adolescent with reference to the teaching of geography in the secondary school. M.Ed. thesis, University of Birmingham, 1964.

Roberge, J. J., & Paulus, D. H. Developmental patterns for children's class and conditional reasoning abilities. *Developmental Psychology*, 1971, *4*, 191–199.

Sells, S. B. The atmosphere effect: An experimental study of reasoning. *Archives of Psychology*, 1936, *29*, 3–72.

Shapiro, B. J., & O'Brien, T. C. Quasi-child logics. *Educational Studies in Mathematics*, 1973, *5*, 181–184.

Thouless, R. H. *Map of educational research*. London: National Foundation for Educational Research, 1969.

Wason, P. C., & Johnson-Laird, P. N. *Psychology of reasoning, structure, and content*. London: Batsford, 1972.

Wason, P. C., & Shapiro, D. Natural and contrived experience in a reasoning problem. *Quarterly Journal of Experimental Psychology*, 1971, *23*, 63–71.

White, S. A. Evidence for a hierarchical arrangement of learning processes. In L. P. Lipsitt & C. C. Spiker (Eds.), *Advances in child behavior development*, Vol. 2. New York: Academic Press, 1965. Pp. 187–220.

CHAPTER 6

The Future of Formal Thought Research: The Study of Analogy and Metaphor

Jeanette McCarthy Gallagher

Temple University
Philadelphia, Pennsylvania

> But I reckon I got to light out for the Territory ahead of the rest....
> —Mark Twain, *Huckleberry Finn*

It is time to move research based upon Piaget's stage of formal thought into new territory. Recent critics of this stage point out weaknesses in various aspects of the combinatorial system and the four-group (INRC) postulated as the structural foundation for a qualitatively different mode of thinking at the time of adolescence. Specifically, one camp in the old territory concentrates on the weaknesses in Piaget's use of propositional logic (for example, Brainerd, 1975; Bynum, Thomas, & Weitz, 1972; Ennis, 1975a,b). Some of the confusion in this area may be attributed to misinterpretations of the aim of Piaget's structuralism: to study children and adolescents not so much as logicians, but as scientists who invent and construct their own understandings (Falmagne, 1975; Stone, 1976).

Quite a different critical approach is taken by Riegel and others (Buck-Morss, 1975; Riegel, 1973, 1975; Wozniak, 1975), who stress the culture-boundness of Piaget's theory. Thus, according to this important camp, Piaget's structural theory may be enriched by a dialectical consideration of the cultural–historical activities within the society of the developing individual.

It is not the intent to review here all the critics of Piaget's stage of formal

77

thought. Rather it is Gardner's (1973) criticism of Piaget's adolescent-as-scientist that is the focus of this paper:

> Formal operations may even at time serve to hinder artistic development, since the tendency to focus on underlying content, to abstract out meaning, to be sensitive to the explicit demands of a task, to proceed in a systematic and exhaustive manner, and above all, to translate problems and questions into logical-propositional terms may all militate against the sensitivity to detail and nuance and the faithfulness to the particular properties of object and medium that are vital for the artist. (p. 308)

In support of Gardner's criticism, it may be noted that applications of Piaget's theory, especially at the formal thought stage have been primarily in science and mathematics. Does this mean that Piaget's theory has little relevance for the understanding of artistic development? As the adolescent grows in the complexity of thinking at the formal thought stage, is a decline in artistic development to be expected? These serious questions lead to a consideration of the need to move formal thought research into new territory.

It is the purpose of this paper to propose two ideas in the hope they may help revitalize research on formal thought. First, it is proposed that the development of the child's and the adolescent's understanding of metaphor and analogy can be linked to Piaget's (1977a) newly emphasized system of correspondences. Related to this first proposal, the notion of correspondences can lead the researcher to a deeper understanding of the system of transformations manifested in research with the traditional tasks at the concrete and formal operational stages. Second, it is proposed that research in metaphor and analogy at the formal thought stage will stimulate a reevaluation of Piagetian theory as a rapprochement between science and the arts,* with results that can perhaps be used creatively by educators and psychologists.

The Meaning of Developmental Epistemology

Before we relate formal operations to the concept of correspondences, it is necessary to examine the meaning of Piaget's unique discipline; genetic (developmental) epistemology. Note that confusion can result from interpreting either of the terms *genetic* or *epistemology* in their traditional senses. *Developmental* is preferable to *genetic* because the latter is sometimes confused with maturational or inherited (*genes*) characteristics (see, for example, Munsinger, 1976). Similarly, epistemology as the study of knowing is to be understood from the controlled or empirical standpoint, that is, the methods of science. Thus, Piaget's area of study is not philosophy, nor does he use the methods of a philosopher.

For the past 50 years, Piaget's empirical study of the development of knowing has been guided by two hypotheses: (a) Knowledge comes from acting upon

---

Arts is used here in the sense of fine arts, including music, literature, etc.

objects and reflecting upon the resulting internalizations of the actions, rather than from merely perceiving the objects. In other words, understandings are structured through meaningful interactions with the environment, not only by verbal explanations or manipulations. (b) Certain actions are internalized mentally and are organized in a structural manner. Mental activity, in a Piagetian sense, is viewed as relational when each new understanding is connected logically in a more complex way to an earlier understanding. Therefore, in both thought and action, the growth mechanism in knowledge must be considered both *retrospective,* drawing upon previous sources for its elements, and *constructive,* inventing new relationships.

Thinking, then, viewed from a Piagetian perspective, is not divided into separate abilities because the individual person constructs or invents understandings through interactions. Consequently, the resulting understandings are richer than those that the environment supplied originally. As knowledge develops, the person is *contributing* to inputs from the environment, instead of permitting the environment to impose itself on the person (Piaget, 1971; 1974 a,b; 1975 a,b,c).

Perhaps a more sophisticated analysis will clarify Piaget's concepts of action and interactions. Piaget, although not always in agreement with the late E. W. Beth of the University of Amsterdam, shows high regard for his work. In their book (Beth & Piaget, 1966), Beth and Piaget reviewed the similarities and differences among the disciplines of logic, psychology, and epistemology. In one important section (pp. 149–153), Piaget summarized what he considers the study of developmental epistemology, using as a base three systems of knowledge. This is a modified outline of the three systems of knowledge summarized by Piaget and the three kinds of relations existing among the systems.

1. *System S:* activities of the subject (subjective or objective reality) that are partially autonomous; that is, psychological knowledge of the subject, by means of experiments, may exist apart from Systems F and E.
2. *System F:* properties (forms and the like) of the object; logic and mathematics, with the system autonomous, since the object is reached by deductive constructions; no need for reference to S or E.
3. *System E:* types of existence or reality of object (for example, physical existence); not autonomous; no direct knowledge of E, always relative to S and conditioned by F.
(4–6.) The relations: *SF, SE,* and *FE.*

Piaget (Beth & Piaget, 1966) explained, "There is thus no direct science of E in the same sense as there is a science of F and a science of S, but only the possibility of an indirect interpretation, connected with the relations, *SE, FE* and consequently *SF.* This is why we propose to call problems relative to the relations *SF, SE, FE* and system E, epistemological" (p. 150). Developmental epistemology is, then, by definition an *interaction* discipline.

Such a schema clarifies why developmental epistemology, at the level of adolescence (and all levels), is not the study of cognitive adolescent psychology, nor the study of the adolescent solving problems in logic, and not even *the study of an adolescent as a scientist,* working for answers in the high-school chemistry laboratory. Logic, the domain of system F, may exist independently of S, and no problem in S is a problem in F. Solutions for problems in S are attained by the competence reached by S (assimilation–accommodation paradigm). Likewise, whatever is asserted in E (the properties of objects) depends upon the assertions in S. The most important rule, *the synthetic rule,* states: "The assertions in S cannot determine the system E without a reference to F, nor can the assertions in F determine it without a reference to S" (Beth & Piaget, 1966, p. 152).

The synthetic rule is familiar to Piagetian scholars: the level of cognitive development (interaction of Systems S and F) controls learning experiences gained from awareness of experiences with objects (System E). In more recent formulations of the model of equilibration or self-regulating mechanisms, the objects themselves may set up resistances, so that understanding characteristics of objects may be a very gradual phenomenon with progressive equilibrations, disequilibriums, and reequilibriums. This is the case in many experiments on the understanding of causality (Piaget, 1971; 1974c; 1975a).

Until recently, Piaget's emphasis in studying the development of knowing was on systems of transformations; that is, to know is to transform. Piaget stressed the importance of transformations at all stages of the child's progression in logicomathematical knowledge. When infralogical areas were studied, such as causality, chance, and probability, the operational structures resulting from the systems of transformations always were shown to interplay and to dominate gradually new understandings. For example, Piaget and Inhelder (1975), in discussing the understanding of probability as a synthesis of chance and deductive operations, stated, "Our present problem is . . . to understand how these operations, once they have been acquired, react on chance, that is, how the subject, in order to assimilate chance with a play of operations, will use the operations so as to understand relative determination which constitutes probability" (p. 231).

Now, with the new emphasis upon correspondences as comparisons that may or may not exist with transformations (Piaget, 1975c; Papandropoulous, 1975), it seems necessary to extend System F (properties or forms of the object) to include rules that are not autonomous, that is, constraints to apply in areas like growth in artistic development. In traditional Piagetian theory, System F represents deductive knowledge, reflecting the autonomy of logic. A simplistic solution seems to be to reorder Systems S, F, and E and their interrelations so that System F includes inductive knowledge. However, the operational structures impose themselves upon inductive processes in such abilities as understanding probability. A strict dichotomy of deductive versus inductive reasoning does not exist in Piagetian theory. Furthermore, such developments as growth in music appreciation seem sterile in an inductive framework.

Piaget's System of Correspondences

What seems a profitable extension of Piagetian theory is to insert growth in artistic knowledge into the system of correspondences. For what is growth in music, art, or literature appreciation and expression but development in the search for comparisons or resemblances? Even across subareas of aesthetics, appreciation develops when, for example, architecture is viewed as symphony in stone or a period's literature is enriched by the study of its music.

A nonautonomous sub-System F (properties of the object) is needed. In creative expression, the subject's activities and the type of the object's existence may alter the object's form. However, System F, the rule system, may not be eliminated. For in the arts, the medium may establish its own constraints. Not all materials are amenable to fine sculpture, nor is each musical instrument capable of a wide range of tone. As the subject interacts with artistic media, the person learns the constraints of that medium and limits the extent of self-expression in that medium.

Gardner's emphasis that formal operations hinder artistic development may be interpreted erroneously as meaning that there are no constraints or *logical* procedures in the broad sense when a person interacts creatively with media. However, each historical age, rightly or wrongly, has established rules for judging the art or music of its period. Innovative artists of each century break from the constraints of the time. However, the study of art history shows that such breaks with tradition have been a logical step from preceding eras.

Before investigating analogy and metaphor in the context of formal thought research, the importance of the system of correspondences in Piaget's theory needs reemphasis. Simple examples of correspondences (or morphisms in mathematics) are the places set at table for each invited guest or a test mark for each student. The relationship formed is called a *mapping*. In the familiar one-to-one correspondence—that is, isomorphism—each element of the first or original set has one, and only one, corresponding element from the second or image set (for further examples, see Dienes, 1971; Dienes & Jeeves, 1970; Skemp, 1971).

One-to-one correspondence is basic to an understanding of the number concept (Piaget, 1952). Only recently, however, Piaget's emphasis has shifted to the importance of making correspondences or comparisons before, or in relation with, making transformations (Piaget, 1975c). For example, a new understanding of the conservation of matter is realized when what is added in one place is said to *correspond* to what is removed from another place. When a ball is rolled into a sausage, the child must understand a displacement, a moving of parts, through grasping the correspondence involved. A realization of the correspondence of what is lost (negative aspects) to what is gained (positive aspects) aids in the transformation; that is, the new knowledge can be assimilated into existing structures.

The example of the balancing of the positive and negative aspects of the conservation of quantity highlights a relationship between correspodences and transformations: how correspondences may set the stage for an understanding of the transformations involved. Another relationship between correspondences and transformations is found when they assist each other to develop mutually. For example, in an experiment by Kamii and Parrat-Dayan (1974), children were asked to determine what actions would be necessary to lower one side of a scale. Younger children answered quite readily that adding (positive aspect) weight to either side would achieve the result. Not until early adolescence did children spontaneously add that taking off (negative aspect) weight from either side would also result in raising the other side. Thus, for the intended result of raising either side, the taking off of weight *corresponded* to the adding of weight. In both of these examples, problems involving clay and a scale, it is as if the equilibration or self-regulation that is necessary is special, for, as comparisons, correspondences have to *coordinate* the positive and negative aspects of a situation so that a deeper understanding of the transformation may be grasped (Piaget, 1977a).

Before elaborating on the study of analogy and metaphor, in relation to Piaget's new emphasis upon correspondences, let us review the meaning of formal thought for an understanding of how correspondences and transformations may develop mutually at this level.

The State of Formal Thought: A Look Behind and Ahead

Piaget's early writing on formal thought (Piaget, 1953; Inhelder & Piaget, 1955) reflected a struggle to integrate various features of the proposed stage. For example, Piaget (1953) stated, "The construction of propositional operations is not the only feature of this fourth period. The most interesting psychological problem raised at this level, is connected with the appearance of a new group of operations or 'operational schemata,' apparently unrelated to the logic of propositions, and whose real nature is not at first apparent" (pp. 20–21). Propositional operations or relations between propositions like implication (if... then) and disjunction continue to receive the greatest attention in formal thought research. In introductions to Piaget's theory, it is not uncommon to find formal thought defined almost exclusively as hypotheticodeductive thinking.

The new group of operations formulated and extended in the 1950s called *operational schemata* sounded like a catchall: combinatorial operations in general (combinations, permutations, aggregations), proportions, mechanical equilibrium, probabilities, correlations, and multiplicative compensations. Then, as now, the combinatorial system was emphasized as the logical basis for the propositional structures, whereas the INRC group was postulated as the logical basis for operational schemata like proportion and correlation. After probing the psychological meaning of these logical structures, Piaget (1953) concluded, "Operational schemata are thus to be thought of as actualized structures, implying the diverse possibilities implicit in the *structured whole,* that is to say, in form of equilibrium of the propositional operations" (p. 42).

The *structured whole* here is the famous INRC group, which now, as we shall see, has moved to the forefront of Piagetian thinking but not to the forefront of research efforts in the area of formal thought. In summary, the links connecting the structures of formal operations were not strong in those early formulations. Lunzer (1965) saw this weakness and set out to correct it.

Lunzer added a thoughtful analysis of the unity of the concrete-operational compared with the formal-operational stage. It appeared that the first group of problems associated with the propositional structures were much easier to solve and thus distinct from those associated with the INRC group. Lunzer (1965) concluded: "The psychological relation between the first group of problems (experimental manipulation of variables) and the second (problems of proportionality and reciprocity), however, is by no means clear" (p. 27). What is important to the current argument is that Lunzer returns again and again to the concept of proportion present at all levels in Piaget's interpretation of formal thought at the adolescent level.

In an effort to find the structural complexities of the reasoning process of formal thought, Lunzer devised an analogy test entitled *How Clearly Can You Think?* (For purposes of clarity, this test will be referred to as the Lunzer analogies test.) The test rationale was based on labeling concrete operations as first-order relations and formal operations as second-order relations. Lunzer argued that the essential feature of formal operations seemed to be second-order relations. By devising an instrument to explore this assumption, he bridged the two basic structures of formal operations, that of the combinatorial system leading to propositions, and the INRC group leading to proportions, reciprocities, and double reference systems.

The Lunzer analogies test contains 20 verbal analogies, 10 numerical proportions, and 10 numerical series problems. The analogies were constructed cleverly to ensure various levels of difficulty:

> COVER is to LID as BOX, INSTRUMENT, NAIL, PLIERS, HAMMER is to TOOL.
> LION is to LAIR as SET, BURROW, DOG is to RABBIT, KENNEL, FOX.
> MILK, CALF, LARGE is to COW as LAMB is to WOOL, SMALL, SHEEP.

Lunzer (1965) tied analogy structure to statement of proportionality:

Thus, an analogy of the form, *leather* is to *shoe* as *wool* is to *cardigan*, necessarily involves three relations: one between the first two terms, a second between the second pair of terms, and, finally, a third (of identity) between the first two relations. In point of fact, the logical structure of such a system qualitatively parallels that of a statement of quantities proportionality:

LEATHER:SHOE::WOOL:CARDIGAN as 3:4::15:20. (pp. 40–41)

Lunzer found that after age 10 there was a sharp rise in performance in numerical analogies and after 11 in the more difficult verbal analogies. He concluded that analogy solution was indeed a formal thought task requiring second-order relations. Lovell (1971) expanded Lunzer's theme, adding evidence from several studies to bolster the position that formal thinking requires *second-degree operations*.

Probably because of lack of norms and standardization, Lunzer's analogy test did not spark much research or theoretical interest. However, as a consequence of revision of Piaget's theory to include emphasis upon correspondences, Lunzer's basic idea may experience rebirth. Regardless, Lunzer should be credited with moving formal thought research in a new direction in a creative attempt at resynthesis and evaluation.

Recent Developments in the Stage of Formal Thought

Reworking the outline of the structures of formal thought comes from Piaget's latest research on causality and consequent restatement of the equilibration model (Piaget, 1972, 1974c, 1975a). Propositional reasoning with the concomitant ability to deal with hypotheses is considered based on a second-order operation, according to Piaget (1972): "It is this power of forming operations of operations which enables knowledge to transcend reality, and which by means of a combinatorial system makes available to it an infinite range of possibilities, while operations cease to be restricted, as are concrete operations, to step-by-step constructions" (p. 47). It follows that the new cognitive possibilities are extratemporal, not tied to *physical displacements* occurring in time as in the concrete-operational stage.

Instead of *operational schemata* as a second general structure, emphasis has shifted to the fundamental structure of the four-group or INRC group. Now the weak link between the two major structures is eliminated:

at the level of the propositional combinatorial system, every operation such as $p \supset q$ implies an inverse N, viz. $p.\bar{q}$, and a reciprocal R, viz. $\bar{p} \supset \bar{q} = q \supset p$, as well as a correlative C, viz. $\bar{p}.q$, which is the inverse of its reciprocal and is reached by permutation of the disjunctions and conjunctions in its normal form. This gives us a commutative group $NR = C: CR = N; CN = R$ and $NRC = I$, whose transformations

are third-order operations, since the operations combined are already second-order
ones. (Piaget, 1972, p. 48)

Clear examples of these transformations have also been given in Piaget and
Inhelder (1969, pp. 316–343). The INRC group is not a simple proportion
because propositions, like disjunctions and conjunctions, are raised to another
order when all the combinations of their inversions, negations, correlations, and
reciprocations are grouped. The INRC group is to be viewed as an operational
structure founded upon previously existing operations. Thus, this structure is far
more complex than the *A is to B as C is to D* model of simple proportion
emphasized by Lunzer. Problems of proportionality, however, have their basis in
the INRC group, as evidenced in problems associated with the balance beam (See
Gallagher & Noppe, 1976; Piaget & Inhelder, 1969).

In summary, then, the propositional system is woven logically by inversions and reciprocities into a far more complex system of the INRC group. What
happens now to Lunzer's formulation? Where are analogies placed in the complexity of adolescent thought?

The Understanding and Usefulness of Analogy as Correspondences or Comparisons

Dawis and Siojo (1972) reviewed the literature of analogical reasoning with
an emphasis on theories of intelligence. They claimed that little could be learned
from philosophers like Aristotle and Aquinas in investigations of the neglected
area of how persons arrive at analogies, that is, how individuals educe relations
and correlates. In a theoretical formulation, Esper (1973) identified the process
of understanding analogies with a stimulus–response association model. Such a
position has been refuted, however, by Achenbach (1969, 1970, 1975), who
demonstrated that a cognitive style of associative responding actually inhibits
analogical reasoning. Unfortunately, Achenbach's important findings are not
linked to a developmental theory, so it is difficult to determine stage sequences,
if any, as analogies increase in difficulty.

The rapid growth in cognitive-development research led to a review of the
philosophical roots of modern psychology (Riegel & Rosenwald, 1975). What
does the cognitive psychologist learn from the ancient, medieval, and modern
philosophical writings on analogy? The psychologist learns how one divides
analogies according to diversity, a term used by scholastic philosophers
(McInerny, 1961; Phillips, 1962; Chapman, 1975). The two main divisions are
analogy of *attribution* (air, food, and exercise, said to be *healthy*) and *analogy of
proportionality*. The latter is subdivided into *metaphorical analogy of proportionality* (the metaphor "The lion is king of beasts" in analogical form becomes:

lion:beast::king:subjects) and *analogy of proper proportionality,* the analogy *par excellence* in Greek usage (as in the scholastic argument: "The life principle in man is to his vital operations as the life principle in plants or animals is to their vital operations"; examples modified from Phillips, 1962).

At first glance, such metaphysical meanderings may seem verbal baggage to the modern psychologist carrying his pocket calculator. A closer analysis of the proposed division of analogy reveals that analogy by attribution corresponds in a qualitative, albeit irreversible, manner with Piaget's structure of classes. The metaphorical analogy of proportionality corresponds with Piaget's structure of relations. Finally, the analogy of proper proportionality is a qualitative, but simpler, correspondent to the INRC group. Piaget now emphasizes that correspondences and transformations are both necessary. In the case of correspondences, however, there is no inverse operation as in transformations. A simple example is the possible inversion of a mathematical proportion (early meaning of *analogy*) such as 2:4::6:12 to 4:2::12:6. However, such inversions are not always possible in a proportional analogy such as race:man::strain:bacteria (example from Wilner, 1964; it is possible that the easy analogies in Wilner's test may be reversible, associative pairings and not true analogies).

What is necessary, then, if we are to view analogies as correspondences is to understand that in both instances the commonalities must be discovered. Piaget (1975c) stressed that seeking resemblances leads to correspondences, not the seeking of differences: "in the case of correspondences, development means finding the closest similarities or the closest resemblances between any two things in spite of their differences" (p. 10). That is the process in the solving and using of analogies.

How useful are analogies? One philosopher of science stresses their widespread use: "Our scientific and linguistic worlds are a tissue of . . . analogical extensions. Although formally invalid, arguments from analogy may be quite useful, acceptable, and revealing or productive of truth" (Sacksteder, 1974, p. 252). It is difficult to force a distinction between the use of an analogy in a figurative manner—that is, to make a relationship more vivid—and the use of analogical inference. The limitations of the latter are associated with establishing causal connections (Copi, 1968).

Development in applications of probability theory and use of Bayesian statistics (Edwards, Lindman, & Savage, 1970; Stilson, 1966; Gottinger, 1974) make the use of analogical inferences more credible. In addition, investigations of classical Chinese philosophy, circa 500–200 B.C., reveal the power and richness of analogic reasoning. Cicoski (1975) stressed that even though propositional logic was developed in late Chou China, as it was in ancient Greece, Chinese philosophy at that time preferred analogic reasoning to validate its assertions (for another opinion see Liu, 1974). Furthermore, according to Cikoski, principles and techniques of modern logic can be used to substantiate the rigor of analogic reasoning.

More importantly, the use of analogies, particularly with metaphors, adds a richness and dimension to arguments and descriptions not possible with ordinary discourse or with propositional reasoning. For example, this quotation from Papert (1973) is like an extended analogy forcing the reader to take a fresh look at complexity and the theory of knowledge:

> Consider how people come to understand how birds fly. Certainly we observe birds, but mainly to recognize certain phenomena. Real understanding of *bird flight* came from understanding *flight;* not birds. Question: to what extent will understanding human intelligence come from understanding *intelligence* versus understanding humans? To push the point take this joke about birds: imagine that people in the last century decided that feathers are the organs of flight because it was discovered that birds cannot fly without feathers; so University Institutes for the study and measurement of feathers were established; just as were so many institutes for the study of neurons existing now. I *do not* suggest that neurologists are wasting their time . . . unless they think that their work is relevant to understanding how the m * * d (an Anglo-Saxon four letter word subject to wide-spread taboos in contemporary society) works, that is, how people think. In this case I say perhaps they are, perhaps they are not, but there is some reason to think they are wasting their time. (p. 3)

In this argument, Papert established a relationship and then argued the absurdity of the result of the proposed relationship.

In addition to adding richness and meaning to discourse, analogies in all the sciences are indispensable: "Even analysis, even the ability to plan experiments, even the ability to sort things out and pick them apart presupposes a good deal of structure, and that structure is characteristically an analogical one" (Oppenheimer, 1956, p. 134).

Although a controversy exists (see, for example, Achinstein, 1963; Braithwaite, 1962; Carloye, 1971) on the use and strength of analogue models in the sciences, there is common agreement that much development in scientific thinking is an outgrowth of the search for similarity of structure. The search for similarity in very different situations, as Oppenheimer (1956) emphasized, is the key usefulness of analogy in science. An important goal in science education, especially for the adolescent, is appreciation of scientific development resulting from explanations based upon analogies and not only on the logic of hypotheticodeductive methods. As Sacksteder (1974) noted, "Analogy is not a relatively poor use of logic; rather logic is a relatively good use of analogy" (p. 252).

Thus, the usefulness of analogy is widespread. Not only do arguments and descriptions with analogies enrich discourse and literature, but analogies also supply a powerful and creative framework for scientific exploration. For Piaget, the system of correspondences in which analogy is placed is not subordinated to the system of transformations. Both are needed and interact at various structural levels. We will return to this point after investigating the place of metaphor in formal thought.

The Understanding and Usefulness of Metaphors as Correspondences or Comparisons

Metaphors, defined as transfer of meaning, are close relatives of analogies (Ortony, 1975; Shibles, 1973). Some metaphors may have an analogical form and some extended analogies contain metaphors. However, the typical analogy takes the form *A is to B as C is to D*. On the other hand, a metaphor is a definition (not to be confused with its close relative, the simile, which uses *like*). Philosophers (see, for example, McInerny, 1961) have stressed the distinctions between analogies and metaphors based upon analyses of structure. Our purpose is to relate both forms of comparison to Piaget's system of correspondences without, of course, implying that the forms are the same or that the terms may be used interchangeably.

Making metaphors, the language of poetry, has been admired by scholars for centuries. Emig (1972), in an enlightening essay on children and metaphor, cited a passage from Aristotle's *Poetics:* "But the greatest thing by far is to be a master of metaphor. It is the one thing that cannot be learnt from others; and it is also a sign of genius since a good metaphor implies an intuitive perception of the similarity in dissimilars" (p. 164).

Recently, interest has heightened in the use of metaphors as teaching devices and as evidence of a special aspect of intellectual functioning. Ortony's (1975) title, *Why Metaphors Are Necessary and Not Just Nice,* is capsulized:

> Metaphors are necessary as a communicative device because they allow the transfer of coherent chunks of characteristics—perceptual, cognitive, emotional and experiential—from a vehicle which is known to a topic which is less so. In so doing they circumvent the problem of specifying one by one each of the often unnameable and innumerable characteristics; they avoid discretizing the perceived continuity of experience and are thus closer to experience and consequently more vivid and memorable. (p. 53)

The assimilation concept in Piagetian theory (Piaget, 1971) is evidenced here in the stress on qualitative restructuring of the known through the incorporation of the unknown to arrive at a new level of understanding.

Cohen (1974) has come closest to the thesis of this essay that the study of metaphors and analogies takes on new meaning within the context of Piaget's system of correspondences:

> Considered abstractly, a metaphor is a mapping of the elements of one set on to those of another. As such it enters into scientific thinking just as it does into archaic

myth-making. A map is a system, the elements of which are in correspondence with the mapped system. The correspondence may take a multitude of forms, which is another way of saying that a map must be isomorphic with the mapped system with respect to some of its features. And just as maps are graded with respect to the detail they display, so metaphors may be graded with the respect to the richness of the correspondence which they hit upon. (p. 419)

The *richness of correspondence* may be aligned with Piaget's (1975a,c) hierarchy of correspondences from the sensorimotor to the operational level when, in the latter case, there may be complex correspondences between disturbances and compensations.

Cohen's (1974) psychological explanation of how metaphor is generated through productive imagination emphasizes mental structuring that is richer than sensory inputs. As was noted, this is a key hypothesis of Piagetian theory on knowledge development. Furthermore, Cohen stated that even though the study of imagination "bristles with difficulties," the *chief mark* of a person's ability to be imaginative is in his constructing metaphors.

Epistemological analyses (Beardsley, 1962; Mackie, 1975) of structures of *interesting* metaphors reveal that in order to understand a metaphor, it is necessary to shift from the *central* meaning of one of the terms and apply its *marginal* meaning to the other term. For example, in the metaphor *Hours are leaves of life* (Billow, 1975), the central meaning of *leaves on a tree* gives way to the marginal meaning of *leaves floating or passing by* as the hours of time in our lives.

Therefore, metaphors are not of the simplistic form *A is B*—that is, identity—but they are complex comparisons.* The shift from central to marginal meaning involves tension elimination. The dissimilarities or tension between the terms (*hours* and *leaves*), although necessarily present, must be set aside so that the person may arrive at grounds for comparison (Ortony, 1975). This shift and tension elimination may be compared with an important characteristic of formal thought: the flexible motion among hypotheses before one settles upon a solution. Such flexibility is related to the concept of decentering on the adolescent level, necessary for both cognitive and social development (Inhelder & Piaget, 1958; Noppe & Gallagher, 1977). Lunzer (1973) coined a term, *acceptance of lack of closure,* for this formal thought ability of remaining flexible rather than becoming impulsive with a quick or easy solution. Lunzer labeled this acceptance of lack of closure as the hallmark of formal thought.

Thus, a survey of contemporary writings by epistemologists and psychologists on the structure and function of metaphors reveals several Piagetian themes. Such analyses support the notion that metaphor, as well as analogies, may be

---

*Note that *complex comparison* is used in recognition of Black's (1962) interaction view of metaphor, as opposed to a simple comparison or substitution view. The dynamics of Black's interaction view is analogous to the coordination of likenesses and differences noted earlier in Piaget's (1975a) expansion of the meaning of equilibration.

placed validly within the system of correspondences to interact with the system of transformation in the process of cognitive development.

•

Proposals for Research in the Development of the Understanding and Appreciation of Analogies and Metaphors

At the outset, it is clear that the understanding and use of analogies and metaphors begin well before adolescence (Gardner, 1973). However, evidence suggests that a shift in complexity in both construction and appreciation of analogies and metaphors begins at early adolescence (Billow, 1975; Gardner, 1975; Gardner, Kircher, Winner, & Perkins, 1975; Gardner & Winner, 1976; Lunzer, 1965; Orlando, 1971). The purpose of this section is to suggest research problems that may assist in the investigation of this shift and that may provide support for the proposed link between Piaget's systems of correspondences and transformations.

The first research area demanding attention is development of validated tests of analogies and metaphors. Careful item and structural analyses are necessary (Gallagher, 1976). The writings of epistemologists and psychologists provide scholarly advice on what are "good" metaphors (see for example, Beardsley, 1962; Cohen, 1974; Ortony, 1975; Stewart, 1973). The analogy tests of Lunzer (1965) and Achenbach (1969, 1970, 1975), although different in construction, have much merit for further research. Recently, Piaget (1977b), in collaboration with Montangero and Billeter, conducted a developmental study of the structural understanding of analogies to clarify the mechanism of reflexive abstraction. In a related study of structural analysis, Gallagher and Wright (1977) devised a scoring system for the written reasons children give in their completion of verbal analogies. It is hoped that such structural analyses will lead to the improvement of test items and consequent developmental studies.

The second research area, logically following from the first, is investigation of the development of understanding of *good* versus *bad* metaphors. For example, at what age level may we expect children to notice the failure in the metaphor *Oranges are the baseballs of the fruit-lover* (Ortony, 1975, p. 50). When vocabulary level is controlled, at what age would we expect children to realize that a literal description such as *Oranges are round* is much more succinct than a clumsy attempt at a poor figurative expression? If we agree with Beardsley's (1962) structural analyses of central versus marginal meaning in good metaphors, then an ability to make such a shift would be supported by the complex proportional system of the INRC group. Thus, it may be hypothesized that the appreciation and production of good metaphors as comparisons or correspondences show a definite increase in early adolescence.

Of course, the *American* question is: Is it possible to teach the appreciation and production of good metaphors? Winner (1975) taught 13 fifth-grade students differences in endings for metaphors (explicit metaphors or similes) with an emphasis upon Gardner's (1974) comparisons between sensory modalities and between psychological and physical domains. The results indicated that preadolescents could learn not only to prefer more appropriate endings but also to produce appropriate figurative endings. It would seem fruitful to expand this research, so that those who were most successful in the use and production of metaphors could be compared with those whose understanding of metaphor seems delayed. How would the successful versus the nonsuccessful subjects perform in Piagetian tasks structurally related to metaphors?

This research question leads to a consideration of a third, perhaps the most important, area of investigation. If correspondences as comparisons are as necessary as transformations in cognitive development (Piaget, 1975c), then it is logical to expect that children who are advanced in the appreciation and production of analogies and metaphors would also be advanced in the solution of Piagetian tasks requiring an understanding of transformations. An attempt (Billow, 1975) to answer this question was confounded by the selection of structurally inconsistent proportional metaphors from children's poetry and works on poetic imagery. In addition, the formal thought task of combinatorial reasoning used by Billow may have been more profitably supplemented by a task from the INRC group, such as the balance problem.

Formal thought research now has advanced beyond the *combinatorial–poker-chip* substage to the use of challenging and creative tasks like those devised by Siegler and Liebert (1975). In addition, careful studies of the traditional tasks first reported by Inhelder and Piaget (1958) validate the proposed transition from concrete to formal thinking (Kuhn & Angelev, 1975; Somerville, 1974). However, more validation studies of tasks based upon the INRC group, involving proportion, are needed. Then it will be possible to investigate interactions between correspondences (analogies and metaphors) and transformations necessary to understand structurally related problems based upon simple and complex proportions and double-reference systems.

A fourth area needing investigation is the relationship between understanding analogies and metaphor and conservation of volume. The late appearance of conservation of volume at preadolescence is caused, according to Piaget and Inhelder (1961), by the necessity of the coordination of three operative groupings that were previously separately formed: conservation of substance, weight, and volume. In addition, understanding volume involves a proportional structure because three dimensions, as well as a double relationship, are involved. Doubling one dimension necessitates the division of the product of the other two dimensions by one-half in order to maintain equality of proportion. It is at the second level or substage of concrete operations at the age of 9 or 10 that a gradually more mature understanding of spatial relations occurs. One needs such awareness of spatial relations to perform in a three-dimensional task such as volume conservation (Gallagher, Wright, & Noppe, 1975). It may be hypothesized that advanced performance in tasks requiring spatial relations, such as conservation of volume, would predict advanced performance on problems involving analogies and metaphors.

A final research area is the study of interrelationships of tasks requiring figurative language. What are the relationships between performance on tests of analogy and metaphor and on tests of appreciation and comprehension of humor at various levels of development? One study (Couturier, Mansfield, & Gallagher, 1975) of a large sample of eighth-grade students investigated the relationships among two tests of humor, two of creativity, and the Lunzer analogies test. Multiple-regression analyses revealed that the understanding of verbal humor in the form of wordplay and jokes is related to performance on the analogies test. The results may be interpreted by an *acceptance-of-lack-of-closure* explanation. A flexible movement among alternatives before settling upon a solution may be required for both understanding humor and solving analogies. More research is needed on the appreciation and production of various uses of figurative language and their relationship to abilities based upon formal-operational structures.

Conclusions Concerning the System of Correspondences as the Link between the Study of the Development of Scientific Thinking and Artistic Thinking

The proposal that formal thought research may be enriched by the study of analogies and metaphors within Piaget's system of correspondences provides answers to three criticisms. First, Gardner's (1973) claim that the *end state* of cognitive development in Piagetian theory is scientific thinking to the neglect of the study of artistic development needs reevaluation. Unfortunately, in Piaget's (1973) most comprehensive attempt to enunciate the pedagogical principles flowing from this cognitive theory, specific points were directed only to the teaching of science. However, in other sections of the work, especially in the argument pertaining to the right to education, Piaget highlighted the need for interdisciplinary approaches at all education levels. For example, in a section on the integration of specialization into wider aspects of culture, he wrote:

> The "general culture" which secondary education is to transmit to the student cannot, as is too often imagined, be restricted to an abstract formation (literary, scientific, or mixed) without roots in the structure and real life of the society as a whole, but must consolidate the different practical, technical, scientific, and artistic aspects of social intercourse into a more organic whole. (p. 70)

Science and mathematics are Piaget's specialties. Because he does not write about teaching art, music, and literature does not mean such cultural areas are unimportant. If the shift in Piagetian theory continues to that of studying the interaction of correspondences and transformations, then we can expect an integration of the appreciation and understanding of all the arts into the mushrooming research in cognitive development in general.

The second area of criticism noted was the interpretation of the formal thought stage as the *end* of growth in cognitive structures. More bluntly stated, after we swing our pendulums, mix our chemicals, and play a little combinatorial poker, if, indeed these are done in the culture under consideration, then the top of the hill is reached and we brace for the aging process! This quotation suggests an approach to formal thought as a *downhill* or even a static-plateau phenomenon, that is, waiting to go *downhill:*

> Very little theoretical attention has been paid to the question of further cognitive evolution in adulthood. Piaget, himself, has indicated that the adult years are not a time of meaningful cognitive change. Piaget and Inhelder (1969, pp. 152–153), state: "Finally, after the age of 11 or 12, nascent formal thought restructures the concrete operations by subordinating them to new structures whose development will continue throughout adolescence and all of later life." In other words, these theoreticians conclude that the stage of formal operations, theorized to be mastered during adolescence, is maintained throughout the remainder of the life-span. (Papalie & Bielby, 1974, pp. 424–425)

The point overlooked in the passage is that the structures proposed by Piaget and Inhelder at all development stages are dynamic, not static (Gallagher, 1977). Growth in richness of use of figurative language—for example, analogy and metaphor as stressed here—may add to both scientific and artistic thinking.

Beth and Piaget (1966) elaborated on the same theme: "From the genetic viewpoint, mental constructions are never complete and the fact that they remain *open* leads us to consider any construction as capable of extending into later constructions" (p. 161). What is needed is a careful look at this open or growth phenomenon in all discipline areas.

An important research area receiving recent attention is the study of cognitive ability in middle and old age (see reviews by Papalia & Bielby, 1974; Hooper & Sheehan, 1977). Concern, however, has not centered upon growth in complexity of cognitive structures during late adolescence and young adulthood before middle age. If a structural theory is by definition a dynamic one, then such concepts as growth in complexity, broadening the ability to make comparisons, and building analytic skills—often associated with the maturation of adult thinking—need operational definitions and research methodology. Although not all-inconclusive, the analysis of the structures of analogy and metaphor, plus the research proposals in this essay, may be the incentive needed for answers to a stagnation model of formal thought.

Finally, the response to the criticism of the weakness in formal thought research in general is a proposal to add another stage beyond formal thought. It is difficult to comprehend how such a solution adds much to an already confused research area. If we are to build on an existing stage, it would seem that the foundation must be firm. Riegel's (1973) description of a final stage of dialectic operations does not include the newer revisions and expansions of Piaget's (1971, 1975a; Gallagher & Reid, in preparation) theory, which clearly includes a dialectic interpretation between and within stages (Youniss, 1974). The fifth stage of problem finding proposed by Arlin (1975) is interesting in its own right outside of a Piagetian framework. Problem finding, emphasized by Arlin, is really an aspect of invention or construction central to Piaget's theory (Beth & Piaget, 1966; Peill, 1975; Piaget, 1973). Thus, each of the Piagetian stages is one of problem finding; to name a fifth stage adds no icing to the cake, let alone spice.

In conclusion, formal thought research needs revitalization. Its end state may include the development of all areas of knowledge. The incorporation of the study of analogy and metaphor into the system of correspondences that interact with the system of transformations gives a new unity to Piagetian theory. The developing adolescent becomes not the logician, nor the scientist, but the inventor, the constructor of his own knowledge on all levels. When the child was small, the mother may have read the story of Huckleberry Finn. The child incorporated the story of the boy and a mighty river into a limited framework.

As the child grew, Mark Twain's theme of everlasting concern with justice was appreciated even more (Trilling, 1962). Later, the adult grasps the metaphor that T. S. Eliot found intertwined throughout *Huckleberry Finn:* "I do not know much about gods; but I think that the river is a strong brown god." In later adulthood and old age, the story takes on new meaning because this person has lived many years and has perhaps a cruel realization of the money god who stands against the river god—a constant theme of conflict and greed in the story. A quotation from Trilling's introduction to *Huckleberry Finn* is a summary of all that this essay has attempted to convey:

> Certainly one element in the greatness of *Huckleberry Finn*—as also in the lesser greatness of *Tom Sawyer*—is that it succeeds first as a boy's book. One can read it at 10 and then annually ever after, and each year find it as fresh as the year before, that it has changed only in becoming somewhat larger. To read it young is like planting a tree young—each year adds a new growth-ring of meaning, and the book is as little likely as the tree to become dull. So, we may imagine, an Athenian boy grew up together with the *Odyssey*. There are few other books which we can know so young and love so long. (p. 502)

And so we return full circle to Huck Finn and strike out with him toward a new territory ahead of the rest.

ACKNOWLEDGMENT

This chapter was prepared with the support of a study leave from Temple University, Philadelphia. The author acknowledges suggestions for changes of earlier drafts from Dr. Howard Gardner, Dr. Mary Ann Yodelis, Illene Noppe, and Julian Weitzenfeld.

References

Achenbach, T. M. Cue learning, associative responding, and school performance in children. *Developmental Psychology*, 1969, *1*, 717–725.

Achenbach, T. M. The Children's Associative Responding Test: A possible alternative to group IQ tests. *Journal of Educational Psychology*, 1970, *61*, 340–348.

Achenbach, T. M. A longitudinal study of relations between associative responding, IQ changes, and school performance from grades 3 to 12. *Developmental Psychology*, 1975, *11*, 653–654.

Achinstein, P. Models, analogies, and theories. *Philosophy of Science*, 1963, *31*, 328–350.

Arlin, P. K. Cognitive development in adulthood: A fifth stage? *Developmental Psychology*, 1975, *11*, 602–606.

Beardsley, M. C. The metaphorical twist. *Philosophy and Phenomenological Research*, 1962, *22*, 293–307.

Beth, E. W., & Piaget, J. *Mathematical epistemology and psychology.* Dordrecht–Holland: D. Reidel, 1966.

Billow, R. M. A cognitive developmental study of metaphor comprehension. *Developmental Psychology*, 1975, *11*, 415–423.

Black, M. *Models and metaphors.* Ithaca, N.Y.: Cornell University Press, 1962.

Brainerd, C. J. On the validity of propositional logic as a model for adolescent intelligence. Paper presented as part of the symposium "New Perspectives on Formal Operations Reasoning," Society for Research in Child Development, Denver, April 1975.

Braithwaite, R. B. Models in the empirical sciences. In E. Nagel, P. Suppes, & A. Tarski (Eds.), *Logic, methodology and philosophy of science.* Calif.: Stanford University Press, 1962.

Buck-Morss, S. Socio-economic bias in Piaget's theory and its implications for cross-cultural studies. *Human Development*, 1975, *18*, 35–49.

Bynum, T. W., Thomas, J. A., & Weitz, L. J. Truth-functional logic in formal operational thinking: Inhelder and Piaget's evidence. *Developmental Psychology*, 1972, *7*, 129–132.

Carloye, J. C. An interpretation of scientific models involving analogies. *Philosophy of Science*, 1971, *38*, 562–569.

Chapman, T. Analogy. *The Thomist*, 1975, *39*, 127–135.

Cicoski, J. S. On standards of analogic reasoning in the late Chou. *Journal of Chinese Philosophy*, 1975, *2*, 325–357.

Cohen, J. Reflections on the structure of mind. *Scientia*, 1974, *109*, 403–425.

Copi, I. M. *Introduction to logic.* London: Macmillan, 1968.

Couturier, L., Mansfield, R., & Gallagher, J. M. Humor, creativity and formal operations in eighth-grade students. Paper presented at the Fifth Annual Symposium of the Jean Piaget Society, Philadelphia, June 1975.

Dawis, R. V., & Siojo, L. T. Analogical reasoning: A review of the literature. ERIC Document Service (ED 077 947).

Dienes, Z. P. *The elements of mathematics.* New York: Herder & Herder, 1971.

Dienes, Z. P., & Jeeves, M. A. *The effects of structural relations on transfer*. London: Hutchinson Educational, Ltd., 1970.

Edwards, W. H., Lindman, H., & Savage, L. J. Bayesian statistical inference for psychological research. *Psychological Review*, 1970, 77, 193–242.

Emig, J. Children and metaphor. *Research in the Teaching of English*, 1972, 6, 163–175.

Ennis, R. H. An alternative to Piaget's conceptualization of logical competence. Paper presented at the meeting of the Society for Research in Child Development, Denver, 1975. (a)

Ennis, R. H. Children's ability to handle Piaget's propositional logic: A conceptual critique. *Review of Educational Research*, 1975, 45, 1–41. (b)

Esper, E. A. *Analogy and association in linguistics and psychology*. Athens: University of Georgia Press, 1973.

Falmagne, R. J. *Reasoning: Representation and process*. Hillsdale, N. J.: Lawrence Erlbaum, 1975.

Gallagher, J. M. Piaget's developmental epistemology and analogy: A return to philosophical roots. Paper presented at the Annual Meeting of the American Psychological Association, Washington, September 1976.

Gallagher, J. M. Piaget's concept of equilibration: Biological, logical, and cybernetic roots. In M. Appel & L. Goldberg (Eds.), *Topics of cognitive development*, Vol. 1. New York: Plenum, 1977.

Gallagher, J. M., & Noppe, I. C. Cognitive development and learning in the adolescent. In J. Adams (Ed.), *Understanding adolescence* (3d ed.). New York: Allyn & Bacon, 1976.

Gallagher, J. M., & Reid, D. K. *Piaget and Inhelder's learning theory*. Belmont, Calif.: Brooks/ Cole, in preparation.

Gallagher, J. M., Wright, R. J., & Noppe, L. Piagetian assessments and concept attainment: Educational implications. In G. Lubin *et al.* (Eds.), *Piagetian theory and the helping professions*. Los Angeles: University of Southern California, 1975.

Gallagher, J. M., & Wright, R. J. Children's solution of verbal analogies: Extension of Piaget's concept of reflexive abstraction. Paper presented in the symposium "Thinking with the left hand: Children's understanding of analogy and metaphor." (Howard Gardner, Chair), Society for Research in Child Development, New Orleans, 1977.

Gardner, H. *The arts and human development*. New York: Wiley Interscience, 1973.

Gardner, H. Metaphors and modalities: How children project polar adjectives onto diverse domains. *Child Development*, 1974, 45, 84–91.

Gardner, H. Children's metaphoric productions and preferences. Paper presented at the Society for Research in Child Development Meeting, Denver, April 1975.

Gardner, H., Kircher, M., Winner, E., & Perkins, D. Children's metaphoric productions and preferences. *Journal of Child Language*, 1975, 2, 125–140.

Gardner, H., & Winner, E. Symbolic competence: The roots of creativity. Paper presented at the Sixth Annual Meeting of the Jean Piaget Society, Philadelphia, June 1976.

Gottinger, H. W. Review of concepts and theories of probability. *Scientia*, 1974, 109, 85–110.

Hooper, F. H., & Sheehan, N. W. Logical concept attainment during the aging years: Issues in the neo-Piagetian research literature. In W. Overton & J. M. Gallagher (Eds.), *Knowledge and development*, I: *Advances in research and theory*. New York: Plenum, 1977.

Inhelder, B., & Piaget, J. *De la logique de l'enfant à la logique de l'adolescent*. Paris: Presses Universitaires de France, 1955.

Inhelder, B., & Piaget, J. *The growth of logical thinking from childhood to adolescence*. New York: Basic Books, 1958.

Kamii, C., & Parrat-Dayan, S. Les contradictions dans les coordinations d'observables (balance). In J. Piaget (Ed.), *Recherches sur la contradiction*, I: *Les différentes formes de la contradiction*. *Etudes d'épistémologie génétique*, XXXI, Paris: Presses Universitaires de France, 1974.

Kuhn, D., & Angelev, J. An experimental study of the development of formal operational thought. Paper presented at the Society for Research in Child Development Meeting, Denver, April 1975.

Liu, S. H. The use of analogy and symbolism in traditional Chinese philosophy. *Journal of Chinese Philosophy*, 1974, *1*, 313–338.

Lovell, K. Some problems associated with formal thought and its assessment. In D. R. Green, M. P. Ford, & G. B. Flanner (Eds.), *Measurement and Piaget*. New York: McGraw-Hill, 1971.

Lunzer, E. A. Problems of formal reasoning in test situations. In P. H. Mussen (Ed.), European research in cognitive development. *Monographs of the Society for Research in Child Development*, 1965, *30*, 19–46.

Lunzer, E. A. Formal reasoning: A reappraisal. Paper presented at the Third Annual Symposium of the Jean Piaget Society, Philadelphia, May 1973.

Mackie, A. The structure of aesthetically interesting metaphors. *American Philosophical Quarterly*, 1975, *12*, 41–44.

McInerny, R. M. *The logic of analogy*. The Hague: Martinus Nijhoff, 1961.

Munsinger, H. The genetics of epistemology: Are concrete operations inherited? Paper presented at the Sixth Annual Conference of Piagetian Theory and the Helping Professions, University Affiliated Program, University of Southern California, 1976.

Noppe, L., & Gallagher, J. M. Creativity and cognitive style: An integrationist approach. *Journal of Personality Assessment*, 1977, *41*, 85–90.

Oppenheimer, R. Analogy in science. *American Psychologist*, 1956, *11*, 127–135.

Orlando, J. E. The development of analogical reasoning ability in adolescent boys. Unpublished doctoral dissertation, University of Michigan, 1971.

Ortony, A. Why metaphors are necessary and not just nice. *Educational Theory*, 1975, *25*, 45–53.

Papalia, D. E., & Bielby, D. D. Cognitive functioning in middle and old age adults: A review of research based on Piaget's theory. *Human Development*, 1974, *17*, 414–423.

Papandropoulous, I. Correspondences: Experimental evidence. Paper presented at the Fifth Annual Symposium of the Jean Piaget Society, Philadelphia, June 1975.

Papert, S. Theory of knowledge and complexity. In G. J. Delenoort (Ed.), *Process models for psychology*. Rotterdam: Rotterdam University Press, 1973.

Peill, E. J. *Invention and discovery of reality*. New York: Wiley, 1975.

Phillips, R. P. *Modern Thomistic philosophy*, Vol. 2. Westminster, Md: Newman Press, 1962.

Piaget, J. *The child's conception of number*. London: Routledge, 1952.

Piaget, J. *Logic and psychology*. Manchester: Manchester University Press, 1953.

Piaget, J. *Biology and knowledge*. Chicago: University of Chicago Press, 1971.

Piaget, J. *The principles of genetic epistemology*. New York: Basic Books, 1972.

Piaget, J. *To understand is to invent*. New York: Grossman, 1973.

Piaget, J. *Adaptation vitale et psychologie de l'intelligence*. Paris: Hermann, 1974 (a)

Piaget, J. *La prise de conscience*. Paris: Presses Universitaires de France, 1974. (b)

Piaget, J. *Understanding causality*. New York: Norton, 1974. (c)

Piaget, J. *L'équilibration des structures cognitives: Problème central du développement*. Paris: Presses Universitaires de France, 1975. (a)

Piaget, J. From noise to order. *Urban Review*, 1975, *3*, 209–218. (b)

Piaget, J. On correspondences and morphisms. Paper presented at the Fifth Annual Symposium of the Jean Piaget Society, Philadelphia, June 1975. (Published in *Jean Piaget Society Newsletter*, Vol. 5, No. 3, Spring 1976, pp. 8–10.) (c)

Piaget, J. (avec Liambey, D., & Papandropoulous, I.). *Correspondances et transformations. Etudes d'épistémologies génétique*. Paris: Presses Universitaires de France, 1977. (a)

Piaget, J. (avec Montangero, J., & Billeter, J.). *Les correlats. L'abstraction réfléchissante*. Paris: Presses Universitaires de France, 1977. (b)

Piaget, J., & Inhelder, B. *Le développement des quantités physique chez l'enfant.* Neuchâtel: De-lachaux et Niestlé, 1961.

Piaget, J., & Inhelder, B. *The psychology of the child.* New York: Basic Books, 1969.

Piaget, J., & Inhelder, B. *The origin of the idea of chance in children.* New York: Norton, 1975.

Riegel, K. F. Dialectic operations: The final period of cognitive development. *Human Development,* 1973, *16,* 346–370.

Riegel, K. F. Toward a dialectical theory of development. *Human Development,* 1975, *18,* 50–64.

Riegel, K. F., & Rosenwald, G. C. (Eds.). *Structure and transformation: Developmental and historical aspects.* New York: Wiley-Interscience, 1975.

Sacksteder, W. The logic of analogy. *Philosophy and Rhetoric,* 1974, *7,* 234–252.

Shibles, W. Variété: L'originalité de Wittgenstein. *Revue Internationale Philosophie,* 1973, *27,* 526–534.

Siegler, R. S., & Liebert, R. M. Acquisition of formal scientific reasoning by 10- and 13-year-olds: Designing a factorial experiment. *Developmental Psychology,* 1975, *11,* 401–402.

Skemp, R. R. *The psychology of learning mathematics.* Baltimore: Penguin Books, 1971.

Somerville, S. C. The pendulum problem: Patterns of performance defining developmental stages. *British Journal of Educational Psychology,* 1974, *44,* 266–281.

Stewart, D. Metaphor, truth and definition. *Journal of Aesthetics and Art Criticism,* 1973, *32,* 213–225.

Stilson, D. W. *Probability and statistics in psychological research and theory.* San Francisco: Holden-Day, 1966.

Stone, J. Piaget's formal thought: A friendly critique. Paper presented at the Sixth Annual Symposium of the Jean Piaget Society, Philadelphia, June 1976.

Trilling, L. Introduction to *Huckleberry Finn.* In Mark Twain, *The Adventures of Huckleberry Finn.* New York: Rinehart Editions, 1948. Reprinted in H. Hill & W. Blair (Eds.), *The art of Huckleberry Finn.* San Francisco: Chandler, 1962.

Wilner, A. An experimental analysis of analogical reasoning. *Psychological Reports,* 1964, *15,* 479–494.

Winner, E. "And Pharaoh's heart hardened . . .": Children's sensitivity to figurative language. Paper presented at the Meeting of the Society for Research in Child Development, Denver, April 1975.

Wozniak, R. H. Dialecticism and structuralism: The philosophical foundation of Soviet psychology and Piagetian cognitive developmental theory. In K. F. Riegel & G. C. Rosenwald (Eds.), *Structure and transformation: Developmental and historical aspects.* New York: Wiley, 1975.

Youniss, J. Operations and everyday thinking. A commentary on "Dialectical operations." *Human Development,* 1974, *17,* 386–391.

CHAPTER 7

Symbol Manipulation Reexamined: An Approach to Bridging a Chasm

J. A. Easley, Jr.

University of Illinois, Urbana–Champaign Campus
Urbana, Illinois

Epistemologists have long sought a firm basis on which to found knowledge. People are *not* firm and mechanical data-processing systems, but quivering masses of sensitive protoplasm. To be sure, our tissues are mechanically integrated with a loosely jointed framework of bone, and they communicate with each other electrically through an exceedingly complex system of neurons, glial cells, and other channels. But as a consequence, we function like trigger-sensitive amplifiers of minute events of both internal and external origin, and we are subject to all manner of delusions and illusions. How can such systems produce, let alone contain, certain knowledge? The answer to this fundamental epistemological problem, from the point of view that dominates Western science and philosophy today, comes to this in brief: individually, man's claims to knowledge are to be mistrusted, but collectively, because of the syntactic and semantic properties of social codes called language, reliable, if not certain, knowledge is possible.

One should not overlook the exciting and important efforts to overthrow and replace this view, which certainly have lessened its acceptance among philosophers recently. The pioneering efforts of Kuhn (1962), Hanson (1958), and Polanyi (1958) paved the way for more recent efforts by Feyerabend (1970), Lakatos (1963–1964), and Bohm (1969) to construct a new philosophy of science and mathematics. However, a new consensus has not, as yet, emerged from the battlefield. Interestingly, much of the current philosophical discussion centers on problems arising from attempts to compare two fundamentally different ways of conceptualizing phenomena. This discussion is also an example of such problems, and so is the present paper.

For the logical or linguistically oriented empiricists and their followers, human languages provide the hope for a solution to this problem through the testing of knowledge claims at several different levels of abstraction. Hempel (1970) provided a recent summary of the logical empiricists' position. Throughout this discussion, the author uses the term *logical empiricist* to refer to psychologists, educators, and others who make assumptions, either tacit or explicit, that correspond to the general characterization given here. At the lowest level is the intersubjective replicability of public events: the sun rises every morning; when one lets go of an object it falls to the ground. At the next level of abstraction are explanatory models: the sun going around the earth; a heirarchy of natural positions for different types of matter; or even more contemporary models. Mathematical principles claim a somewhat higher level with a variety of theories about such abstract models as number systems and spaces (points, lines, and planes) with which to express the laws of the explanatory models. At the third level, we find all manner of formulas and theories about the concrete and abstract sets of entities at the second level. At the highest level, we find a collection of what are called *metalanguage theories*, systems of principles that govern the use of the object languages in the mathematical theories and model construction. Here we find not only systems of symbolic logic, which typically function to check the consistency of theories, or the logical validity of arguments and proofs by symbol manipulations, but also methods or strategies for empirical inference—for example, principles of statistical inference—which apply mathematical theories and models to test the correlations of events at the lowest level for departure from randomness.

In this view, then, there is an essential interaction between the free creation of conjectures or hypotheses on the one hand (an internal process variously considered random, methodical, or a creative mystery of the human spirit) and, on the other hand, the external rational reconstruction and mechanical checking of hypotheses or conjectures syntactically for consistency with each other and semantically for consistency with public events. Sometimes these opposing processes are identified as the *context of discovery* and the *context of demonstration*.

Piaget, however, following Darwin's evolutionary psychology (Ghiselin, 1973), accepts the knowledge man has developed as an expression of biological structures and processes. In discussions with Piaget in 1968, this author recalls several questions that Piaget expressed. These are paraphrased here. For Piaget the question is *not*, How do mathematics and logic help man acquire knowledge? but rather, How do the natural processes of thought observed in man explain the development of the magnificent edifices of mathematics and logic? A second question of Piaget's is, How can formal and abstract systems such as mathematics and logic, given their biological origins, have anything to contribute to the development of knowledge about the structure of atoms, or the size of the universe, matters that apparently lie outside the domain of raw experience and the survival of primitive man? Can epigenesis explain such a remarkable adaptation as logical and mathematical symbol manipulation?

For example, Piaget explains the origin of the conviction of the necessity of certain mathematical relations by an appeal to the general aspect of self-regulation at all levels of biological development (Piaget, 1971, pp. 321–329; 1972, p. 10). This explanation avoids the modern version of preformation found in transmission genetics, in which every biological aspect of an organism is considered to be derived from its genes. However, a clearer conception of what is meant might be obtained if we invoke the conceptions of developmental genetics or even of molecular genetics. Meanwhile, the best we can do to grasp this explanation is to employ a crude analogy. Conviction of the necessity of transitivity arises after many years of development, so we are not interested in the self-regulation of the zygote before any of the species characters have been formed. We might, however, take a function like breathing to be one connected with a more general aspect of self-regulation than, for instance, picking up a luscious pear and biting into it. So transitivity carries a greater conviction of both the necessity of doing an action, the greater difficulty in stopping it, and a greater conviction in the expected consequences of doing it. Analogously, if the conception of and belief in transitivity of a particular relation can be traced to some general self-regulation of the organism, it carries greater certainty than does a belief, for instance, that all crows are black, which presumably is formed more by external patterns. It would appear that if the child's conception of length depends on somewhat different action schemes than does his conception of weight, then, if he has a conviction of the transitivity of longer than, shorter than, lighter than, and heavier than, this conviction that having a greater or lesser quantity is necessarily a transitive relation arises from deeper regulations in the organism than the action schemes associated with those particular quantities. It is as though a quantity cannot now be conceived that is intransitive, no matter what action schemes generate it.

Piaget's program for developing a biological epistemology to answer these fundamental epistemological problems has been carried remarkably far in the work of the many experiments carried out with his collaborators in Geneva. Some major lines of human intellectual development have been carefully drawn and documented in a truly impressive array of experiments, ranging from the schemes of infancy that coordinate sensorimotor activity, through the rapid development of language, a perceptually dominated preoperational stage, and the period from 6 to 12 years of age, during which systems of concrete operations become competent in broader and broader areas, culminating only at about 13 years of age in the stage of formal operations. The key structure in the last stage appears to be the INRC group, which integrates into a dynamic unity the four basic operations that have been developing independently during the previous period.

Speaking of preoperational thought, Piaget and Inhelder (1958) say:

> On the dynamic side, these regulations [between perceptions and actions] take the form of the corrections and adjustments inherent in the child's action. These latter regulations foretell the advent of operational processes in orienting the child's actions toward reversibility. Although they do not result in complete compensations, such regulations do thrust a small wedge of potential transformations (i.e., elementary processes based on "possibilities" as distinct from "reality") into a type of cognition which is still almost completely bound to reality (either in the sense of external perceptual reality or in the sense of imagined actions). (pp. 247-248).

This may be expressed in the following way: dynamic coordinations anticipate the concrete operations (Identity, Reversibility, Negation, and Correlation), which in turn are integrated into the INRC group at the stage of formal operations.

It is most important to keep the dynamic process of Piaget's operations in mind, because the formal aspects of formal thought are easily assimilated into the logical empiricist's system, a process that robs them of the dynamic creative life processes that underlie them. One can find many other passages that make little or no sense to the logical empiricist, for whom operations are procedures or relations, but do make sense as references to the dynamic character of operations, conceived biologically. For example, "The equilibrium field of concrete operations is limited in the sense that, like any equilibrium, the characteristics of such operations are determined by the compensation of potential work (operations) compatible with the system links; however, these links are limited both by the form of the operations involved and by the actual content of the notions to which they are applied" (Inhelder & Piaget, 1958, p. 249). The reference to potential work is an analogy with physical chemistry, and the last part of the sentence clearly separates out the form of the operations and their content, which are the aspects most psychologists have attended to, the only aspects that can be assimilated into the logical empiricists' framework.

The potential for formal thought, which requires the clinical interview to demonstrate its existence (since tests may or may not invoke it), is also given a dynamical character in the following:

> From the point of view of physics, we know that a state of equilibrium is characterized by compensation between all of the potential modifications compatible with the links of the system. Even in experimental physics—i.e., in the science relating to reality in its most material aspect—the notion of possibility plays an essential positive role in the determination of the conditions of a state of equilibrium. To the extent that psychology feels the need to consider states of equilibrium as well, it is thus *a fortiori* indispensable to resort to the notion of possiblity expanded into the notion of "potential" actions or mental transformations (in the sense that the physicist uses when he speaks of potential acceleration or potential energy). (Inhelder & Piaget, 1958, p. 256)

When a physicist adopts the term *potential* to refer to *electromotive force* or *electrostatic tension,* he makes explicit its dynamic connotation, which can be overlooked in the static image of a stone resting on a table, whose potential acceleration or potential energy can be calculated without any feeling of dynamism. Similarly, Piaget's references to "a complete combinatorial system of hypotheses," "propositional logic," and the "INRC group of transformations" assimilate too easily to the relatively static, or at best procedural, conceptions of the logical empiricists and thus lose all feeling for their dynamical character, alluded to in the above quotation.

In much the same way as Felix Klein showed how transformation groups can generate geometries, from Euclid's to general topology, Piaget shows how the INRC group is capable of generating the 16 binary combinations of propositions in symbolic logic. The clearest formulation is to be found in Grize (1971), but Piaget (1952) has also provided a further expansion of this exponential series of sets of logical formulas. It also supports a complete combinatorial system for analyzing representations, and the hypotheticodeductive method with its all-but-one strategy. In Piaget's view, we are not required to believe that every person accepts logical or methodological principles as a guide, any more than that every logician or methodologist behaves in accordance with the principles that he makes explicit in his work. But Piaget's view does imply that such logical or methodological behavior can potentially emerge in any person who has reached the stage of formal operations, at least on an occasion or two and perhaps with a good deal of help, but without requiring training in the principles of logic or the rules of scientific method. Inhelder and Piaget (1958) remarked, "Only the operations actually at work in a given situation are for the moment 'real'; the others are merely potential" (p. 257). Furthermore, not only do the operations of Piaget's theory function to generate systems of logical syntax that can be used to test hypotheses or conjectures, but they function generatively in the context of discovery as well (Inhelder & Piaget, 1958, pp. 58, 250–251, and *passim*). They are adaptive, not only in the sense of providing general principles of symbol manipulation for evaluating whatever claims to knowledge emerge, but in the sense also that they provide a tendency to develop certain beliefs about the physical world, for example, the conservation of physical quantities such as volume. This conception of the internal, developmental operations appears to challenge seriously the logical empiricists' view accepted by most psychologists, and it is natural that Piaget's findings have in turn been challenged by them.

Shortly after Inhelder and Piaget's *The Growth of Logical Thinking* appeared in English translation (1958), Richard Anderson (1965) attempted to teach the all-but-one strategy to children who were well below the age at which formal operations were said to appear. That is, he taught them to change one variable at a time in certain kinds of concept-formation problems and to test whether manipulating each independent variable had any effect on the dependent variable. In situations in which the independent and dependent variables were clearly evident and there was an external memory available, children learned to solve conjunctive-concept puzzles by this mechanical procedure and could transfer their skill to new problem materials. Some of the tasks in *The Growth of Logical Thinking,* however, did not meet these conditions, and these children did not transfer the procedure to these tasks successfully. It is clear that Anderson conceived of this strategy as a rule for the manipulation of symbols (e.g., an external memory system) for familiar variables. In Inhelder and Piaget's examples and discussion, however, there is no such limitation on their conception of this strategy. Thus, we are entitled to conclude that they were describing a broader cognitive structure than the one that Anderson succeeded in developing in his subjects.

Within a decade after Inhelder and Piaget had announced that children "cannot handle propositional logic" until they reach the stage of formal operations, Shirley Hill (1961), O'Brien and Shapiro (1968), and Ennis, Finkelstein, Smith, and Wilson (1969) gave younger children tests of logic and found that they did substantially better than chance would allow. The children were presented with sets of premises and asked to choose, among several alternatives, the one that was a valid inference from the premises (or in some cases the one that was invalid). On the basis of their scores, it was concluded by Hill that the children could handle propositional logic somewhat better than guessing, though not perfectly. Relatively few adults can make a perfect score on such a test. O'Brien and Shapiro and Ennis *et al.* concluded that this ability was largely limited to one category of problems. Knifong (1972, 1974), however, pointed out that many of the correct answers in these tests were the only choice available consistent with what Piaget had called *transductive logic,* characteristic of the 5- to 7-year-old's thinking, and others were consistent with Grouping I, a structure available to most children above 7 years of age. "Transduction is a form of reasoning which proceeds from particular to particular without generalization and without logical rigour" (Piaget, 1959, p. 186). So the test results described above do no damage to Piaget's theory.

It appears that a clear discussion of the question whether formal thought could be characterized in linguistic terms (Inhelder & Piaget, 1958, p. 252) has been ignored by those persons who have so interpreted it or even identified it with the logical syntax of language. We read that "it is possible to get correct reasoning about simple propositions as early as the seven–eight year level, provided that these propositions correspond to sufficiently concrete representations." This correspondence is a factor that has not been strictly controlled in the studies under review. Anderson's identification of external memory comes closer than Ennis's suppositional versus factual test items (Ennis *et al.,* 1969, p. 56). The authors then went on to define propositional logic itself in a nonlinguistic way, when they said:

> in spite of appearances and current opinion, the essential characteristic of propositional logic is not that it is a verbal logic. First and foremost, it is a logic of all

possible combinations, whether these combinations arise in relation to experimental problems or purely verbal questions. Of course, combinations which go beyond a simple registration of data pre-suppose an inner verbal support; however, the real poser of propositional logic lies not in this support but rather in the combinatorial power which makes it possible for reality to be fed into the set of possible hypotheses compatible with the data. (p. 253)

This definition removes the entire basis of the criticism by Ennis *et al.* (1969), for that is explicitly and totally based on the ''Whorfian assumption that understanding of the concept of one-way implication is closely related to the use of the one-way interpretation of the word 'if' '' (p. 5).

Quite apart from the controversy described above, Joseph Hoffman (Easley, 1964b) found that 12-year-olds, in supplying conclusions to *modus ponens* items, showed a substantial difference in the two cases formed by reversing the order of premises. When a conditional statement was preceded by the statement of its antecedent, there were far fewer children who wrote its consequent than when the conditional statement preceded the statement of the antecedent. This shows that the basis for the response is something different from *modus ponens*. These and other experimenters have all interpreted logic mechanically, as a system of rules for symbol manipulation, a syntax of metalanguage rules governing inferences in the object language, not as an organizing system of dynamic cognitive structures.

In the early 1960s, Patrick Suppes developed a computer system at Stanford that checked proofs in symbolic logic as they were constructed, step by step, by the student (Suppes & Binford, 1965). In 1964, a similar system for proofs in algebra was developed on the PLATO system at Illinois by Easley, Gelder, and Golden (1968). With his system, Suppes successfully taught children below the age of formal operations to do proofs in mathematical logic. Since they also learned to translate English sentences into the form of symbolic logic, they would presumably have been able to make a mechanical application of the rules they had learned on the computer to solving logic problems like those on the tests described previously. Again, we see a purely mechanical conception of logic, but also a conception of learning that separates the context of discovery and the context of demonstration. Piaget's view of a generative logic would not only be consistent with Descartes's and Polya's conception of proof (1962), that ''every step follows intuitively from a previous step,'' but would also have to account for mistakes and false moves. Even the steps later rejected as invalid are also generated from previous steps by an intuitive process of some kind. Thus, it is the mechanical epistemology, but not Piaget's, that requires a sharp distinction between the two contexts.

Many other examples could be given that demonstate that the dominant response to Piaget's work has involved a retranslation of one or more of his key ideas into a form more compatible with the logical empiricist's point of view. For example, when Easley (1964a) explicated Piaget's experiment on relative motion (the snail on the board), he attempted to reduce the structure of the INRC group to a table of its operations, forgetting the dynamic character of the group implications described in Inhelder and Piaget's discussion of the formal-level child's response.

It is interesting to note that those comments, made on the closing day of the Berkeley conference (Ripple & Rockcastle, 1964) as a lengthy and unscheduled question to Piaget about whether young children who appear to understand relative motion have achieved the stage of formal operations, were prompted in part by the author's curiosity about his unhappiness with logical empiricism reflected in an incident that had occurred just a few days earlier. Meeting Piaget for the first time, and attempting to make serious conversation with him in halting French, the author mentioned an interest in epistemology and, when asked whose epistemology he found interesting, he mentioned the name of Rudolf Carnap. Piaget's face fell noticeably, but he recovered with a generous comment. This author did not forget his shock that he had erroneously thought Piaget's work compatible with Carnap's logical empiricism. So fascinated had this author been by the experiments themselves and by Piaget's logical and mathematical models of thought, that, like most American psychologists and educators, the author had assimilated what he had read of Piaget's writings to the logical empiricist's position that he held at that time and had ignored what would not so assimilate.

Although Inhelder and Piaget, in describing concrete and formal operations, often emphasize the mathematical and logical structures that characterize the newly emerging intellectual potential, they apparently do not forget the dynamic aspects of these operations. Thus, in explaining why the operations on weight lag several years behind operations of length, they wrote:

> This is because it is more difficult to order serially, to equalize, etc., objects whose properties are less easy to dissociate from one's own action, such as weight, than to apply the same operations to properties which can be objectified more readily, such as length. Thus, from the standpoint of content, the "potential transformations compatible with the system links" which determine the boundary line between real and possible operations are still more limited than is implied by the form of the operations involved. (Inhelder & Piaget, 1958, pp. 249–250)

Here is implied a reason for the delay of formal operations. It is not that the child cannot manage the forms earlier but that other cognitive processes, especially action schemes, are sometimes so powerful that they override the weaker operations on form. When, as in Anderson's experiment, strong action schemes are avoided by the choice of content (color, form, and position attributes), the all-but-one strategy can be mastered. It will not, however, transfer to the pendulum problem, in which strong action schemes (pushing, feeling the pull of the weight, etc.) dominate. It seems that one can then add that formal operations, as a stage, are a level of growth in which operations on form are strongly enough organized to be able to override action schemes and other competing structures.

This potential for overriding perceptions and actions linked tightly to the situation must then be the dynamical reason for what Inhelder and Piaget have described as the key procedural characteristic of formal thought, that is, the reversal of direction between *reality* and *possibility;* instead of the derivation of a rudimentary type of theory from the empirical data, as is true in concrete inferences, formal thought begins with a theoretical synthesis implying that certain relations are necessary and thus proceeds in the opposite direction (Inhelder & Piaget, 1958, p. 251). Note that the language of Inhelder and Piaget in describing this property of formal thought is completely consistent with the logical empiricist's conceptual system.

Many examples having to do with concrete operations also show that the interpretation of the findings of Inhelder and Piaget is commonly colored by logical empiricism. This raises the serious question of whether these two points of view can have any fruitful interaction. If they can, it must be more open and involve a more serious consideration of both points of view instead of each proponent's imposing his own view of logic and scientific method on the dialogue and thus distorting what the other has to say.

One first-order approach to the problem of bridging two radically different points of view is to establish an independence of the major categories of thought of each view from those of the other. There is a sense in which these two points of view are incommensurable and the chasm between them unbridgeable. If Kuhn is correct about the incommensurability of pre- and postrevolutionary scientific paradigms, Hempel's effort to connect them with bridging principles is doomed. Our efforts to bridge this chasm may ultimately fail for a similar reason; however, becoming aware of the chasm is a value gained that is to be preferred over the common tendency to identify the two sides. The grid in Figure 1 arrays the major categories of each view in orthogonal positions so that their interactions can be examined. A naive view identifies the two sets in one-to-one correspondence, considering, in effect, only the cells of the main diagonal. Concrete operations become object-language operations and formal operations become metalanguage operation on operation. The distortions of both views that result are serious, and they will not be entirely cured by a consideration of the other cells in the grid; but as a heuristic exercise, they may be useful.

We have already seen a number of phenomena that are candidates for one or more of the off-diagonal cells. For example, the all-but-one strategy that Anderson was able to teach young children is more mechanical in nature than Inhelder and Piaget's formal operations, but it may resemble concrete operations or preoperational processes. Since it functions in the context of solving concept-formation problems as a metalanguage operation on statements in the object language, it belongs in the top row and is therefore off the main diagonal. Similarly, the type of preoperational reasoning called *transductive logic* may

	1 SENSORIMOTOR SCHEMES	2 PREOPERATIONAL STRUCTURES	3 CONCRETE OPERATIONS	4 FORMAL OPERATIONS
1 METALANGUAGE PRINCIPLES OF INFERENCE		TRANSDUCTIVE LOGIC USED ⟶ IN LOGIC TESTS	ANDERSON'S LIMITED ALL-BUT-ONE STRATEGY	
2 OBJECT-LANGUAGE MATHEMATICAL OBJECTS				POLYA'S PLAUSIBLE REASONING LAKATO'S PROOFS AND REFUTATIONS
3 MODELS OF SCIENTIFIC AND MATHEMATICAL OBJECTS				INRC GROUP (BALANCE, SHADOWS, ETC.)
4 OBSERVATIONS OF EVENTS, REPLICATIONS, SEQUENCES, ETC.				INHELDER AND PIAGET'S ALL-BUT-ONE STRATEGY (PENDULUM, FLEXIBLE BARS, ETC.)

FIGURE 1

show itself, at least in the case of logic tests, as an operation on the object language. It can therefore appear in the second cell of the top row. There may be no serious contenders for the top left cell—metalanguage sensorimotor processes—if we consider whole tasks. However, we should not overlook, perhaps, that there are sensorimotor coordinations involved in symbol manipulation at any level, for example, arranging the symbols in a line and reading them from left to right. A game like WFF'N PROOF (developed by Allen, 1965) probably involves all the cells of the top row except the one called "Formal operations," in which it might naively have been placed simply because manipulating logical symbols is considered formal. In Piaget's view, it is the formation of a general system of representations for the formal aspects of a problem and using that representation to generate and control the testing of hypotheses that is called formal.

The idea suggested by the right-hand column of the grid that formal operations might involve any level of abstraction is a helpful one. The descriptions in *The Growth of Logical Thinking* seem to involve only the lowest two levels, that is, the subjects are operating on visual images of their experiences, certain replications, etc., or they are operating on models of the physical systems themselves. However, in mathematics, generating new conjectures and testing them in the manner described by Polya (1954) and Lakatos (1963–1964) is clearly formal operations within the middle two levels, both the mathematics theory level and the mathematical models level. To fill the top right cell, we need a kind of problem solving that generates theory at the metalanguage level, that is, metalanguage applied to metalanguage. Similarly, we expect to see the creative process working at every level.

Now, to fill in other cells of the grid is entirely possible, but we must go on to examine the limitations of this preliminary venture we have made toward bridging the chasm between the two points of view. One possible defect of the grid has surfaced, namely, the fact that only the context of demonstration is treated by the logical empiricist's view, whereas the two contexts are not separated in Piaget's view. Although Inhelder and Piaget have discussed these two functions as sequential, in the parts of interview protocols presented no clear separation is evident. It seems clear that the same cognitive structures are involved in both functions, so the apparent separation seems purely for purposes of discourse (Inhelder & Piaget, 1958, pp. 75–76, 157–158, 250–251). This lack of commensurability is present in every cell and has resulted in the attributing of generative processes to the vertical columns and the process of testing to the horizontal, a procedure that separates the two views more than they should be, according to Piaget's view. They should be allowed to interact in the testing process, as was barely suggested by the remarks about the upper-right-hand cell, where the two versions of "logic" and method intersect.

This is not the only alternative. Witz and Easley have considered others (Witz & Easley, 1972), and Witz has embarked on the monumental task of remapping Piaget's program from the ground up, that is, developing mathematically rigorous models of sensorimotor schemes for infant behavior and then adding to the system new, more powerful structures to simulate observed behavior in detail as the subject grows older (Witz & Easley, in press).

The point most neglected from Piaget's viewpoint, though it is implied in his fundamental questions discussed at the beginning of this paper, is the power of the notational systems used in mathematics. One cannot simply say that the mathematician writes down whatever comes into his head. He devises clever notational systems, in which the precise way of abbreviating and condensing is of the utmost importance. A good notational system aids enormously in the reasoning process, which means that it draws on natural or learned tendencies in symbol manipulation. It is interesting in this connection that Davis and Ginsberg (1971–1972) have undertaken to study the ways in which children use the notation of arithmetic. A study in progress by Erlwanger (1973) at Illinois has also convinced this author that the development of children's mathematical-symbol manipulation cannot be understood from the logical empiricist's point of view. The following remarks are merely intended to whet the appetite and to suggest how, within one of the other cells of the grid, a deeper synthesis of the two points of view is possible.

It would seem that it is a mistake to assume that statements of the form 2 + 2 = 4 or 1/2 + 1/2 = 1 or 15/5 = 3 have a semantic basis of meaning for the child in the number system. As Aristotle noted, not all familiar quantities are addable. Twin A is 2, and Twin B is 2, but how does bringing them together make four? One half of an apple plus one half of a pear does not make one of anything. Not all quantities are divisible either: 15 degrees Farenheit is pretty cold for Illinois winters, but what does it mean to divide that temperature by 5? Three what?—is what? When we already understand ages, halvings, and temperature, we use number language intelligibly in everyday conversation. But when children encounter number exercises in school, semantic limitations on number operations may not be experienced. The number–numeral distinction is rarely maintained, and some other things that may be called *numberals* are manipulated, more like sticks and stones, involving something like the structures of concrete operations. That is, adding two objects to a collection would be a concrete operation if it had an inverse and other specified properties of operations. Adding 2 and 4 to get 6 is an abstract operation (there is nothing concrete to do), but writing a 6 after the equals mark when one is confronted with "4 + 2 =" is a concrete act. Writing or saying "5/15 = 3" involves a concrete operation in the many children who do so, because with a perverse kind of reversibility they often identify 15/5 and 5/15—the same two *numberals* and the same operation.

A bright fifth-grader named David who had a reputation for good work in school mathematics told me that 1.60 was the same as 1.06, because it didn't matter if you put a zero in front of the 6. He admitted that if you were thinking of money, a dollar and sixty cents was clearly more than a dollar and six cents. But, he insisted, for anything else, like gallons of gasoline, for instance, 1.60, which he called one and sixty-hundreths gallons, was the same as 1.06, which he called one and six-tenths gallons. It seems clear that David had no very clear system of rational numbers in mind that he was naming, nor did he have any clear conception of decimal fractions (numerals); instead he thinks of physical or economic quantities and operates on *numberals* to express his feelings about these quantities.

There are, we submit, many other concrete operations involved in the performing of calculations of the standard sort in elementary-school arithmetic, and they are especially evident when children have difficulty with applications—that is, solving word problems. Borrowing, carrying, bringing down zero, lining up decimal points, and arranging partial products in multiplication are all candidates for research as preoperational or concrete-operational thought.

In conclusion, the examples of research on formal operations discussed not only show the deep differences that exist between Piaget's point of view and that of the dominant scientific approach today but also indicate the great loss that would result if all of Piaget's findings were simply translated into a logical empiricist's framework. Certainly, it would represent a failure of Piaget's life program to reorient epistemology toward the biological, evolutionary view. On the other hand, there are many ways in which the role of symbol manipulation in thought needs to be taken more seriously.

The time is ripe for taking the evolutionary view of human life more seriously, for the mechanical epistemology that has dominated psychology is properly criticized for being demeaning and does not do justice to our experience as persons. However, to bring about a consensus and, in Kuhn's terms, a scientific paradigm in the field of human cognition will require recognition of the positive accomplishments of both views. Probably no one person is going to accomplish a synthesis singlehandedly because of the great disparity that exists in epistemology, but perhaps a number of us could do it within the next decade if we make it a major priority.

References

Allen, L. E. Toward autotelic learning of mathematical logic by the Wff'n Proof games. *Monographs of the Society for Research in Child Development,* 1965, *30,* 29–41.

Anderson, R. C. Can first graders learn an advanced problem-solving skill? *Journal of Educational Psychology,* 1965, *56,* 283–294.

Bohm, D. Science as perception-communication. A talk recorded on tape for the University of Illinois Symposium on Philosophy of Science, March 1969.

Davis, R. B., & Ginsberg, H. (Eds.). *Journal of Children's Mathematical Behavior,* Winter, 1971–1972, *1,* 1.

Easley, J. A., Jr. Comments on the INRC group. In R. E. Rippel & V. N. Rockcastle (Eds.), *Piaget rediscovered.* Ithaca, N.Y.: Cornell University, Department of Education, 1964. Pp. 109–111. (a)

Easley, J. A., Jr. What's new in the test file? *UICSM Newsletter,* February 1964, *No. 14,* 37–39. (b)

Easley, J. A., Jr., Gelder, H. M., & Golden, W. M. *A PLATO program for instruction and data collection in mathematical problem solving.* University of Illinois, Coordinated Science Report, R-185, January 1964. (CERL reprint, December 1968).

Ennis, R. H., Finkelstein, M. R., Smith, E. L., & Wilson, N. H. *Conditional logic and children.* Cornell Critical Thinking Readiness Project, Phase IIC, Final Report, August 1969.

Erlwanger, S. Benny's conception of rules and answers in IPI mathematics. *Journal of Children's Mathematical Behavior,* 1973, *1*(2), 7–26.

Feyerabend, P. K. Against method: Outline of an anarchistic theory of knowledge. In M. Radner & S. Winokur (Eds.), *Minnesota studies in the philosophy of science, IV: Analyses of Theories and Methods of Physics and Psychology.* Minneapolis: University of Minnesota Press, 1970.

Ghiselin, M. T. Darwin and evolutionary psychology. *Science,* March 1973, *179,* 964–968.

Grize, J.-B. *Logique Moderne.* Fascicule II, Paris: Gauthiers-Villars, 1971.

Hanson, N. R. *Patterns of discovery.* Cambridge, England: Cambridge University Press, 1958.

Hempel, C. G. On the "standard conception" of scientific theories. In M. Radner & S. Winokur

(Eds.), *Minnesota studies in the philosophy of science, IV: Analyses of theories and methods of physics and psychology*. Minneapolis: University of Minnesota Press, 1970.

Hill, S. A. A study of logical abilities in children. Unpublished doctoral dissertation, Stanford University, 1961.

Inhelder, B., & Piaget, J. *The growth of logical thinking from childhood to adolescence*. New York: Basic Books, 1958.

Knifong, J. D. A Piagetian analysis of logical abilities of young children. *Journal of Structural Learning*, 1972.

Knifong, J. D. Logical abilities of young children—two styles of approach. *Child Development*, 1974, *45*, 78–83.

Kuhn, T. S. *The structure of scientific revolutions*. Chicago: University of Chicago Press, 1962.

Lakatos, I. Proofs and refutations. *British Journal for the Philosophy of Science*, 1963–1964, *14*, 1–25, 120–139, 221–245, 296–342. (Reprinted: Cambridge University Press, 1976.)

O'Brien, T. C., & Shapiro, B. J. The development of logical thinking in children. *American Educational Research Journal*, 1968, *5*, 531–542.

Piaget, J. *Essai sur les transformations les opérations logiques: Les 256 opérations ternaires de la logique bivalente des propositions*. Paris: Presses Universitaires de France, 1952.

Piaget, J. *Judgment and reasoning in the child*. Paterson, N.J.: Littlefield, Adams & Co., 1959.

Piaget, J. *Biology and knowledge: An essay on the relations between organic regulations and cognitive processes*. Chicago: University of Chicago Press, 1971.

Piaget, J. Problems of equilibration. In J. M. Gallagher & R. H. Humphreys (Eds.), *Piaget and Inhelder on equilibration*. Philadelphia: Jean Piaget Society, 1972.

Polanyi, M. *Personal knowledge: towards a post-critical philosophy*. London: Routledge, 1958.

Polya, G. *Mathematics and plausible reasoning* (2 vols.). Princeton, N.J.: Princeton University Press, 1954.

Polya, G. The teaching of mathematics and the biogenetic law. In I. J. Good (Ed.), *The scientist speculates*. London: Heinemann, 1962.

Ripple, R. E., & Rockcastle, V. N. *Piaget rediscovered*. Ithaca: School of Education, Cornell University, 1964.

Suppes, P., & Binford, B. Experimental teaching of mathematical logic in the elementary school. *The Arithmetic Teacher*, 1965, *12*, 187–195.

Witz, K. G., & Easley, J. A., Jr. *Analysis of cognitive behavior in Children*. Final Report, Grant No. OEC-0-70-2142(508), U.S. Department of Health, Education, and Welfare, 1972.

Witz, K. G., & Easley, J. A., Jr. A new approach to cognition. In Van den Daele, L., Pascual-Leone, J., and Witz, K. G. (Eds.), *Neopiagetian perspectives in cognition*. New York: Academic Press, in press.

PART III

SOCIAL COGNITION

CHAPTER 8

Interface between the Behavioral and Cognitive-Developmental Approach to Research in Morality

Roger V. Burton

State University of New York at Buffalo
Buffalo, New York

Philosophers and social theorists in every period of recorded history have devoted much discussion to moral conduct, not only to what it is but to how parents and teachers might encourage or unintentionally interfere with its development in the young. In spite of the attention directed to morality throughout the ages, there was relatively little empirical investigation of this domain until this century. The landmark studies were those conducted by Hartshorne and May, *Studies in the Nature of Character* (1928, 1929, 1930), and by Piaget, *The Moral Judgment of the Child* (1932). These two classic studies represent quite contrasting theoretical points of view.

The Behavioral Approach

Hartshorne and May were struck by the lack of empirical evidence on actual conduct, and being greatly influenced by Thorndike's pragmatic orientation of attacking a psychological question directly (the research was in fact under Thorndike's immediate supervision at Columbia University), they decided that in studying morality, they should focus their research on methodological considerations. Their rationale was that

> Only by building a broad foundation of statistically usable data can the science of human behavior, as distinct from the art of studying and improving individuals, be

developed. . . . (p. 7) The first question to ask is, "What did the subject do?" Until
this question is answered in quantitative terms so that what he did is clearly known,
there is little use in going on to ask why he did it, and still less use in speculating
whether he is to be blamed or praised. (Hartshorne & May, 1928, p. 11)

Accordingly, the definition of honesty for their research program was intrinsi-
cally linked to overt behavior. To qualify as an acceptable test, the situation had
to tempt the child to do something for personal gain that he or she would not want
others to know about. The crucial part of their definition of honesty was the
element of deception: an attempt to conceal one's behavior and/or the intention of
one's action.

With this frame of reference, many tests were produced, skillfully and
creatively, using techniques developed in the field of psychological testing and
measurement. With the high standards they set for their tests, procedures, and
sampling, these investigators provided an admirable model for studying an unex-
plored and complex domain of behavior.

Hartshorne and May concluded from their analyses of the correlations
among the tests that there was little evidence for the existence of a general trait of
honesty, a conclusion labeled the *doctrine of specificity*. They based this conclusion on the fact that the correlations tended to be low among the tests and that the
magnitude of any particular correlation was related to the apparent similarity
between the two tests. They interpreted the data as demonstrating that honesty
was determined mainly by conditions in the test situation rather than by any
unified character trait. The implication was that the morality of an individual, at
least as being relevant to actual moral conduct, would not be reflected by any
single index of his or her behavior.

It should be noted, however, that the model of personality traits they rejected was an extreme position of individual consistency. It required any test of
honesty to correlate highly with any other test of honesty and to be an excellent
predictor of the individual's behavior in any other test and under all conditions.
In fact, they recognized that there was some generality demonstrated in the data
by the tendency for all correlations to be positive, no matter how different the
tests and the situations.

To reconsider the implications of this doctrine of specificity, the original
intercorrelations of their data can be reanalyzed with multivariate methods (Burton, 1963). Both principle component and Guttman simplex analyses provided
evidence of a single general factor accounting for 34–43% of the common variance. Although certainly not an *all-or-none* trait of moral conduct, it did demonstrate a modest proclivity for individuals to differ in their general resistance to
temptation. A theoretical model proposed to account for the data hypothesized
that the differences in consistency of cheating across the tests reflected varying
amounts of generalization along two potentially independent gradients of
generalization. The first was a physical-stimulus gradient of similarity that would

account for the tendency for tests of the same type and in the same setting to correlate rather highly. For example, the average correlation for the academic-achievement tests in their study correlated 0.68, compared with the average correlation across all tests of only 0.23. The other gradient, and the factor hypothesized as contributing most to individual consistency of behavior across the various tests, was a conceptual gradient, especially involving mediation by verbal labels. It was proposed that this central, conceptual mediation would account for variability within individuals to be consistent across quite physically different situations and kinds of moral conduct. The consistency of any individual's moral conduct, then, depended both on the degree to which the tests were physically similar and administered in similar settings and also on the degree to which the individual had learned to perceive the tests as belonging to the same conceptual class of events, that is, as all being tests classified as situations involving moral conduct or honesty. The model attempted not only to *explain* the data that were then available but, in addition, to predict what might be the learning experiences that would lead to some individuals' being relatively consistent in their moral conduct and to others' being quite unpredictable and variable in each situation.

Subsequent experimental evidence has clearly supported the contribution of cognitive structure to the learning and performance of moral conduct. The results of experiments by Aronfreed, Walters, Parke, Cheyne, and Burton clearly demonstrate the influence of providing cognitive structure during the learning to inhibit a tabooed response and suggest how this structure serves to mediate moral conduct when the child must exert self-control. The results of these studies are complex. But they can be summarized as demonstrating that the provision of appropriate cognitive structure or reasoning, at a level of complexity that the child can understand and accept, greatly enhances the effectiveness of disciplinary techniques. Furthermore, the well-established effects of certain parameters of punishment, such as intensity and timing, can be exceedingly modified. For example, under conditions of low cognitive structure, such as would be the case with a preverbal child, the earlier the administration of punishment in the sequence of the child's performing the unacceptable act and the greater the intensity of the punishment, the greater will be the suppression of that behavior.

By contrast, when it is possible to add reasoning to the disciplinary action and to explain precisely what it was that the child did that was wrong, why it was wrong, and what alternative action was desired, the effects of intensity and timing tend to cancel out and perhaps even to reverse (Parke & Walters, 1967; Cheyne, 1972). There is also evidence that with a given complexity of a discrimination problem—and many moral dilemmas present difficult discriminations for children—there is an optimal level of motivation for learning the problem (e.g., Aronfreed & Leff, 1963; Cheyne, Goyeche, & Walters, 1969; Walters & Parke, 1965). The addition of clear instructions or reasons for restricting certain actions simplifies learning. Furthermore, a most important finding for parents is that the situation in which the child was deviant can be re-created verbally, and disciplinary action can be taken that may then be effective in deterring further deviance (Andres & Walters, 1970). However, the situation and the child's actions must be adequately described, and the punishment must be timed to coincide with the deviant act in order for this technique of delayed discipline to be effective.

In this brief historical review of behavioral studies on moral conduct, it seems clear that there has been a gradual but increasing concern on the part of the behaviorally oriented investigators to consider the cognitive concomitants of the moral behavior that is the major focus of their research. The direction of these studies is to explore the factors that contribute self-directive properties to knowledge of the moral code, that produce resistance to temptation not only in the short run but also over time, and that transfer to other facets of moral conduct. These questions lead the behaviorist inevitably into greater involvement with the cognitive context that has been established during the history of the child's learning self-control in a temptation situation.

The Cognitive-Developmental Approach

Although Piaget's emphasis and reputation for studying morality was on the cognitive rationales given for moral judgments, it is worthwhile noting that he too began his studies of morality by observing behavioral conformity to rules in a marble game. It is especially interesting that Piaget considered the behavioral stages of marble playing separately from the stages described for the children's attitudes toward the rules of the game. This separation seems unlike current Piaget in that the need for concrete action in the processes of assimilation–accommodation of a cognitive structure seems such an intrinsic part of his general theory of intellectual development. The importance of the interplay and feedback between direct manipulation of objects and the cognitive manipulation of concepts involving these material objects, or direct sensory experiences, as essential for the attainment of the more abstract levels of thought is continuously stressed.

Perhaps the reason for this separation in his exploration of morality was due to the seeming lack of agreement betwen what the child said and what he or she did, between "words and deeds," to use Bryan's expression (Bryan & Walbek, 1970). In describing the stages for rules and the verbal attitudes toward them, Piaget proposed four stages for the behavior involving rules and only three stages for the verbalized, cognitive domain. In the first stage for both facets, the child uses marbles as play objects or manipulanda with no awareness of rules. With greater language development and social awareness, the child begins to imitate the way others play the game. He or she now describes the rules as absolute, fixed, and inviolate, and yet he or she flagrantly bridges and ignores the rules whenever necessary to obtain egocentric wishes. In spite of knowledge of what the rules are, the child clearly has not understood their implication for prescribing and proscribing certain actions for his or her play.

In beginning school, the child increasingly plays his or her games with peers, gradually experiencing the constraints that they place on his or her behavior and in turn insisting that they too abide by the rules. Coinciding with these environmental experiences, Piaget suggested that the third stage for behavior begins and the second cognitive stage is most clearly represented. Although the child is aware that the rules involve social interaction, abiding by the rules is still imposed by others: the child is kept honest by the surveillance of his or her peers, and he or she in turn keeps them in line. The rules are not yet part of his or her own, internalized (or interiorized) standards. Any suggestion that new rules be applied is unacceptable since they would not be fair.

Finally, the child plays by the rules as just part of the game itself. The child also perceives the rules as convenient guidelines that are mutually agreed on and that may be modified or completely changed. At this period, there seems to be a flip-flop from the earlier correspondence between action and words. Whereas earlier, the rules were immutable and yet violated constantly, rules are now seen as flexible and yet are adhered to. What is the explanation for this seeming lack of isomorphism between words and deeds? What are the links tying together the belief in rules as absolute, in immanent justice, and in moral realism with actual behavioral deception? How is it that the perception of rules as being historically arbitrary, as being easily changed whenever there is mutual agreement, supports strict adherence to them? Also what is the correspondence between these facets assessed in the social situation compared with the relation between the child's words and his or her obeying the rules when not under surveillance, that is, when he or she has to apply the rules to herself or himself? These questions still need to be answered.

It is when the simple choice of following or breaking the rules of a game is left behind and attention is focused on the moral basis that the person provides for actions that should or should not be taken in a situation that we come to the familiar format of the cognitive-developmental approach, especially as represented in the extensions of this approach by Kohlberg (1964). The moral judgment of a respondent is based not on what he or she does but on his or her use of certain ethical principles to describe contrasting actions portrayed in stories depicting moral dilemmas. For the development of moral judgment, Piaget reduced the number of stages even further: a primary stage of *moral realism, moralism of constraint,* or *heteronomous morality*—in general, a stage similar to the second stage in attitudes toward rules—and a second stage variously labeled *morality of cooperation, reciprocity,* or *autonomous morality*. The dimensions hypothesized as discriminating these stages were mainly immanent justice, intentions versus consequences, and retribution versus restitution. Many studies have demonstrated that there is an age-related progression for these dimensions, although these studies also provide evidence that the relation across dimensions is about the same as found for the Hartshorne and May tests of honesty (e.g., Johnson, 1962; Harris, 1970). Furthermore, many studies clearly demonstrate the same kind of situational determinants operating for moral-judgment assessments as are found for moral-conduct tests. Consistency of moral judgments depends on factors common to the different dilemmas, such as similarity of the item formats (Breznitz & Kugelmass, 1967), the extent to which the same dimensions are involved (Johnson, 1962), the degree to which children are familiar with the content of the items (Magowan & Lee, 1970), and the clarity of the item in distinguishing the intentions of the central figure from the consequences of his actions (Armsby, 1971). Thus, the empirical support for the assumption that morality assessed through moral judgments is unidimensional is about the same as that found by Hartshorne and May for moral conduct.

The Overlap between Approaches

As previously indicated, research in the behavioral tradition has increasingly incorporated attention to cognitive structures in order to increase the understanding of the acquisition and performance of moral conduct. Unfortunately, in this author's opinion, those following Piaget's cognitive-developmental approach have not followed up the questions that his initial work raised regarding the correspondence between the cognitive and behavioral facets of morality and have focused almost solely on moral judgment *per se*. Nevertheless, what is the evidence for correspondence between the verbal and behavioral assessments of morality? Interestingly, one of the most substantial findings for correspondence between moral knowledge and conduct was provided by Hartshorne and May, who reported a correlation between the summary scores on the behavioral tests and the summary scores on the knowledge tests approaching 0.40. Later studies, however, have been extremely variable. Some correspondence has been reported by Kohlberg (1965) between his principled level and conduct in the Milgrim obedience situation, and yet Podd (1972), using the same measures, found none. Perhaps the most interesting study as far as suggesting what might be the relation of judgment in directing behavior was reported by Krebs (1967). Although sometimes cited as demonstrating correspondence between moral judgment and behavior, the data are more complex. A positive relation was found if moral judgment was first assessed and then a temptation test followed. If assessed after the temptation test, however, moral judgment was *negatively* related to honesty. These data suggest a cognitive-dissonance interpretation. Once having stated high levels of moral principles, the person then makes his or her behavior consonant with that commitment. After having complied with the rules, by contrast, one makes his or her judgment consonant with his or her behavior, portraying a greater rule orientation, which tends to be a *law-and-order* stage. Subjects who cheat subsequently consider all of the reasons that would justify breaking prescriptions, and this increased consideration of extenuating circumstances makes their moral judgments more complex and likely to be judged at a higher level. The important issue is that it was the moral conduct that greatly influenced the moral judgments. These findings are very similar to those that children portray in deviation doll-play stories following a temptation test: cheaters portray more parental fixing and less punishment, whereas children who are honest project an increase in punishment and less indulgence on the part of parents (Burton, 1971).

Overall, there is some relation between measures of cognitive orientation regarding moral conflicts and a person's actual behavior; but the small magnitude of overlap, whenever it is demonstrated, suggests that the primary determinants of the verbal responses to moral dilemmas may well be different from the major determinants of overt behavior in specific situations. Yet the evidence that correspondence increases with age indicates that people become more integrated as they reach adult status and may react more consistently across their verbal and overt behavior.

When the developmental aspects of the two approaches are considered, it has generally been concluded that moral judgment is correlated with age but that moral conduct is not. Therefore, moral judgment is a cognitive-developmental variable, whereas moral conduct does not meet the requirement. Yet, this conclusion seems due to differences in the methods used to assess the association. If consistency of moral conduct is the measure, there is a correlation with age (Hartshorne, May, & Shuttleworth, 1930). Since this score involves a sampling of many conduct measures, similar to the rating for an individual's moral judgment, it seems more appropriate as a measure of the developmental character of moral conduct. The evidence that consistency of moral conduct is developmental may well be as strong as is that for moral judgments (Holstein, 1973).

In conclusion, data provided within both approaches indicate that the two research orientations can profit from each other. Furthermore, to ignore contributions because they come from a different approach and orientation can only hinder advancement in our understanding of this domain, the importance of which is manifested in the immoral conduct recently exposed by the Watergate and Ellsberg cases. The directive properties of cognitive structure have been demonstrated by controlled experimental and field studies, and yet many questions are left unanswered. Why is there such low correspondence between overt moral behavior and the cognitive measures of moral knowledge, judgment, and attitude? We must explore the conditions determining when cognitive structure directs behavior, as well as when it does not. The evidence clearly indicates that cognitive knowledge or advancing moral judgment is not sufficient to result in moral conduct. Studying moral judgment for its own sake may be a *cul-de-sac* and, even worse, misleading, since there is the implicit assumption that moral judgments are related to what people do when faced with moral decisions. Behaviorists study schedules of reinforcement, hierarchies of learned responses, and instrumental behavior. These concepts are used to explain how child-rearing practices may change over the socialization history of the child in order to be appropriate to his or her level of development (Burton, Maccoby, & Allinsmith, 1961; Yarrow, Campbell, & Burton, 1968). The language is quite different, but there seem to be strong parallels with the way that Piaget and Inhelder (1966) discuss the development of structures that change from simply passively organizing events that the child experiences to permitting him or her to predict and thus to direct his or her behavior. If we are willing to translate the terminology of the two schools, certainly the questions that both orientations are asking involve similar problems. The time is long overdue for a rapprochement, a sympathetic attempt by each school to profit from the point of view of and contributions made by the other.

References

Andres, D., & Walters, R. H. Modification of delay of punishment effects through cognitive restructuring. Proceedings, 78th Annual Convention, Vol. 5, Part 1, American Psychological Association, 1970. Pp. 483–484.

Armsby, R. E. A reexamination of the development of moral judgments in children. *Child Development*, 1971, *42*, 1241–1248.

Aronfreed, J., & Leff, R. The effects of intensity of punishment and complexity of discrimination upon the learning of internalized suppression. Unpublished manuscript, University of Pennsylvania, 1963.

Breznitz, S., & Kugelmass, S. Intentionality in moral judgment: Developmental stages. *Child Development*, 1967, *38*, 469–479.

Bryan, J. H., & Walbek, N. H. The impact of words and deeds concerning altruism upon children. *Child Development*, 1970, *41*, 747–757.

Burton, R. V. Generality of honesty reconsidered. *Psychological Review*, 1963, *70*, 481–499.

Burton, R. V. Correspondence between behavioral and doll-play measures of conscience. *Developmental Psychology*, 1971, *5*, 320–332.

Burton, R. V., Maccoby, E. E., & Allinsmith, W. Antecedents of resistance to temptation in four-year-old children. *Child Development*, 1961, *32*, 689–710.

Cheyne, J. A. Punishment and "reasoning" in the development of self-control. In R. D. Parke (Ed.), *Recent trends in social learning theory*. New York: Academic Press, 1972.

Cheyne, J. A., Goyeche, J. R. M., & Walters, R. H. Attention, anxiety, and rules in resistance-to-deviation in children. *Journal of Experimental Child Psychology*, 1969, *8*, 127–139.

Harris, H. Development of moral attitudes in white and negro boys. *Developmental Psychology*, 1970, *2*, 376–383.

Hartshorne, H., & May, M. A. *Studies in the nature of character,* I: *Studies in deceit.* New York: Macmillan, 1928.

Hartshorne, H., May, M. A., & Maller, J. B. *Studies in the nature of character.* II: *Studies in service and self-control.* New York: Macmillan, 1929.

Hartshorne, H., May, M. A., & Shuttleworth, F. K. *Studies in the nature of character,* III: *Studies in the organization of character.* New York: Macmillan, 1930.

Holstein, C. B. Moral judgment change in early adolescence and middle age: A longitudinal study. Paper presented at the Society for Research in Child Development meeting, Philadelphia, 1973.

Johnson, R. C. A study of children's moral judgments. *Child Development,* 1962, *33,* 327–354.

Kohlberg, L. The development of moral character and moral ideology. In M. L. Hoffman & L. W. Hoffman (Eds.), *Review of child development research,* Vol. 1. New York: Russell Sage Foundation, 1964.

Kohlberg, L. Relationships between the development of moral judgment and moral conduct. Paper presented at the Society for Research in Child Development meeting, Minneapolis, 1965.

Krebs, R. L. Some relationships between moral judgment, attention, and resistance to temptation. Unpublished doctoral dissertation, University of Chicago, 1967.

Magowan, S. A., & Lee, T. Some sources of error in the use of the projective method for the measurement of moral judgment. *British Journal of Psychology,* 1970, *61,* 535–543.

Parke, R. D., & Walters, R. H. Some factors influencing the efficacy of punishment training for inducing response inhibition. *Monographs of the Society for Research in Child Development,* 1967, *32,* 1, Serial No. 109.

Piaget, J. *The moral judgment of the child.* New York: Harcourt, Brace, 1932.

Piaget, J., & Inhelder, B. *L'image mentale chez l'enfant.* Paris: Presses Universitaires de France, 1966.

Podd, H. Ego identity status and morality: The relationship between two developmental constructs. *Developmental Psychology,* 1972, *6,* 497–507.

Walters, R. H., & Parke, R. D. The role of the distance receptors in the development of social responsiveness. In L. P. Lipsitt & C. C. Spiker (Eds.), *Advances in child development and behavior,* Vol. 2, New York: Academic Press, 1965.

Yarrow, M. J. R., Campbell, J. D., & Burton, R. V. *Child rearing: An inquiry into research and methods.* San Francisco: Jossey-Bass, 1968.

CHAPTER 9

From Adolescence to Adulthood: The Rediscovery of Reality in a Postconventional World

Carol Gilligan and Lawrence Kohlberg

Harvard University
Cambridge, Massachusetts

> [E]ach new mental ability starts off by incorporating the world in a process of egocentric assimilation. Only later does it attain equilibrium through a compensating accommodation to reality. (Piaget)

The formally operational adolescent lives in a world of possibility. Between the concrete and traditional structures that anchored his childhood world and the choices that will define his adulthood lies the expansive universe of the hypothetical. Fascination turns from what is to what might or could be, and as the alternatives proliferate, it becomes clear that formal operations can lead from adolescence to infinity or, perhaps, to adolescence infinitely. Standing at this peak of cognitive assimilation, the adolescent has been proclaimed both metaphysician and philosopher; no longer a child, he is not yet an adult, and our interest lies in the nature of the transition from adolescence to adulthood as it occurs in the moral realm. We begin at that place in development where the hypothetico-deductive mind of the adolescent turns to morality and questions not only the content but also the premises of a conventional moral philosophy. Our concern is with the nature of these questions and with the various forms of their resolution.

We will begin by reviewing recent findings concerning the relationship between formal operational thinking and moral development, then consider the problem of moral relativism and the nature of postconventional moral judgments, and finally discuss the relationship between moral and ego development in late adolescence.

The questioning of what has been assumed to be the given—the awareness of alternatives to an established system of beliefs—differentiates a scientifically oriented from a traditional culture (Horton, 1970). However, within a scientifically oriented culture, such awareness is contingent upon the development of formal operational thought. Although moral judgment is not the mere application of logic to situations of interpersonal conflict, Piaget's logical structures do set limits on moral reasoning. The attainment of a particular stage of logical operations is thus a necessary though not a sufficient condition for the development of a parallel structure in the moral realm.

Like other new cognitive structures, formal operations are acquired gradually, and three levels can be distinguished and shown to be sequential. Kohlberg and Colby (1977), have found that the three levels of formal thought correspond to moral Stages 3, 4, and 5, respectively. (For a summary of stages, see Appendix.) Stage 3 moral judgment requires cognitive processes that are transitional between concrete and formal operations; Stage 4 moral judgment requires low-level formal operations; and Stage 5 and 6 moral judgment require high-level formal operations. While individuals may show the logical operation without its parallel in moral judgment, they almost never show the moral stage without its hypothesized logical prerequisite.

Interesting evidence for this relationship between logical and moral stages comes from the finding that attempts at moral education—that is, at fostering or accelerating moral development—depend for their success on the presence of the underlying logical operations (Kohlberg and Colby, 1977). In a study assessing the effects of educational intervention on moral development, a comparison was made of the logical levels of those subjects originally completely conventional who showed some use of Stage 5 thinking on the posttest as opposed to those who showed no acquisition of Stage 5. Of the 10 subjects who manifested Stage 5 thinking, 9 were fully or predominantly formal operational on both pretest and posttest. The one exception, although predominantly concrete, did show some formal thought on both pretest and posttests. Of the 14 subjects who did not acquire any Stage 5 reasoning, 3 were predominantly formal and 11 were predominantly concrete. The probability of this distribution's occurring by chance is 0.0013.

However, while formal operations are thus a necessary prerequisite for principled moral reasoning, they also make possible the questioning of morality itself in a way hitherto inconceivable. The ability to go outside the given, to see it as only one possibility among many, both real and hypothetical, allows for a new kind of criticism. From a conception of the ideal can ensue various forms of rejection of the real, all revolutionary ideologies having their destructive as well as their Utopian components. This tension between the actual and the possible, between the real and the ideal, has always been the center of a reflective adolescence, and in our studies of adolescent moral judgment, we see the various manifestations of this tension in the moral realm.

The progress of moral development entails the questioning of convention, which leads the individual out of the world of his childhood into an exploration of alternatives which eventuates in the discovery of a principled basis for adult ethical commitments. At the peak of this developmental arch lies the timeless universe of possibility where reflection is most free from the constraints of choice—the world, that is, of adolescent moral philosophy.

While the sequence of moral stages is invariant and their logical ordering clear, the process of stage transition at the higher levels of moral development (i.e., from conventional to principled judgment) is made more complex by the phenomenon of adolescent relativism. The hallmark of the relativist is the unease he manifests when asked to make a moral judgment. The terms *right* and *wrong* stick in his throat, and his typical response is either to question their meaning or to assert their meaninglessness. Such questioning is metaethical in that it stands outside the realm of normative ethical judgment and inquires into its premises. Logically, it is conditional upon the capacity for abstraction made possible by formal operational thought. Psychologically, it goes along with the penchant of reflective adolescents to question the given and challenge assumptions that they cannot endorse as their own.

Relativism, as a phenomenon in moral development, was first identified by Kohlberg and Kramer in 1969. Among their longitudinal subjects, they found a small group whom they labeled *extreme relativists* and considered as regressors. Rejecting conventional moral reasoning on the basis of a relativistic awareness that any given society's definition of right and wrong, however legitimate, is only one among many, both in fact and in theory, these subjects, instead of moving ahead from Stage 4 to Stage 5, reverted to what sounded like a resurrected Stage 2 moral philosophy of instrumental hedonism. Consider their responses to the following dilemma:

> In Europe, a woman was near death from a very bad disease, a special kind of cancer. There was one drug that the doctors thought might save her. It was a form of radium that a druggist in the same town had recently discovered. The drug was expensive to make, but the druggist was charging ten times what the drug cost him to make. He paid $200 for the radium and charged $2,000 for a small dose of the drug. The sick woman's husband, Heinz, went to everyone he knew to borrow the money, but he could only get together about $1,000 which was half of what it cost. He told the druggist that his wife was dying, and asked him to sell it cheaper or let him pay later. But the druggist said, "No, I discovered the drug and I'm going to make money from it." Heinz got desperate and broke into the man's store to steal the drug for his wife. (Kohlberg & Gilligan, 1971, p. 1072)

Bob, a junior in a liberal private high school, says in response to the question as to whether Heinz's theft was right or wrong:

There's a million ways to look at it. Heinz had a moral decision to make. Was it worse to steal or let his wife die? In my mind I can either condemn him or condone him. In this case I think it was fine. But possibly the druggist was working on a capitalist morality of supply and demand (p. 1073)

Asked "Would it be wrong if he did not steal it?" he replied:

It depends on how he is oriented morally. If he thinks it's worse to steal than to let his wife die, then it would be wrong that he did. It's all relative; what I would do is steal the drug. I can't say that's right or wrong or that it's what everyone should do. (p. 1073)

Bob started the moral-judgment interview by wondering if he could answer any questions because he "questioned the whole terminology, the whole moral bag." He went on:

But then I'm also an incredible moralist, a real puritan in some sense and moods. My moral judgment and the way I perceive things morally changes very much when my mood changes. When I'm in a cynical mood, I take a cynical view of morals, but still whether I like it or not, I'm terribly moral in the way I look at things. But I'm not too comfortable with it. (p. 1073)

Here are some other juniors from an upper-middle-class public high school:

Dan: Immoral is strictly a relative term which can be applied to almost any thought on a particular subject . . . if you have a man and a woman in bed, that is immoral as opposed to if you were a Roman a few thousand years ago and you were used to orgies all the time, that would not be immoral. Things vary so when you call something immoral, it's relative to that society at that time and it varies frequently. [Are there any circumstances in which wrong in some abstract moral sense would be applicable?] Well, in that sense, the only thing I could find wrong would be when you were hurting somebody against their will.

Elliot: I think one individual's set of moral values is as good as the next individual's. I think you have a right to believe in what you believe in, but I don't think you have a right to enforce it on other people.

John: I don't think anybody should be swayed by the dictates of society. It's probably very much up to the individual all the time, and there's no general principle except when the views of society seem to conflict with your views and your opportunities at the moment, and it seems that the views of society don't really have any basis as being right and in that case, most people, I think, would tend to say forget it, and I'll do what I want. (pp. 1073–1074)

Conceived by Kohlberg & Kramer (1969) as a regression, this form of relativistic thought was seen as impeding moral development, a roadblock on the way from Stage 4 to Stage 5. It was scored 4-1/2, 2, 5-2, 4-2, and the confusion in the numbers reflected the uncertainty as to its proper place in the developmental conception. This kind of relativism was, however, distinctly adolescent in its penchant for dichotomies. In its stark, all-or-nothing formulation, if conventional morality is relative, then all morality is relative, and everyone should do his own thing. In the absence of morality, *authenticity* prevails—if there is no general moral code to which one can adhere, then at least one can strive to be true to one's self.

The developmental assumption underlying Kohlberg's original position was that the relativistic suspension of moral judgment would be resolved with the discovery of moral principles that were universal in their application and hence could provide a rational basis for moral choice in a postconventional, heterogeneous world. It was the adolescent's search for such principles that we urged the educator to take seriously if he wished, following Dewey, to foster development (Kohlberg & Gilligan, 1971). In part, the urgency of this message stemmed from the realization that an arrest of development at this point could lead to the moral defiance of a Nietzsche or a Raskolnikov or, in its milder form, to an asocial, amoral hedonism. However, for the longitudinal subjects, such fears were groundless. The forces of development that led 20% from upstanding convention to moral nihilism eventually set them all to rights. Every single one of the *retrogressors* had returned by age 25 to the moral fold, with more Stage 5 social-contract principle and less Stage 4 convention than in high school. In sum, this 20% were among the highest group at high school, the lowest in college, and again among the highest at age 25. Moral relativism and nihilism, no matter how extensive, seemed to be a transitional attitude in the movement from conventional to principled morality.

These findings support the conception of relativism advanced by Turiel (1973), a conception that views it not as regressive but rather as transitional, arising out of the Stage 4 identification of morality with convention. While the relativist seems to be rejecting morality itself, he nevertheless holds onto the term *moral,* as a careful reading of the examples will show. It is the morality of convention that is being cast aside, and the essence of the transitional process consists in the sorting out of this confusion. Both the difficulty of doing this and the struggle to do so is well illustrated in the following reply of a college student to the question "What do you mean by the term *morality* or *moral?*"

> I haven't really thought about that. The problem is that I have a tendency to revolt against morality in the sense of matters, social matter, sexual; in other words, things put forth by my parents. Therefore, I don't really, I haven't really formulated any morality for myself yet because I am still in the process of casting off what I don't believe to be proper attitudes. My greatest fear is the morality, I suppose it is morality, of the great mass of people being imposed on me. I fear that more than the authority of an individual, and so I am still casting around for my own, what is moral in all of those matters.

The interviewer, himself casting around, goes on to say, "Well, one thing that occurs to me is that you are telling me that you don't know what the content of your morality would be yet. Can you tell me what it is structurally?"

> Structurally? Well, I think I just have to go and formulate a very simple definition or just say that, that I have no real moral, nothing is immoral which does not injure anyone else. Beyond that, despite what is commonly accepted by society, if you are the only person involved, then nothing is really immoral. In your relations with other people I would have to say that, as I have said, if you don't injure anyone else, don't interfere, block anyone else from what they are intent upon doing, then it can't be called immoral no matter what it is. In these instances where you do, where your conception of what you want to do or ought to do infringes upon the rights of others . . . I don't know, that's difficult, I haven't decided. I have to decide these cases individually, and I might tend to look to something else than morality. Some other justification.

What this statement elucidates is the impossibility of any longer making moral judgments on the basis of convention, the search for some alternative mode of moral judgment, and, in the absence of such, the attempt to resurrect an individual point of view toward the solution of what are now only very ambivalently seen as moral conflicts.

While it is clear from the foregoing example that the discovery of moral principles would solve the problem posed by this form of adolescent relativism and enable the student to be moral in terms that he could see as his own, other evidence indicates that the discovery of principles does not necessarily put an end to metaethical questioning. Evidence of questioning that signified what was conceived to be a different kind of relativism began to show up in interviews of college students and among members of that group whom Keniston (1970) politely terms *youth*. What distinguishes these individuals from the previous relativists is their ability to understand and articulate a principled moral philosophy. Fishkin (1973), interviewing British university graduates, some of them among the perpetually uncommitted, found an extreme form of relativism that was manifested in a complete refusal to make moral judgments. Asked if Heinz was right or wrong in stealing the drug, they questioned not only the possibility of answering that question but the premises of the question itself—that is, the meaning of morality. *Right* and *wrong* were seen as scientific rather than moral terms and as such could be used to answer questions about means but not questions of ends. There may be a *right* (successful, effective) way to save a life, but it is impossible to say whether or not it is *right* (good) to do so.

This suspension of moral judgment may be part of a more general suspension of commitment, thus comprising the moral or ideological component of a full-blown Eriksonian identity crisis. Fishkin's subjects, unable to find any more meaning in life than they found in morality, chose to refrain from societal or personal commitments and preferred, in effect, to live apart. This type of relativism, and the prolonged identity crisis and moratorium that may accompany it, may be seen as a failure of accommodation, an inability to integrate an abstract and generalized conception of the ideal with the inevitable limitations of any particular commitment or choice.

Evidence for this interpretation comes from interviews with college and graduate students who are in the process of attempting to make this kind of accommodation. Having worked out the logic of a postconventional or principled moral philosophy, their concern is with reconciling this logic with the particularities of their own experience and thus with bringing their moral philosophy, which was forged against the constraints of the ideal, back into the world of the real.

The moral development represented by the achievement of Stages 5 and 6 consists of an elaboration of moral principles that are seen to constitute a universally valid basis for resolving moral dilemmas. The essence of these principles is that they are both universalizable and reversible—that is, valid anywhere and from any point of view. However, while they represent the logically most adequate conception of justice and equity, they may require for their application an assimilation of reality to the clean world of the hypothetical dilemma, an assimilation based on the formal Piagetian assumption of "all other things being equal" (Inhelder and Piaget, 1968). Just as the person in the midst of an identity crisis may entertain, for a time, the question "Who am I?" in a universe of seemingly unconstrained choice, so too in moral development, we see evidence of this same process of purification (Sennett, 1970). Faced with the new problems of sexuality and moral responsibility yet lacking experience in dealing with them, the adolescent seeks to maintain control by relying on reason to order an unfamiliar world in which the potential for chaos seems at times to be alarming. In doing so, he assimilates the discrepant and tries to bring reality into line with his philosophy.

However, the tension between the order of pure reason and the disorder of experience comes to the surface in the attempt to integrate an abstract conception of justice with the particularities of everyday life. A second-year law student, reflecting on his own moral development, illustrates this process:

> . . . I think I tried to take a paradigm of abstract moral values, that I roughly tried to develop. I sort of worked out in my mind what I personally considered to be the most important aspects of life and I sort of ranked them one to ten. That is sort of what it looked like and then I would sort of try to apply that paradigm to any particular situation that I saw, try to figure out how I thought morally it should come out. I think today, and I think this is partly due to the fact that I am older and probably due to the fact that my education has changed me, the education in the last year of law school, I look at each situation and now I try to extract the moral problems involved in a given situation, and rather than trying to pigeon-hole a certain situation, I try to find out what those problems are. To tell the truth, I don't think about those problems as much as I did four years ago anyway, that whole paradigmatic approach is just not part of the way I operate any more.

He describes an earlier crisis of relativism that, by comparison, points up the distinctively different nature of his present struggle:

> During my sophomore year, I rejected morality completely. I did, in the freshman year
> and in the sophomore year, a lot of talking about huge theoretical moral constructs and
> systems, and during the end of my sophomore year, I got into some experiences which
> led me to the conclusion, not very much based on reasons, that morality was by and
> large a lot of bunk, that there was no right or wrong whatsoever, that people did things
> that were givens of experience and it was beyond anyone's judging power not only to
> determine whether any person's acts were right or wrong, but to determine whether
> there was a right or wrong. I read a lot of Kant, obviously, so he really got to me in
> those days, and I don't think that is a position I have totally rejected either . . . after the
> relativism, I started reading Marx a lot . . . and stopped thinking in moral terms, or I
> stopped thinking in abstract moral terms as I had been thinking. I think during the first
> couple of years, I went from a position of very abstract, sort of universalistic moral
> concepts to, on the other hand, a sort of nihilistic rejection, to sort of worrying about
> more immediate problems.

While the conception of the moral is retained as an ideal, its application is now sought in terms of the immediate realities of human interaction. This is a resolution very much in process; the moral is defined, albeit with a lingering relativistic qualification, as follows:

> Sometimes I think of a truly moral existence, if there is such a thing, as being, relating
> to any person one comes across . . . not as instrumentality and manipulator, not as a
> means, but relating to that person as an end in himself and essentially as a human
> being and nothing more and nothing less.

Responding to the Heinz dilemma, this student now saw the moral problem as arising not from Heinz's theft but rather from the druggist's failure to consider the wife's life as an end in itself rather than as a means to his own profit.

The tension between the universal and the particular that the process of accommodation attempts to reconcile is illustrated by another study that provides data on the development of sex-role concepts (Ullian, 1973). These data indicate that, in young children, perceptions of sex roles are descriptive, full of detail about the way things are. At the conventional levels of development, these descriptions take on prescriptive valuation, and statements about what men and women or boys and girls *do* turn into injunctions as to what they *should do*. When the development of postconventional thought makes possible the assessment of conventions on the basis of the underlying principles they reflect, the "is" of existing sex-role stereotypes comes to be judged against the "ought" of what is considered just and equitable treatment of the sexes. But the fascination with the power of the idea of equality may lead to the assimilation of reality to principle, to the obscuring from view of all differences between men and women in the name of equality. It is only through the accommodation of principles of equality to the actuality of sex differences that it becomes possible to understand what equity or justice for men and women would in fact entail.

Thus, in the process of accommodation lies the recovery of detail, the rediscovery of the finite and the particular. And the equilibration, which signifies the development of an adult moral sense, would then consist of integrating an ideal conception of justice with knowledge of the realities of human social experience.

We are currently conducting a follow-up study of college students who, three years ago, took our course on moral and political choice, a course in which we explicitly dealt with ethical relativism in the hopes of fostering the development of principled moral judgment. In reinterviewing these students, we are interested not only in the success of that effort but also in learning more about the relationship between moral and ego development in late adolescence. More specifically, we are interested in the ways in which moral development affects and is affected by life choices. Thus our attention turns to the relationship between moral judgment and moral action, and to the role of experience in moral development.

A preliminary look at these interviews suggests that while there is often a rough correspondence between moral and ego development in that conceptions of both self and morality may be described as being either conventional, relativistic, or principled, there are some interesting variants of this pattern. In some students, we see a moral philosophy that is fully principled but that neither touches nor is touched by the rest of their life. In others, we find evidence of a considerable struggle to reconcile principles with experience, where the process of accommodation eventuates in a transformation of moral judgment itself (Gilligan and Murphy, 1977). While it is clear that these data will provide some answers to our questions regarding the transition from adolescence to adulthood, it is equally apparent that for others we will have to wait until we have among our subjects people further into life.

For the moment, we conclude that there is a relativism or a methethical questioning possible at each of the higher stages of moral judgment, that what is questioned is the conception of morality characteristic of that particular stage, and that at the principled stages, this questioning comes out of the attempt to reconcile principles with experience.

In the world of tradition, morality provides ready-made answers to the questions of how to live and what to do. The formally operational adolescent has the capacity to seek new answers to these questions and thus to conceive a better world. If, however, such conceptions are to be more than hypothetical, they must be taken back into the universe of experience and tested against the actual constraints of reality. Otherwise, moral development stops in the egocentric isolation of a perpetual adolescence, and the *morality* of pure reason comes to resemble the *authenticity* of pure madness where

The falsities of an alienated social reality are rejected in favor of an upward psychopathic mobility to the point of divinity, each one of us a Christ—but with none of the inconveniences of undertaking to intercede, of being a sacrifice, of reasoning with rabbis, of making sermons, of having disciples, of going to weddings and to

funerals, of beginning something and at a certain point remarking that it is finished
(Trilling, 1971, pp. 171–172).

ACKNOWLEDGMENT

Support for Carol Gilligan's work was provided by a grant from the Spencer
Foundation.

APPENDIX

Definition of Moral Stages*

I. Preconventional Level

At this level the child is responsive to cultural rules and labels of good and
bad, right or wrong, but interprets these labels either in terms of the physical or
the hedonistic consequences of action (punishment, reward, exchange of favors)
or in terms of the physical power of those who enunciate the rules and labels. The
level is divided into the following two stages:

Stage 1: *The punishment-and-obedience orientation.* The physical consequences of action determine its goodness or badness regardless of the human
meaning or value of these consequences. Avoidance of punishment and unques-
tioning deference to power are valued in their own right, not in terms of respect
for an underlying moral order supported by punishment and authority (the latter
being stage 4).

Stage 2: *The instrumental-relativist orientation.* Right action consists of that
which instrumentally satisfies one's own needs and occasionally the needs of
others. Human relations are viewed in terms like those of the market place.
Elements of fairness, of reciprocity, and of equal sharing are present, but they are
always interpreted in a physical pragmatic way. Reciprocity is a matter of "you
scratch my back and I'll scratch yours," not of loyalty, gratitude, or justice.

II. Conventional Level

At this level, maintaining the expectations of the individual's family, group,
or nation is perceived as valuable in its own right, regardless of immediate and

*Reprinted from: Kohlberg, L. The claim to moral adequacy of a highest stage of moral judgment. *The
Journal of Philosophy*, 1973, *70* (18), 631–632.

obvious consequences. The attitude is not only one of *conformity* to personal expectations and social order, but of loyalty to it, of actively *maintaining,* supporting, and justifying the order, and of identifying with the persons or group involved in it. At this level, there are the following two stages:

Stage 3: *The interpersonal concordance or "good boy—nice girl" orientation.* Good behavior is that which pleases or helps others and is approved by them. There is much conformity to stereotypical images of what is majority or "natural" behavior. Behavior is frequently judged by intention—"he means well" becomes important for the first time. One earns approval by being "nice."

Stage 4: *The "law and order" orientation.* There is orientation toward authority, fixed rules, and the maintenance of the social order. Right behavior consists of doing one's duty, showing respect for authority, and maintaining the given social order for its own sake.

III. Postconventional, Autonomous, or Principled Level

At this level, there is a clear effort to define moral values and principles that have validity and application apart from the authority of the groups or persons holding these principles and apart from the individual's own identification with these groups. This level again has two stages:

Stage 5: *The social contract, legalistic orientation,* generally with utilitarian overtones. Right action tends to be defined in terms of general individual rights, and standards which have been critically examined and agreed upon by the whole society. There is a clear awareness of the relativism of personal values and opinions and a corresponding emphasis upon procedural rules for reaching consensus. Aside from what is constitutionally and democratically agreed upon, the right is a matter of personal "values" and "opinion." The result is an emphasis upon the "legal point of view," but with an emphasis upon the possibility of changing law in terms of rational considerations of social utility (rather than freezing it in terms of stage 4 "law and order"). Outside the legal realm, free agreement and contract is the binding element of obligation. This is the "official" morality of the American government and constitution.

Stage 6: *The universal-ethical-principle orientation.* Right is defined by the decision of conscience in accord with self-chosen *ethical principles* appealing to logical comprehensiveness, universality, and consistency. These principles are abstract and ethical (the Golden Rule, the categorical imperative): they are not concrete moral rules like the Ten Commandments. At heart, these are universal principles of *justice,* of the *reciprocity* and *equality* of human *rights,* and of respect for the dignity of human beings as *individual persons* ("From Is to Ought," pp. 164–65).

References

Fishkin, J. Personal communication, 1973.

Gilligan, C., & Murphy, J. M. The philosopher and the "Dilemma of the Fact." Unpublished Manuscript, 1977.

Horton, R. African traditional thought and western science. In *Africa, 37,* 50–71, 155–187. Also reprinted in M. Marwic. *Witchcraft and Sorcery.* Harmondsworth, England: Penguin Books, 1970.

Inhelder, B., & Piaget, J. *The growth of logical thinking from childhood to adolescence.* New York: Basic Books, 1968.

Kenniston, K. Youth: A "new" stage of life. *American Scholar,* Autumn, 1970, 631–654.

Kohlberg, L. Continuities in childhood and adult moral development revisited. In P. B. Baltes & L. R. Goulet (Eds.), *Lifespan developmental psychology,* 2nd ed. New York: Academic Press, 1973.

Kohlberg, L., & Colby, A. The relation between cognitive and moral stages. In L. Kohlberg (Ed.), *Moralization: The cognitive developmental approach.* New York: Holt, Rinehart, and Winston, 1977.

Kohlberg, L., & Gilligan, C. The adolescent as a philosopher: The discovery of the self in a post-conventional world. *Daedalus,* Fall, 1971, *100,* 1051–1086.

Kohlberg, L., & Kramer, R. Continuities and discontinuities in childhood and adult moral development. *Human Development,* 1969, *12,* 93–120.

Piaget, J. *Six psychological studies.* D. Elkind (Ed.), tr. by A. Tenzer. New York: Random House, 1968.

Sennett, R. *The uses of disorder.* New York: Vintage Books, 1970.

Trilling, L. *Sincerity and authenticity.* Cambridge, Mass.: Harvard University Press, 1971.

Turiel, E. Stage transition in moral development. In R. L. Travers (Ed.), *Second handbook of research on teaching.* Chicago: Rand McNally, 1973.

Ullian, D. The development of masculinity and feminity. In B. Lloyd, & J. Archer (Eds.), *Exploring sex differences.* New York: Academic Press, 1976.

CHAPTER 10

Adolescence, Egocentrism, and Epistemological Loneliness

Michael J. Chandler

University of Rochester
Rochester, New York

Previous research by this author and others (Chandler, 1972, 1973; Chandler & Greenspan, 1972), which can only be alluded to here, concerns the assessment and remedial training of various social and interpersonal skills in adolescents who, counter to normative expections, have failed to acquire certain habits of thought characteristic of formal-operational intelligence. The young persons typically used in these studies were children who had failed in their initial attempts to conform to adult social expectations and had been labeled as delinquent or mentally ill. To gain some better understanding of these troubled children, the researchers made attempts to chart their progress along several lines of sociocognitive development, focusing particularly on the status of their efforts to differentiate themselves from and define themselves in relation to others.

Within the context described above, these studies centered primarily on the ability of these children to decenter or departicularize the focus of their conceptual concerns and to take and coordinate the roles and points of view of others. Not surprisingly, these atypical young persons regularly show marked developmental lags and are often persistently egocentric in ways more characteristic of and appropriate to better socialized children much younger than themselves.

In order to attempt some better understanding of the significance of these developmental delays, it is necessary to understand not only where these children have been but where they are or should be going. What is present and potential at the beginning of development and the growth process that follows is, according to Piaget (1972), only made evident if one begins at the end and examines the outcome or end state of this process. Progress can be measured only in terms of destinations, and only when the full realization of the child's capacity is achieved are we able to read backward in time and grasp with any clarity the coherence or lack of coherence of the preceding events. For this reason, much of the subsequent discussion will center on some of the complexities of the more usual forms of adolescent development in general and the process of self–other differentation in particular rather than on the particulars of the disturbed children with whom we typically deal.

Despite his own insistence that development is best understood when viewed in the light of its own consequences, Piaget has focused the majority of his creative efforts on earlier developmental stages. Mature cognition, in the shape of formal operational thought, is the least researched and perhaps the least understood facet of his theory (Dulit, 1972). Several papers in this volume are devoted in one way or another to attempting to gain some better understanding of this difficult problem area. This paper will be restricted to a discussion of a single, but central, piece of this puzzle, the problem of self–other differentation. In particular, what is considered here are some of the personal and social consequences of the adolescent's disquieting discovery of the private and privileged character of his own and others' thoughts and feelings, of the recognition of his own ultimate subjectivity, and the "plurality of solitudes," which will be referred to here as *epistemological loneliness*. Prior to discussing the concept of epistemological loneliness, we will make some general comments about Piaget's theoretical model and then review, in an abbreviated form, some of the developmental milestones that he has charted in the course of self–other differentiation.

Piaget's developmental theory is, within certain limits, generally understood to be a dialectic growth model. In this model newly acquired mental structures serve to resolve intellectual and interpersonal dilemmas of earlier stages by consolidating once isolated and seemingly contradictory experiences and, at the same time, to create in their wake new dilemmas or contradictions, which are not resolved until the next juncture in development is reached (Riegel, 1973). The symmetry inherent in this dialectic model is, however, somewhat jeopardized when the child enters into what is described as the last of his major developmental stages. The emergence of formal-operational thought should, like the styles and structures of cognition that precede it, both create as well as solve certain important conceptual problems and generate in its wake a set of disequilibrating forces that may, without the benefit of some new and reparative revolution in cognitive organization, continue without resolution. The achievement of formal operational solutions to the problem of self–other differentiation may, and often does, precipitate for the adolescent a sphere of disequilibration for which few if any nonregressive solutions are possible. The double-edged character of these cognitive accomplishments serves to dampen the enthusiasm with which adolescents embrace their own newly acquired conceptual skills, to discourage them in their attempts to consolidate their intellectual gains, and at times, to derail entirely their subsequent developmental progress. In order to be clear about this, we will first step back from the period of adolescence and review some of what Piaget and others have said about the problem of self–other differentiation in earlier developmental periods.

The process of self–other differentiation, as it begins to occur in infancy, is, according to Piaget (Piaget, 1929; Piaget & Inhelder, 1956), a process of literal physical disentanglement in which the young child gradually establishes the boundaries of his own person and learns where his own body begins and ends. Prior to this accomplishment, infants are prone to taking exploratory, get-acquainted bites of their own seemingly disembodied hands and feet, frequently attempt to magically influence objects at a distance, and mistakenly assume responsibility for events initiated by others. By the end of the sensorimotor period, however, most infants have acquired a reasonably accurate understanding of the geographic limits of their own bodies and, at least on the plane of action, have more or less successfully differentiated themselves from the animate and inanimate objects around them.

For Piaget, the active erection of functional body boundaries is, however, only the first step in a very long process of defining the differences between self and other (Looft, 1972). As the focus of the child's concerns shifts to a more representational plane, the entire process of self–other differentiation must again be repeated in the spheres of thought and feeling. The preoperational child, while he has a reasonable understanding of his own physical integrity, remains almost totally ignorant of and is confused by the uniqueness of his mental representations. During the preschool years, children routinely assume that their thoughts and feelings are identical to and coextensive with the thoughts and feelings of others. This representational failure in self–other differentiation, which Piaget has labeled as *egocentrism,* has been shown to persist in one form or another at least until adolescence (Elkind, 1967).

As the child moves into the period of concrete operations, he begins to develop the analytic capacity to recognize that things may be subject to different interpretations and that others may see things or feel about things differently from himself. Still, according to Feffer (1960), such children typically lack the skill necessary to decenter the focus of their concerns and to coordinate such multiple perspectives. Rather, in a serial fashion, the child succeeds only in sequentially shifting from one noncoordinated point of view to another. Yet, because of his burgeoning perspective-taking skills and because of his increasing ability to reason rationally about events, he does, during this concrete-operational period, begin to piece together the realization that if two people think differently about the same thing, then someone may very well be wrong. This loss of certainty has a range of far-reaching consequence and has been described by a variety of theorists. This is the period of the clay-feet phenomenon, when old truths are challenged and parents and other local deities begin to falsify their previously unquestioned omniscience. This turn of events is well captured in a quote from a book by Edmund Groose (1909, pp. 33–34) entitled *Father and Son: A Study of Two Temperaments:*

> My mother always deferred to my father and in his absence spoke of him to me as if he were all wise. I confused him in some sense with God; at all events I believed that my father knew everything and saw everything. One morning in my sixth year, my mother and I were alone in the morning room, when my father came in and announced some fact to us. I was standing on the rug, gazing at him, and when he made this statement, I remember turning quickly, in embarrassment and looking into the fire. The shock to me was as that of a thunderbolt for what my father said *was not true.* . . . Here was the appalling discovery, never suspected before, that my father was not as God and did not know everything. The shock was not caused by any suspicion that he was not telling the truth, as it appeared to him, but by the awful proof that he was not, as I had suspected, omniscient.
>
> The theory that my father was omniscient or infallible was now dead and buried. He probably knew very little; in this case he had not known a fact of such importance that if you did not know that, it could hardly matter what you knew. (Elkind, 1973a, p. 109)

One by-product of the concrete-operational child's emerging sense of ideological relativity implicit in the preceding quotation is the growing realization that if some people are right, then others are inevitably wrong. Under such circumstances, it becomes a matter of paramount importance to be on the winning side. Differences of opinion may be tolerable, but only so long as it is always someone else who is wrong. This defensive sense of certainty, which Elkind (1973a) has labeled "cognitive conceit," permits the imposition of an assumptive reality on the world and allows the concrete operational child to harness in part the ambiguity created by his or her own increasing analytic skill. The effectiveness of this technique for arbitrating differences of opinion by fiat is, however, like other interim developmental solutions, relatively short-lived. It is not possible to grow in rationality without becoming increasingly impressed by the arbitrariness of one's own hypotheses, and as the child moves closer to acquiring a formal operational mode of thought, the assumption that one is always right can no longer be maintained.

One of the principle accomplishments of the adolescent period and the emergence of formal operational thought is this gradual realization that persons all view the world from individualized and idiosyncratic perspectives and that there is no simple criterion of objectivity by which to arbitrate this diversity of points of view: "Each person is a center of another orientation to the objective world, a center of another arrangement of the universe" (Laing & Cooper, 1964, p. 108). This manifold of perspectives refuses epistemological unification and constitutes, as has been pointed out, the irreducible specificity of life: "Each particular perspective, each particular point of view, that is, precisely, each person, is the center of his own world, but not the center of anyone else's world—although many people long and strain to make it so. Each point of view is an absolute and at the same time, absolutely relative'' (Laing & Cooper, 1964, pp. 11–12).

Faced with this growing recognition, the child gradually begins to move closer to the understanding that objectivity, rather than being an as-yet-undiscovered secret, is instead what Piaget has called ''the recognition of the universality of subjectivity'' (Piaget & Inhelder, 1956). The initial recognition of this uncertainty principle is not, however, equivalent to its wholehearted acceptance, nor is it at all obvious how one is to cope with, let alone take pleasure in, this ultimate relativity. This growing realization is instead typically accompanied by a sense of uneasiness that is hard to shake off. There is a gradual dawning of an awareness of what Sartre (1965) called a ''plurality of solitudes''—that each person's point of view relentlessly cancels out the viewpoint of another. This potentially ominous and isolative awareness is what we have chosen to call a *sense of epistemological loneliness*. This loneliness and sense of estrangement are the legacy of the disequilibration that formal operational thought wills to the already embattled adolescent. If, as Piaget has suggested, formal operational thought is the last major structural revolution in cognitive development, then we can anticipate no radical developmental solution to the emotional havoc created by one's own incontestable epistemological solitude. Without a new brand of redeeming cognitive reorganization waiting in the wings, what sort of solutions are available to the adolescent, and how is he to come to terms with his loneliness?

We are not convinced that a solution, at least a nonregressive solution, does exist for this problem. There have nevertheless been a great variety of public and private solutions posited—some of which are seized upon by adolescents in sufficient number that an enumeration of them may help us understand part of the complexity of this age group. Several examples follow.

The Search for a Negotiated Consensus: The Peer Group as an Enclave of Common Conviction

Having stumbled upon this rat's nest of divergent opinion, the adolescent must decide how he is to mediate these divergent views and relate them to his own. One available means of doing so is to search out a group of peers and negotiate a consensus with them. This cliquishness and press toward conformity that often characterize groups of adolescents have been subject to a variety of interpretations (Elkind, 1973b). Some have understood this phenomenon as a response on the part of adolescents to external pressure and exclusionary practices emanating from the adult culture. Without attempting to discount the realities of such external pressures, we would, by contrast, wish to emphasize a more internal locus of this pressure toward peer-group conformity.

In this view, adolescents, faced with the specter of isolation and epistemological loneliness, often voluntarily constitute themselves into social collectives and pledge to differ from one another in as few ways as possible. By binding themselves together into a univocal social whole, they ward off the sense of estrangement that accompanies their new-won sense of subjective relativity and create an enclave of common conviction. Sartre described this process as the creation of a figment part of the self that is defined exclusively in terms of others and that creates a domain in which the individual becomes as one with the everybodies and shares their common fate (Nordstrom, Friedenberg, & Gold, 1967, p. 131). Within such an imposed consensus, the peer group becomes the measure of all things, and deviations either by the self or by others threaten this delicate group solution. Under such circumstances, any chink in the unified ideological front must be expeditiously dealt with or loneliness will begin to trickle back in.

Prejudice and Stereotypy

One method of warding off the threat imposed by individuality is to blur out of focus the distinctness that characterizes separate persons and to treat them as abstract, stereotyped entities that are mutually intersubstitutable (Sartre, 1965). Stereotyping in this sense is a means of bracketing a number of human beings together into a kind of fictitious social *Gestalt* and relating to that collection as if it were a single individual. Through such stereotyping maneuvers, common among adolescents, the threat of individuality is warded off through an act of perpetual negation (Elkind, 1967).

In pursuit of a group consensus, one's own ill-advised attempts at individuation may constitute as serious a threat as the individualizing efforts of others and must be treated with equal harshness. The self becomes a source of public embarrassment to be hidden away or legislated out of existence.

Efforts to impose an artificial consensus need not necessarily take the form of large peer-group movements, and individual adolescents may seek to achieve some less ambitious sense of communality. The search for intimacy that frequently characterizes older adolescents and young adults (Erikson, 1968) may be partially understood as a retreat from a search for group agreement and a retrenchment in a plurality of two.

Ideological Imperatives and the Wholesaling of Opinion

The need for some sense of ideological companionship need not necessarily take the form of legislating agreement within one's own peer group. Certain adolescents may more effectively achieve a sense of communality by opting into some prepackaged world view that advocates a particular set of religious or secular ideologies. What for some adolescents takes the form of a crisis of estrangement or a struggle for group consensus becomes for others what Elkind (1973b) has described as an endemic search for faith.

For some, this takes the form of religious conversion (Heise, 1972), in which the fallibility of human judgment is exchanged for a direct pipeline to divine wisdom. Such conversion experiences are not, however, limited to the adoption of a formal religious faith, and many adolescents also achieve enlightenment through some more secular but noncritical conversion to the canons of some science or some humanistic faith, such as the perfectibility or infinite adaptability of mankind (Elkind, 1973b). All of the forms of secular and non-secular conversion share in the common assumption that differences in opinion are symptomatic of routine but correctible errors in human judgment that serve to becloud the truth of the matter. Special guidance (in the form of divine enlightenment) or special caution (in the form of methodological rigor) is assumed to provide an adequate corrective for these human shortcomings. Philosophical realism provides a powerful ally to persons who opt for this well-worn solution.

Abstraction

One almost universal, and for that reason less easily identifiable, method employed by adolescents in their efforts to minimize the idosyncrasies of their world is simply to do what persons at the formal operational level do best: think abstractly.

Abstract thought, through a kind of selective attention and inattention, provides a means of denying, or at least circumventing, a variety of potential contradictions and identifying similarities at the cost of obscuring differences. For all of its other much-lauded attributes, abstract thinking is a powerful tool for lopping off awkward differences of opinion and imposing a kind of elegant, if somewhat syncretic, consensus.

Riegel (1973), drawing upon a Hegelian frame of reference, has recently argued against the view that abstract reasoning, with all of its cavalier selectivity, should be regarded as the ultimate in cognitive achievement. According to this view, a slavish adherence to the classical principle of identity, which maintains that facts or opinions should not contradict one another, is an unnecessary and peculiarly nonhuman standard of judgment. Within a more Hegelian model, contradiction, rather than being treated as a limitation to overcome, is seen as a necessary condition of all thought and provides the dynamic necessary to prompt all cognitive growth and development. Riegel (1973) argued, although not, we think, against Piaget, that cognitive maturity depends not on abstraction but upon a new kind of concretism in which all available contradictory views and perspectives are preserved and held in what Carmichael (1966) has described as an "awkward embrace." Within this view, it is not necessary that an individual equilibrate all available conflicts. Instead, it is possible to live with, thrive upon, and eventually come to take pleasure in these contradictions. Through this recognition of the irreconcilable, a person comes to capture the one more significant truth of the situation: that being different, lonely as it may be, makes all the difference. This ultimate irony is not based upon a sense of isolation or separateness but is founded, rather, on a sense of one's immersion in and dependence on a world of others. "True irony," is, according to Kenneth Burke, " ... not 'superior' to the enemy. True irony, humble irony, is based upon a sense of fundamental kinship with the enemy, as one *needs* him, is *indebted* to him, is not merely outside him as an observer, but contains him *within,* being consubstantial with him" (Burke, 1954, p. 514, in Carmichael, 1966). Given all this, one wonders less why some troubled adolescents approach formal operational thought slowly, or reluctantly, or not at all.

References

Burke, K. *Grammar of motives*. New York: Prentice-Hall, 1954.

Carmichael, D. Irony: A developmental and cognitive study. Unpublished doctoral dissertation, University of California, Berkeley, 1966.

Chandler, M. J. Egocentrism in normal and pathological childhood development. In F. J. Mönks, W. W. Hartup, and T. deWit (Eds.), *Determinants of behavioral development*. New York: Academic Press, 1972.

Chandler, M. J. Egocentrism and antisocial behavior: The assessment and training of social perspective taking skills, *Developmental Psychology,* 1973, *9,* 1–9.

Chandler, M. J., & Greenspan, S. Ersatz egocentrism: A reply to H. Barke. *Developmental Psychology,* 1972, *7,* 104–106.

Dulit, E. Adolescent thinking à la Piaget: The formal stage. *Journal of Youth and Adolescence,* 1972, *1,* 281–301.

Elkind, D. Egocentrism in adolescence. *Child Development,* 1967, *38,* 1025–1034.

Elkind, D. Cognitive structures in latency behavior. In J. C. Westman (Ed.), *Individual differences in children*. New York: Wiley, 1973. (a)

Elkind, D. Culture, change, and their affects on children. *Journal of Social Casework,* 1973, *54,* 360–366. (b)

Erikson, E. *Identity: Youth and crisis*. New York: Norton, 1968.

Feffer, M. H. The cognitive implications of role taking behavior. *Journal of Personality,* 1960, *28,* 383–396.

Gasse, E. *Father and son: A study of two temperaments*. London: Heineman, 1909.

Goodman, P. *Growing Up Absurd*. New York: Random House, 1960.

Heise, D. *Personality and socialization*. Chicago: Rand McNally, 1972.

Laing, R. D., & Cooper, D. *Reason and violence*. London: Tavistock, 1964.

Looft, W. R. Egocentrism and social interaction across the lifespan. *Psychological Bulletin,* 1972, *78,* 73–92.

Nordstrom, C., Friedenberg, E., & Gold, H. *Society's children: A study of resentment in the secondary school.* New York: Random House, 1967.

Piaget, J. *The child's conception of the world.* New York: Humanities, 1929.

Piaget, J. Intellectual evaluation from adolescence to adulthood. *Human Development,* 1972, *15,* 1–12.

Piaget, J., & Inhelder, B. *The child's concept of space.* London: Routledge, 1956.

Riegel, K. F. Dialectic operations: The final period of cognitive development. Paper presented at the biennial meeting of the Society for Research in Child Development, Philadelphia, March 1973.

Sartre, J. *Being and nothingness.* New York: Philosophical Library, 1965.

PART IV

APPLIED RESEARCH

CHAPTER 11

The Function of Reading in the Transition to Concrete and Formal Operations

Hildred Rawson

The Ontario Institute for Studies in Education
Toronto, Ontario, Canada

Introduction

The study reported in the first part of this paper was designed to uncover relationships between corresponding cognitive operations under two sets of conditions: first, in situations in which logical operations in conservation, classification, deduction, induction, and probability reasoning are required in response to concrete-verbal stimuli; then in situations in which these operations are required in reading. The study was exploratory. The purpose was to examine the extent to which cognitive operations in the categories assessed are likely to be available equally to 9- to 10-year-old children in the two situations, concrete and reading.

The concrete-verbal tests used in the study were adapted from tests originally designed by Piaget and Inhelder, and by Matalon. They are referred to here as the *Concrete tests*. The *Stories tests* were based on stories constructed by the examiner. The comparability of the paired items was checked using the formulas of symbolic logic. Preliminary questions on the stories ensured that the child had read and could recall the information essential for the operations required.

The statistical procedures applied in the analyses of the data included product–moment correlations and canonical correlation for assessing relations within the data and between the Concrete and Stories data taken as wholes.

Following this study, levels of cognitive functioning of children of comparable potential who were *not* learning to read were examined. The responses of children 10–15 years old appeared to indicate a level of thinking skill below that of the 9- to 10-year-old children in the earlier study.

The program for reteaching underachieving readers was designed to coordinate, as far as possible, instruction in reading and the development of operational thinking. Outcomes and procedures of that program are described here.

Recently an experiment in reteaching underachieving grade four children in a school system was conducted in cooperation with a doctoral student (1976).* Some outcomes and procedures of that study are also presented.

Implications for the transition from concrete level reasoning to formal operations are discussed as well.

Relations between Cognitive Operations in Concrete and in Reading Situations

The study of the relations between cognitive operations in concrete and reading situations was based on a sample of 100 children, 50 boys and 50 girls, drawn from a population of 563 children entering grade five in 13 schools in a western Canadian city. The mean age of the children in the sample was 9 years, 10 months.

The reading comprehension levels of these children was assessed by use of the *STEP Reading Test, Form 4B*. The mean percentage of correct responses on the 70 items of this test was 68.5. The mean number of items correct was 48, and the standard deviation was 8.6. The average IQ estimate of the children in the sample, based on the *SRA Primary Mental Abilities Test*, was 109.7.

The subjects were tested individually, first on the set of seven stories (the Stories tests) and again, after a period of two weeks, on the Concrete tests. In the administering of the Stories tests, silent reading of a story was followed by an interview with the child consisting of preliminary questions and test questions with no marked transition between them. All preliminary questions were answered correctly, with assistance if necessary. Concrete test interviews were similarly conducted, with questions identifying the materials being followed by test questions. The Concrete test materials were arranged at five stations in a large semicircle in an open classroom. The interviews were conducted in the child's school. They were tape-recorded and typed for scoring.

Five categories of operations were assessed: conservation, including conservation of substance, weight, and volume, each at three levels of complexity, defined by the number and extent of the changes in shape and distribution of the

---

*Janice Baker is a doctoral candidate at The Ontario Institute for Studies in Education. The chairman of the committee for this study is Dr. Michael Orme of The Department of Applied Psychology.

material of one or both objects; classification, including class-inclusion relations and the construction of the multiplicative class; deduction; induction; and probability. Explanations were elicited for each decision and inference.

The readability level of each of the seven stories of the Stories tests was estimated by use of the Dale–Chall readability formula based on a total story. The mean readability grade score was 4.6. The range of the readibility grade scores was 4.4–5.0.

The reliability of the *STEP Reading Test* was determined by calculations based on the Kuder–Richardson formula 20 using total scores of the 100 subjects on the 70 items of the test. The reliability coefficient obtained was $r_{xx} = 0.85$.

Test–retest coefficients of correlation obtained for the Concrete and Stories tests were $r_{xx} = 0.74$ and 0.72 respectively ($n = 13$). A number of factors may have affected the measurement of the reliability of these tests. The questions presented tended to be an instructional experience for children approaching an understanding of the operations assessed, and these questions were likely to be answered correctly on retest. In addition, the teachers reported that when the children returned to the classroom, they continued to discuss solutions to the test questions that interested them.

The mean percentage of correct responses obtained for each of the 5 categories assessed by the Concrete and Stories tests is shown in Table 1. The results in Table 1 suggest that the mean percentage of correct responses for each of the categories measured by the Concrete tests was generally higher than that obtained for the corresponding categories in reading (Rawson, 1969).

Results on subtests of each of the categories assessed will now be described.

Conservation

The Concrete tests of conservation were adapted from those described in *Le développement de quantités physiques chez l'enfant* (Piaget & Inhelder, 1962).

TABLE 1
Mean Percentage of Correct Responses, Concrete and Stories Tests
($n = 100$)

Category	Concrete mean %	Stories mean %
Conservation ($n^a = 27$)[a]	54	35
Classification ($n = 19$)	64	27
Deduction ($n = 17$)	53	51
Induction ($n = 6$)	47	34
Probability ($n = 6$)	56	49
Average ($n = 75$)	56	39

[a] n^a = number of test items in the category.

Table 2 shows the mean percentage of responses that correctly stated that the substance, weight, and volume of two objects—for example, two balls of plasticine—originally equal, were "the same" after deformations that included changes in the shape and the distribution of the material. Each of these conservation tasks was presented at three levels of complexity. At the first level of complexity, one of the two equal objects was deformed by one action resulting in a change of shape with the substance remaining continuous, that is, object $A_1 \rightarrow A_1'$, one ball of clay $\rightarrow$ is "doughnut." At the seond level of complexity, one object is deformed by one action, a ball $\rightarrow$ a "snake," and the seond object was deformed by two actions, a ball cut into small cubes and distributed over an area so that the substance became discontinuous, $A_1 \rightarrow A_1'$; $A_2 \rightarrow A_2''$. At the third level of complexity, material was distributed in space with change in visibility over time, for example, sugar dissolved, popcorn exploded, $A_2 \rightarrow A_2'''$.

It may be seen in Table 2 that the mean percentage of responses *asserting* conservation at each level of complexity in the Stories tests was consistently lower than for the corresponding items on the Concrete tests, with the exception of volume at the third level of complexity Stories. The averages of the mean percentages on the Concrete tests were comparable to results reported by Piaget and Inhelder (1962) and by Lovell & Ogilvie (1960, 1961).

Table 3 shows the mean percentage of responses *asserting and defending* conservation of substance, weight, and volume. Explanations could be at level zero. In the Stories test, for example, the following response was scored 1 for the decision and zero for the explanation:

> He gave the chickadees and the sparrows and the jays just the same amount to eat because they were all cold and hungry.

Logical explanations could be based on *reversibility* (the objects could be returned to their original shape without loss); on the *principle of transitivity* ($A_1 = A_2$; $A_2 = A_2'$; $\therefore A_1 = A_2'$); or on the inference, *modus ponens:* premise I, given:

TABLE 2

Mean Percentage of Responses Asserting Conservation at Levels of Complexity I, II, III ($n = 100, n = 3$ at Each Level of Complexity)

Subtests	Concrete conservation Mean % Level of complexity				Stories conservation Mean % Level of complexity			
	I	II	III	Average	I	II	III	Average
Substance	94	88	60	80	72	53	66	64
Weight	88	78	54	73	40	34	44	40
Volume	65	68	33	55	43	49	51	48

TABLE 3
Mean Percentage of Responses Asserting and Defending
Conservation of Substance, Weight, and Volume ($n = 100; n = 9$)

Subtests	Concrete conservation Mean %	Stories conservation Mean %
Substance	64	43
Weight	57	27
Volume	40	36

$A_1 = A_2$; premise II, a tautology, if nothing is added and nothing removed, the amount of a substance, its weight, etc., remains the same; premise III, an observation: nothing is, in fact, added or subtracted by the transformation; inference: therefore, they still must be the same.

Again, the scores on the reading tests appeared to be lower than on the concrete tests. It appears that identical logical operations in conservation are more difficult in reading than in concrete experimental situations, even when the information in reading also refers to concrete situations and the child has just rehearsed verbally what he read in response to preliminary questions. The *décalages* suggested by these findings would imply that operations in conservation considered to be established beyond extinction in concrete test situations may not be assumed to be similarly available in reading. Comprehension in reading can be expected to be affected by a delay in the generalization of an operation to the different medium.

Classification

The materials and test items for the Concrete tests of classification were adapted from those originally described by Inhelder and Piaget (1964). For the corresponding Stories items, two stores were used: one, an account of ducks returning to the prairie in the spring, for assessing class-inclusion relations; the second, a description of "A City of Long Ago," required the construction of the multiplicative class, *A yellow raft,* the adjective–noun construction. The first story, the story of ducks returning, begins like this:

> The first birds to arrive in the spring are the ducks, and the first ducks are the pintail.
> The pintail arrive in flocks of hundreds. . . . They settle on the wheat fields and feed
> there until the ice has melted on the ponds. . . .

Predicates (Table 4) describe the properties of members of a class: "Pintail and mallard *are pond feeders,* " "Birds *are feathered creatures*"; for class inclusion a response is "more birds than ducks; ducks are birds too."

Table 4 shows the mean percentage of correct responses on subtests of the

TABLE 4
Mean Percentage of Correct Responses, Subtests of Classification
(*n* = 100)

Subtests	Concrete classification Mean %	Stories classification Mean %
Class inclusion (*n* = 8)	73	24
Multiplicative class (*n* = 6)	48	27
Predicates (*n* = 6)	60	30

concrete and stories tests of classification. The results shown in Table 4 suggest that scores obtained on the Stories tests of classification were considerably lower than those obtained on corresponding test items on the Concrete tests.

It appears that recognizing class-inclusion relations in reading involves considerable restructuring of the information presented. In the Story test, the child read:

... birds ... are ducks. ...
ducks ... are pintail.

If he was unable to abstract criterial properties and construct the superordinate and subordinate classes on this basis, he was likely to respond as follows to such questions as, "Are ducks birds?" "Are there more ducks or more pintail on the prairies in the summer?"

Ducks aren't birds. They're better than birds, they swim and fly.

There'll be more pintail than ducks. It said in the story the pintail arrive in flocks of hundreds.

It appears that identical logical operations in classification are more difficult in reading than in concrete stimulus situations, even when the information in reading is rehearsed orally. In the testing situation, if a child hesitated in response to a preliminary question, or if his response was inaccurate or incomplete he was instructed to reread the passage orally, a word not recognized was pronounced for him and the preliminary question was repeated. The preliminary questions elicited essential information and encouraged the recall of experiences:

What kind of birds come back first in spring?
What kind of ducks come first?
Where do the pintail get their food before the ice melts on the ponds?
How do they get their food, have you watched them?
What do they look like when they're feeding?

Questions for which the answers were given in the text were not difficult for these children. It was the questions that required operations in classification, the

Piagetian-type questions, that made clear the limitations in their understanding of the materials they read.

Deduction

The materials and the test items for the Concrete tests of deduction were designed to replicate Matalon's study of deduction (1962). Both the "Village" and the "Lights" test materials from that study were used. The results obtained on the Concrete tests are considered to be comparable to those reported by Matalon.

Corresponding Stories test items were based on two stories. One describes a pioneer doctor and his young son driving with horses and a sleigh across a frozen river in a blizzard. They are trying to find a cut in the river bank on the other side in order to reach a patient. Additional questions were based on the story, "The Ducks Arrive in Spring," referred to above.

The mean percentage of correct responses on subtests of the Concrete and Stories tests of deduction is shown in Table 5. A correct inference and its logical justification was scored 1.

The results in Table 5 suggest that inferences based on *modus ponens* and *modus tollens* were likely to be about equally available in concrete and reading situations as measured by these tests. *Modus tollens* appeared to be the more difficult operation in each situation. In the Stories tests, an inference based on *modus tollens* was required in response to this question:

There are no ducks on the prairie. $\sim$ D: (no ducks).
Has the ice melted on the ponds? IM? or $\sim$ IM? IM: ice melted.
How did you know that ? $\sim$ D & (IM $\rightarrow$ D) $\rightarrow$ $\sim$ IM.

A corresponding test item from the Concrete tests of deduction, the "Lights" test, is the following:

This light switch works by a rule. The rule is, "If the red light is on, the green light is on". R $\rightarrow$ G (demonstrated). The child repeats the rule. The windows are closed, so the lights are not now visible.

TABLE 5
Mean Percentages of Correct Responses, Subtests of Deduction
($n = 100$)

Subtests	Concrete deduction Mean %	Stories deduction Mean %
Modus ponens ($n = 3$)	97	86
Modus tollens ($n = 3$)	71	67
Undetermined ($n = 4$)	21	13
Possible ($n = 6$)	65	48
Not possible ($n = 4$)	55	70

The green light is *not* on. ~ G
What about the red light? Is the red light on, or is it off?
~ G & (R → G) → ~ R

The negative statement in the premise and the negative form of the inference may explain some of the difficulty of operations based on *modus tollens*. In the "Lights" test, only one child declared, "I can't tell if I don't *see.*" He was persuaded to try.

An inference was *undetermined* when a conclusion did not necessarily follow from the given premises. In the story of the blizzard, for example, a statement, such as "There is a house in front of them," could mean that they had reached the patient, but not necessarily. The horses could have turned in the storm and gone home, a possibility suggested in the story. In the Concrete "Lights" test, the inference was *undetermined*—that is, "One cannot know"— in this situation:

Rule: "If the red light is on, the green light is on."
The green light is on. What about the red light? What is the rule?
What about the red light? Why is that?

In the inferences *possible* and *not-possible,* two propositions were to be considered for compatibility. If each proposition was possible and the two were mutually possible, they were compatible. In the story of the blizzard, the following statement was read and rehearsed in the preliminary questioning, "If they find the cut in the river bank, they will reach the patient's house." The possible and not-possible inference questions included these:

Is it possible to *not* find the cut and *not* get the patient's house?
How is that possible (not-possible)? (The question repeats the decision.)

Is it possible to *find* the cut and *not* get to the patient's house?
Would you explain how that is not possible (possible)?

These inferences required a judgment of the possibility that each statement could be true and that together they could also be true. It is interesting that the *non-possible* inference was generally answered correctly in the Stories tests (Table 5). It may have conformed to the children's hopes for a happy ending. The ability to judge the possibility and the compatibility of statements that are not statements of reality appears to anticipate operations at the formal level. The 9–10-year-old children in this study did not appear to question that one could reason from hypothetical premises or from contrary-to-fact premises.

Induction and Probability

The Concrete tests of inductive and probability reasoning were adapted from tests described by Piaget and Inhelder in *The Origins of the Idea of Chance in*

Children (1951, 1975). In this study, Piaget and Inhelder postulated that the development of operations in inductive and probability reasoning are dependent on the prior acquisition of class-inclusion relations, including disjunctive class relations, and the notion of the irreversibility of chance distribution. These operations are also dependent, they point out, on ability to accept evidence even when the evidence is in conflict with expectations. Later developments in inductive reasoning Piaget and Inhelder considered to be associated with flexibility in constructing and testing hypotheses and greater rigor in what is accepted as necessary and sufficient evidence. Judgments of probability at the formal level, they suggest, depend on the convergence of concrete level operations of chance with developing concepts of proportion, combinations and permutations.

Bocheński (1965) describes a sequence in which operations in induction are likely to be performed, and this sequence was followed in the presentation of questions in the Concrete and Stories tests of induction. First, preliminary questions assisted the child in assembling specific relevant observations. An appropriate response to these observations was "surprise," that is, an alert recognition that an entirely "new" situation now existed. Questions then suggested a search for an explanation—in this case, a search for the intervening constant altering a chance situation. The final questions elicited a statement of an inductive inference and its justification.

The intervening constant producing a new situation in the Concrete tests was an invisible magnet placed in one of a set of 8 black blocks (Piaget & Inhelder, 1951). The blocks were identical in appearance but of three different weights. The situation that was altered by the introduction of the magnet was the probability distribution of the points at which a freely moving spinner at the center of a board was observed to come to rest. The 8 blocks were placed symmetrically on colored wedges around this spinner.

The children usually proposed and tested a number of hypotheses to account for the fact that the spinner now stopped at one point only—hypotheses, such as "It's this heavy (or this medium heavy) block that makes the spinner stop here," or "The spinner always stops here because these two blocks are next to (or opposite) each other." By testing and eliminating these hypotheses and by confirming a hypothesis, such as "It's something in this block," the children succeeded in identifying the intervening constant.

The new and surprising situation in the Stories test concerned the dramatic changes described in the story when some boys return to a familiar cave they have been exploring. The cave is now silent and still; no bats fly screaming over their heads; their candles go out at the entrance to the cave; a chipmunk turns away from the cave and hides under a stone; an eagle flies overhead. The preliminary questions rehearsed these observations. The recognition question then was, "Are things really different at the cave on this day, or are the boys just imagining things?" The subsequent questions required the construction and testing of hypotheses to account for the differences "on this day"; the statement of an inductive inference; and the validation of the inference.

A number of children insisted that the boys were just imagining things (Table 6). A few explained it this way, "It's not really different, their mothers told them not to go into caves." Others recognized the situation as new but offered no explanation. Others gave a separate explanation for each observation. In that case an attempt was made to suggest that the observations could be related events:

> You say the wind blew the candles out. Would your explanation account for the other things that happened?

> Could you suggest an explanation that might account for other things that happened?

If the child then offered an explanation to account for at least two of the observations and also recognized its limitations

> A wild animal in the cave could make the bats go away and it would scare the chipmunk too... but that wouldn't make the candles go out...

the response was scored 6, as indicating an understanding of how inductive thinking could be conducted.

The following response was scored 10 (Table 6):

> It's different all right, they're not just imagining something. The bats are gone, maybe dead, the candles don't stay lit like they used to, and that chipmunk, he won't go in there either... Say, I just remember. I put a match in a bottle once... There's got to be something the matter with the air in there... candles need air to burn, and the bats need air too... it's the air all right!

The mean percentage of correct responses on the subtests of inductive reasoning is shown in Table 6.

It may be seen in Table 6 that almost 90% of the subjects correctly described the situation as "different" in the concrete situation, and approximately 70% did so in reading. Fewer succeeded in constructing hypotheses to account for the observed differences and still fewer supported an inference either by experiments

TABLE 6
Mean Percentage of Correct Responses, Subtests of Inductive
Reasoning (n = 100)

Subtests	Concrete induction Mean %	Stories induction Mean %
Recognition (n = 2)	87	69
Hypotheses (n = 3)	36	20
Inductive inference (n = 5)	20	13
Total induction (n = 10)	48	34

or by subsuming the inference under a law of nature. The number of items in each of the subtests of induction was small, which severely limited the possibility of generalizing from the results.

The Concrete tests of probability assessed notions of random distribution, uniform chance distribution, and the quantification of probability. The materials used were described by Piaget & Inhelder (1951). The Stories tests of probability assessed understanding of conditional probability, that is, the probability that Event B will occur given that Event A has occurred. The story describes a series of independent chance events. The child was to refer these events to past experience in considering the likelihood of a future occurrence of these events in just this sequence. Since each event in the story is the outcome of a set of multiple interacting forces, the probability is zero.

The sequence of events described in the story occurs after Mary gets off the school bus. She trips and falls . . . she notices a green snake crossing the path; then she sees a flock of crows settling in an old tree, and she arrives home to find her mother making muffins. The questions were:

> Do you think "these things" could happen just like this again tomorrow when Mary gets off the school bus? Next week . . . ? Can you explain why things like this are (not) likely to happen again just like this tomorrow? Next week?

A number of the responses suggested almost complete acceptance of the possibility of a recurrence of the events in the same sequence. Other responses seemed quite mature:

> Not possible! Life's not like that. It's a little different every morning from the time you brush your teeth!

The mean percentage of correct responses on the Concrete and Stories tests of probability was 56 and 49, respectively. It is, of course, difficult to generalize since there were only six test items in each situation, and the Stories items were based on one story.

A statistical analysis of the data obtained for the five categories of operations measured by the Concrete and Stories tests will now be presented.

Statistical Analyses

The matrix of product–moment correlations between the 10 categories of the Concrete and Stories tests is presented in Table 7.

It may be seen in Table 7 that the strongest relation within the data was between the Concrete and Stories tests of conservation ($r = 0.44, p < 0.001$), suggesting that approximately 20% of the variance of the Stories tests of conservation was predictable by the Concrete tests of conservation. Of the 25 intercorrelations between Concrete and Stories tests, 11 were significant. Five of these appeared to be highly significant. There appears to be a tendency for significant

TABLE 7

Product—Moment Correlations between Categories of the Concrete and Stories Tests
$(n = 100)^a$

Category		2	3	4	5	6	7	8	9	10
Conservation	1	25^c	24^c	-01	19^b	44^d	25^c	21^b	06	05
Classification	2		29^c	11	16	20^b	13	23	26	07
Deduction	3			17	26^c	25^c	13	39^c	09	02
Probability	4				11	23^b	07	13	17	19^b
Induction	5					15	-01	25^c	21^b	-02
Conservation	6						25^c	39^d	27^c	08
Classification	7							31^c	06	14
Deduction	8								22^b	01
Probability	9									-10
Induction	10									

^{a}Decimal points and diagonal elements are omitted.
$^b p < 0.05$
$^c p < 0.01$
$^d p < 0.001$

correlations to be based on conservation and deduction. The range of the variance predictable by corresponding test scores was from 19.4% ($r = 0.44$), Concrete and Stories conservation, to negligible ($r = 0.01$).

Significant correlations occurred within the Concrete data, and within the Stories data. The range of the variance predictable within the Concrete data was from 8.4% ($r = 0.29$), Concrete conservation and classification, to negligible ($r = 0.01$); the variance predictable within the Stories data was from 15% ($r = 0.39$), Stories conservation and deduction, to negligible. It appears that a limited process of generalization of the logical operations assessed was under way within each situation.

The pattern of observed correlations suggests that some of the operations contributed a greater amount than others to the prediction of the variance common to the two sets of tests. This may be clearer from the weights assigned to the different categories in the assessment of the maximum possible relation between the two sets of data taken as composites.

In the calculation of the maximum possible relation between the two sets of data taken as composites, one significant canonical correlation was obtained ($R_c = 0.549$, $p < 0.01$). The weighting system for this canonical correlation is presented in Table 8.

The canonical correlation obtained ($R_c = 0.549$) may be seen in Table 8 to be based primarily on Concrete and Stories conservation. The weights assigned were 0.808 and 0.912. Concrete probability and Stories deduction also contrib-

TABLE 8
Canonical Correlation between the Two
Composites, Concrete and Stories, Based on
Scores on the Categories Assessed ($n = 100$)

Canonical correlation	0.549
Chi-square	49.85
Degrees of freedom	25
Probability	<0.01

Test	Normalized weights[a]
Concrete data	
1. Conservation	808
2. Classification	210
3. Deduction	248
4. Probability	421
5. Induction	254
Stories data	
6. Conservation	912
7. Classification	218
8. Deduction	316
9. Probability	143
10. Induction	−016

[a]Decimal points are omitted.

uted to the prediction of the maximum correlation, but to a lesser degree (0.421 and 0.316). The contribution of Stories probability and of Stories induction to maximizing the relation between the two composites appears to have been negligible (0.143 and −0.016) on the basis of these tests.

The maximum correlation between the composites ($R_c = 0.549$) indicates that approximately 30% of the total variance was common to the two sets of tests. Conservation, Concrete and Stories ($r = 0.44, p < 0.001$), accounts for 20% of this common variance, leaving the remaining 10% to be accounted for by classification, deduction, induction, and probability.

This result lends support to the view that the relation between the two sets of data, while significant, is not strong and that the greater part of the variance common to the tests taken as composites can be accounted for by a single cognitive category—conservation.

The variance not common to the two sets of tests, that is, 70% of the total variance, can be accounted for in part by error and by the limitations of the tests, in part by elements unique to each test situation. The variance unique to each test situation included solutions not equally available to subjects in the Concrete and

Stories situations, that is, to differences in the difficulty of solving identical logical problems from information presented in concrete situations and in reading.

Alternative Explanations

In the concrete situations, differences in difficulty were observed, as expected, between operations in different domains—between, for example, conservation of substance and conservation of weight (Table 3). Results in Tables 3–6 indicate that differences also occurred within a *single* domain in each of the categories assessed. These differences were associated with the change of medium from concrete to the printed page, for example, between operations in class inclusion in concrete situations and in reading (Table 4).

Alternative explanations for differences in performance within a single domain were possible. Some of the differences could be explained by differences in the demands made by the input in the two cases. In reading, there would be greater need for imaging and for an ability to hold and consider information presented in propositions. A related explanation also appears to be consistent with the data and with Piaget's concept of cognition as action abstracted and internalized as schema. In this view, operational thinking would develop in concrete situations with manipulable materials, acquiring stability and integration at this level before attaining the degree of generality and mobility needed for an interpretion of information in the more abstract medium of print. An extension of this explanation is possible. The relationship between cognitive operations in concrete and reading situations could be considered to be one of mutual facilitation, with levels of performance in each medium, in part a function of interaction between operations becoming available in either situation. The extent of this interaction could be seen as a facilitative factor in learning to read. Inadequate provision for interaction—infrequent cognitively-oriented questions in either situation—could be a limiting factor in the rate of development of operational thinking during the critical years preceding the transition to formal operations.

Natural Development or Acceleration?

Is intervention necessary to ensure normal cognitive development? Is acceleration justified? Is it possible?

Piaget recognizes difficulties in accepting acceleration as an alternative to "natural development." He raises the question "whether progress obtained independently from natural development can serve as a basis for new spontaneous constructions, or whether the subject who passively receives information from the adult will no longer learn anything without such help..." (Piaget, in

Inhelder, Sinclair, & Bovet, 1974). Clearly as Inhelder points out, it will be important to avoid "telling," to construct questions carefully, to provide for the active involvement of the child in situations that "resemble in some way" those in which natural development occurs. However, under present conditions, natural development may not be relied on to provide the intellectual skills required for coping with the demands of elementary and secondary curricula. The evidence is strong and accumulating. Initial delays persist and seriously interfere with academic progress. Studies by Elkind (1962) and Tower & Wheatley (1971) showed that only 60% of college freshmen interviewed believed that the volume of a ball of clay remained constant when the ball was rolled into a sausage. Renner *et al.* (1976) report the results of interviews with a sample of 588 students, grades 7–12, aged 12 to 19 years. Only 14 students, 2.4% of the total sample, could be called fully operational. Combining the number of students who scored within the early concrete operational group with those whose scores indicated a fully concrete operational level, 75.3% of the students in the secondary schools could be considered, at best, concrete operational. Renner *et al.* continue: "This is a stage of intellectual development, which Piaget's data have told him children begin to leave at about 11 years of age, and from which they have emerged by age 15."

At grade 7, Renner *et al.* report, 83% of the sample of 96 students interviewed still scored within the concrete level; at grades 9 and 10, 82% and 73% obtained similar scores; at grades 11 and 12, 71% and 66% continued to function within the concrete operational level. The authors find these data "devastating" when compared with the topics in the secondary-school curriculum that require abstract thinking.

Herron (1975) suggests returning concrete-level college students to the point at which changes in cognitive structure apparently came to a halt by providing concrete experiences, concrete models of abstract concepts. He would undoubtedly agree that questions will be needed—questions that challenge the dominance of perception and require the defense of logical decisions. There may be a further problem. Is it possible to assume that operational thinking as it becomes available in concrete situations will be generalized to reading?

The possibility of a facilitative association during the elementary-school years between learning to read and the discovery of cognitive operations in concrete situations suggests that a program that includes an orientation to the development of operational thinking concurrently in concrete and reading situations could be of assistance to children learning to read and to children who find reading difficult.

Two attempts to develop and evaluate such a program are described. The first, extending over a period of 10 years, involved some 250 children, aged 8 to 16 years, referred to the Educational Clinic, The Ontario Institute for Studies in Education (OISE); the second was conducted in 1976 within a school system.

A third is planned for the fall of 1977, also in a school system. In this study, teachers themselves will undertake the teaching. This would seem to be a more direct approach, if it proves successful, to the problems of the underachievers present in most classrooms.

The Clinical Study

The performance of the children referred to the Educational Clinic on concrete tests of cognitive operations in conservation and classification was low in comparison with the results obtained for children learning to read (Tables 2, 3, 4). Some 9- to 15-year-olds *asserted* conservation for substance at levels of complexity I and II, tasks the children learning to read succeeded in at the 94 and 88 mean percentage levels and justified at the 64 and 57 mean percentage levels (Tables 2 and 3). In classification, most of the underachieving readers correctly grouped a pile of counters on the basis of color and shape. Some, however, hesitated, then grouped on the basis of number, 3-3-3-3, rejecting 4 of the red circles from the class of circles. Presented with 2 classes of red counters, 7 red circles and 3 red squares, very few recognized the inclusion relation ''more red ones.'' Progress was generally rapid, as questions were repeated in comparable concrete and verbal situations, in reteaching the code, and in comprehension in reading (outlined in discussing the school study). Questions could be extended to include conservation of weight, volume, area, length, distance, speed, and, for some of the 15-year-olds, conservation of energy.

Table 9 presents the means of the differences calculated from individual differences between pre- and posttest grade scores and the range of these differences for each of three age groups. A mean difference of 1.7 in grade scores represents a mean difference of 1 grade, 7 months for the group as a whole as measured by the test indicated; a range of 1.4 to 2.5 represents the range of mean differences in grade scores within the age group. The results reported in Table 9 indicate mean gains in grade scores following 20–22 hr of clinical instruction, 1 hr a week over a period of approximately 5 months during 1972–73.

The progress suggested by the results shown in Table 9 is encouraging. Could comparable results be obtained in teaching groups of underachieving readers in a school setting? A project under the auspices of the Halton County Board of Education was designed to explore this possibility. The study was undertaken in cooperation with Janice Baker, doctoral candidate, OISE. Baker proposed and designed the study, established the sample, conducted the pre- and posttesting, scored the results, and videotaped the sessions. She is now completing an analysis of the data and will study the records of the instructional sessions in relation to outcomes. The writer was the instructor.

TABLE 9

Means and Ranges of the Differences between Pre- and Posttest Grade Scores on a Series of
Standardized Reading Tests ($n = 50$; $n = 20$; $n = 12$)

Age group	Schonell Word Reading		Gilmore Oral R Accuracy		Silent reading tests			
					Vocabulary		Comprehension	
8–9 years	1.4	0.5–2.4	1.0	0.6–2.3	1.7	1.4–2.5[a]	1.9	0.7–3.9[a]
($n = 20$)								
10–12 years	2.0	0.7–4.3	2.3	0.5–4.6	1.3	0.6–2.1[b]	1.3	0.6–2.7[b]
($n = 18$)								
13–15 years	2.5	0.7–4.2	2.7	0.8–4.6	1.9	0.10–4.0[c]	1.9	1.0–4.2[c]

[a]*Gates–McGinitie Reading Tests,* administered by the school six weeks after clinical instruction discontinued.
[b]*Metropolitan Achievement Tests.*
[c]*Nelson Reading Test.*

A report of the procedures used in establishing the sample and assigning subjects to treatment and control groups and a statistical analysis of pre- and posttest achievement scores has been prepared (Baker & Orme, 1977). Excerpts from this report are presented below.

The School Study

From a random sample of 16 schools representative of each of the socioeconomic levels within the jurisdiction of the Board of Education, a population of 618 grade four students who had been assessed on both a group standardized test of intelligence* and a reading achievement measure† was established. Of the 618 students, 97 met the criteria set for reading (at least one year below the fourth grade norm on all three subtests of the Gates–MacGinitie; a total raw score of less than 45 out of a potential 152). Forty-six of these 97 students scored below the 85 IQ cut-off criterion for identifying candidates for the study. To explore the possibility that all 97 students were in fact of average ability, two additional measures of ability were administered—a short form version of the *Wechsler Intelligence Scale for Children* and the *Goodenough–Harris Draw-a-Person Test.*

From the pool of 97 students who met the criteria for inclusion, 18 matched pairs were randomly assigned to the treatment and control Group One. Control Group Two students consisted of six grade four pupils involved in an alternative corrective reading program. One-way analysis of variance indicated no signifi-

The Otis–Lennan Mental Ability Test.
†*The Gates–MacGinitie Reading Test.*

cant differences in age, intelligence, sex, or in two measures of reading achievement (speed and accuracy, and vocabulary). There were significant differences on the *Comprehension Subtest* of the *Gates–MacGinitie*. These differences, however, were in favor of the two control groups.

The 18 members of the treatment group were assigned to 3 groups, 6 children in each group. Each group received 18 hr of instruction, 1 hr each week for a period of 5 months, from the middle of January to the end of May, 1976.

Analysis of covariance between three groups, using pretest scores as covariate, was used to determine differences between the 3 groups.

Table 10 shows the results of the analysis of differences on the *Piers–Harris Children's Self-Concept Scale.** The results indicate that there were significant gains in self-concept.

Table 11 shows the results of the analysis of covariance between the 3 groups calculated from the total raw scores on the *Gates–MacGinitie Reading Tests*. Scores on the 3 subtests on this test: vocabulary, speed and accuracy, and comprehension are included in the total score. It appears in Table 11 that gains in reading in the treatment group are significantly higher than for the controls, as measured by the Gates–MacGinitie. Results on each of the subtests of this test indicated gains significantly higher for the treatment group.

A measure of progress in spelling for each of the three groups was obtained using the *Metropolitan Achievement Test-Spelling*. Gains in spelling shown in Table 12 are significantly higher for the treatment group than for the control groups.

The program of instruction for the treatment group will now be described.

Reading Instruction and the Development of Cognitive Operations: A Piagetian and Linguistically Oriented Program

In an instructional program designed to coordinate the development of cognitive operations and learning to read, two possibilities are of concern. The first is that there may be a level of cognitive functioning that is a necessary though not a sufficient condition for learning to read and that potentially able children may be functioning below this necessary operational level. The second is the possible contribution of learning to read to the development of these operations. Understanding messages in reading has been seen to involve operations in conservation and classification, in probability and inferential reasoning (Table 1)—operations discovered in concrete experimental situations. Are comparable operations effective in the mastering of the printed code? The printed code has been considered to have a predictable relation to speech (Venesky, 1970; Chomsky, 1968). Concrete

*Additional statistical information is available from Janice Baker, OISE.

TABLE 10

Analysis of Covariance between Three Groups on Piers–Harris
Children's Self-Concept Scale-Norms

Source	Mean % (pre)	Mean % (post)	F ratio	Significance of F
Treatment ($n = 18$)	33.50	74.86	4.64	.01
Control$_1$ ($n = 18$)	54.61	50.10		
Control$_2$ ($n = 6$)	66.83	51.13		

cognitive operations may be applicable in understanding elements and relations within the code: elements such as the consonants, consonant clusters, and vowels; morphophonemic elements and stress patterns; relations, including the meaning of a word as a class name (Anglin, 1970); the structures of sentences (Lyons, 1975; Halliday, 1975); and of discourse (Grimes, 1975). In this case, the code could provide an opportunity to challenge pre-operational thinking and extend emerging cognitive operations to a more abstract situation.

Cognitive Operations and the Printed Code

The function of cognitive operations in mastering elements of the printed code will now be considered. First, the consonants.

Consonants. The *production* of consonantal sounds is not the concern; children master this at an early age. What may be important is an awareness of how this is done: *cognizance* is Piaget's word, the linking in consciousness of action and concept (Piaget, 1976). For most children, the association of sound

TABLE 11

Analysis of Covariance between Three Groups on
Gates–MacGinitie Reading Test-Total Raw Score

Source	Mean % (pre)	Mean % (post)	F ratio	Significance of F
Treatment ($n = 18$)	33.22	55.52	18.13	.001
Control$_1$ ($n = 18$)	35.66	40.48		
Control$_2$ ($n = 6$)	36.16	43.64		

TABLE 12
Analysis of Covariance between Three Groups on *Metropolitan Achievement Test*-Spelling Raw Score

Source	Mean % (pre)	Mean % (post)	F ratio	Significance of F
Treatment (n = 18)	12.22	30.43	38.50	.001
Control₁ (n = 18)	17.11	17.17		
Control₂ (n = 6)	16.33	20.89		

and symbol appears to be a matter so easily accomplished that the risk may be adult interference with the child's competence. Underachieving readers also learn consonant–symbol associations, but their continued attention to the matter, their reversals, their confusion of g/c, d/t, and so on suggest that they have learned in some nonspecific, unproductive manner. It is the *features* of a consonant sound that are represented by a symbol, features traditionally described as *points of articulation*, allowing for other features, such as voice, nasal, vocalic, back, front, and continuant, to be associated features. A printed symbol represents a particular set of these features: the letter *b*, for example, represents the distinctive features consonantal, anterior (front), voice; the letter *l* represents the distinctive features vocalic, consonantal, anterior, coronal (tongue tip raised and retracted toward the hard palate), continuant (Chomsky, 1968).

Since the child pronounces these consonant sounds and discriminates between them in the speech of others, he need only become aware of a minimal set of distinguishing features, and then give this set a name—its name as a consonant letter. The operation is comparable to one in classification: the abstraction of criterial properties, and identifying and naming the class and the superordinate class in which it is included.

An operation in conservation will also be involved in an initial study of the consonants. The name and the set of distinguishing features identifying a consonant sound may be seen to be conserved with changes in the position and in the shape of the symbol, as in lower case and upper case, print and script. For example, the distinguishing features represented by the letter *m* in remember, Mark, music, charm; *ch* as /ch/ in church and Charles, and alternatively as /k/ in echo, school, Christmas.

Identification of the distinguishing features of consonants can proceed at a rapid pace—"putting together what belongs together," and naming the class is effective in recall (Miller, 1956):

> Everyone say "music." Get ready to say "music," don't say anything, just get ready.
> I'm ready. What touches? Make the first sound you way when you say "music."

Listen. Put your hands over your ears and listen. Hear it? /m__ __ __ __/. Put your fingers on your throat and say /m/. Do you feel the vibration? You are using your voice box.

Tell me when I say a word that does not begin with the sound /m/: museum, matches . . . lunch. . . .

Say "come" . . . what touches? Listen. Put your hands over your ears and listen . . . say "go" . . . listen. . . . Say "fun" . . . Say "van". . . .

Questions in classification are included:

What do you call the marks you use when you write your name?
What is a letter?
Is this a letter? Why not? It's an interesting mark. . . .
Is this a letter? m.
How did you know that?

Spelling in the beginning is writing the letter for the first consonant sound pronounced in a word, for example, the *f* of fantastic, the first letter in baseball, museum. . . . Children check each letter, after it is written, with a model on the chalkboard, and "edit" their work. They begin to comment on an error they may have made: "I wrote a *c* for a *g,* and you said game." Other voiced-whispered confusions may occur. Since children are editing their work as the lesson proceeds, each child's work is perfect at the end of the exercise.

Lax Vowels. Vowels are voiced sounds. Lax vowels are pronounced with the face and other muscles relatively related. Space is shaped but without closure. To assist the child in discrimination and recall, five lax vowels are presented as a class of speech sounds, in the sequence high front to low back:

i   e   a   o   u

A gesture, the hand moving downward from the lips to the throat as each vowel is pronounced, reinforces awareness of the position from which each vowel is spoken.

A word such as *top* is written on the chalkboard and a procedure similar to *blending* is used in listening for the vowel sound:

Put your mouth this shape (pointing to t). If you move your tongue very fast, you can say the consonant sound and the vowel sound right together. Are you ready? Try it. Feel how fast your tongue moves. You have a clever tongue!

Say /tŏ/ again. Hold it! Now close the vowel sound with the whispered /p/: tŏ — p.

Before spelling a word, the child pronounces it quietly and selects the vowel he hears from the row of vowels on the chalkboard. Decisions are checked before spelling to avoid an error. Spelling now includes words such as:

shut   dish   sand   left   camp

The -ck spelling rule may be inferred by examining occurrences in a set of one-syllable words: truck, rink, stick, lock, broke, brick, then trek. The operation involves assembling and grouping observations in a search for the environments in which the -ck spelling occurs, and stating the principle involved, that is, an inductive operation. More is accomplished than arriving at a simple rule to eliminate spelling errors. It is expressed in the child's exclamation, "I know what it is! I have it. You spell it -ck in words like that and it comes right after a lax vowel." "Words like that" the children call "one-beat" words, "you speak once." They gesture the "beat," indicating a one-syllable word.

Alternative spellings of the lax vowels, /ŏ/, /ŭ/, /ĕ/, and /ə/, are examined, and patterns noted:

dr*a*w	cr*a*wl	*au*thor	t*ou*gh
en*ou*gh	r*ea*dy	inst*ea*d	w*ea*ther
*a*like	*a*round	*a* book	

Consonant Clusters.   Consonant clusters at the beginning of English words present an interesting regularity. One subclass begins with a consonant (C) or two consonants (CC) followed by an *l* or *r*.

bl, cl, fl, gl, pl, sl, spl
br, cr, dr, fr, gr, spr, str

A second group begins with the letter *s:*

sc, sk, sch, sp, st, sm, sn, sw

A third group is nonregular, a class with few members:

dw, tw, qu, x /ks/ /gs/

Children discover these regularities by consulting a dictionary, or by sorting a set of cards. They "put together what belongs together" on the basis of a common characteristic. Discrimination proceeds as for the single consonants. Spelling will include words of the form C C(C) V C(C). Consonants in sequences at the end of a one-syllable word are treated as single consonant sounds in sequence. Initial consonants and consonant clusters are spoken *with* the vowel; consonant sounds that *follow* the vowel are spoken in sequence.

Inflectional Suffixes.   Inflectional suffixes are syntactic features indicating tense, agreement with a third person singular subject, number, and comparison. They are presented as a group:

-ing -ed -s -es -er -est

Children apply these suffixes, in general correctly, to word classes to which they may be added in speaking. They now examine these words in print, note the meanings that the suffixes contribute to a word, and the reliable pattern that applies when adding them to one-syllable words. The pattern to be discovered is

"1, 1, 1 and you double." If the word is *one* syllable (you speak once), has *one* vowel, and *one* consonant after the vowel, double the last consonant and then add the suffix. Children will find the proviso to the rule later: Double if the suffix begins with a vowel, but *not* if the suffix begins with a consonant.

nets   sadly   cupful

Children now write by ear and by rule, words of the form:

hidden   running   dashing   getting
brushing   springing   slipped
bigger   trucking   thicker

Tense Vowels. In speaking the tense vowels, the muscles of the throat, and to some extent other muscles, are tensed. Children will be familiar with the pronunciation of *open* tense vowels in one-syllable words:

go   no   me   so   you   I   to

and perhaps in two-syllable words in which the tense vowel is stressed:

ópen   músic   méter   Ápril   ísland

Tense vowels also occur as clusters: apart as in *ride;* together as in *rain.* The clusters "apart - with - *e*" may be presented as a group:

i+e   e+e   a+e   o+e   u+e

The possibility that a pattern is followed in the addition of inflectional suffixes to words ending in -e is considered. A series of words containing V + e are presented with suffixes added. Hypotheses are suggested and checked against new evidence. It is noted that the final -e is retained if the suffix begins with a consonant:

careful   useful   useless

Tense vowel clusters are also written "together." The first vowel written is regularly pronounced by name:

dream   tried   clay   stain   throw

The vowel *ie* may be pronounced by the name of the second vowel:

chief   thief   believe   fiend

A few vowels are "non-regular," neither vowel is pronounced by name:

eu/ew   oo/u + e   oi/oy   eigh   ou/ow (round, how)

Children may search for instances of the spelling -*eigh*-. Then they may find 5 words and their derivatives:

eight   weight   freight   sleigh   neighbor

Other regularities will be observed by the children:

> If two or more spellings of a tense vowel are available, one spelling regularly occurs *within* a word, the other at the end of the word: noise, toy.

> Inflectional suffixes are added directly to a word ending in a tense vowel:

> seeing   skiing   canoeing,
> playing   throwing   (but threw)
> played   journeying

R-Controlled Vowels. The children search for instances of r-controlled vowels in the materials they are reading. They find several members of this class of vowels that are pronounced /er/ as in her:

> ir   ar   er   or   ur   ear-   our-

> world   *ear*th   *lear*n   arm*or*   doct*or*   cour*age...*

Others:

> ar   or   -air   -are   -ary   err

are likely to be "different." Context clues and the "echo" effect (hearing the words spoken recently by an adult in conversation) are helpful.

R-vowels are another instance of the opportunities presented by the code for encouraging flexibility in thinking—the ability to shift from an initial decision to consider alternatives. Introducing all or a considerable number of the members of a class at one time has these advantages: it provides a stimulus toward organization for recall; it introduces the notion that in learning one is alert to recurring patterns; it suggests the need for flexibility in deciding a particular case, taking into account "environment" and context.

Children may experiment with placing the vowels within a hierarchical structure, naming the classes and subclasses, and listing members included in each class. An example of a structure of this kind is shown in Figure 1.

The Sentence. Children are reading and examining sentences as they study the code. They frequently begin by describing a sentence in this way:

> It begins with a capital and ends with a period. Many sentences do. What comes between these signals is, of course, the sentence, "judgments about such matters as who did it, who it happened to, and what got changed" (Fillmore, 1968, p. 24).

For an initial understanding of the sentence, a link between semantics and syntax is attempted. In the sentence,

> The robins are building a nest in our tree.

the questions are:

> *Who* is building a nest in our tree?
> *What* are the robins doing?

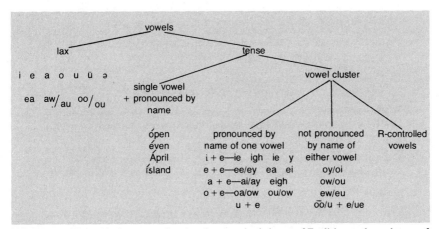

FIGURE 1.   Hierarchical structure showing classes and subclasses of English vowels, and some of the members of each subclass.

So the sentence has two parts. The children read the sentence, gesturing the two *parts*—an arm extended to the left, and an arm extended to the right. A *frame* placed above the sentence indicates that the whole is a sentence, an *S*. Lines from the *S* identify the two parts, somewhat as a gesture:

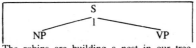

The parts are given names, categorial names, NP VP, and names that refer to each part in a particular sentence—the part that is the subject of this sentence, and the part that is the predicate of this subject.

The NP VP is identified in sentences spoken by the teacher and by the children:

The mother robin is bringing mud for the nest.
The father robin is carrying sticks.
The children are watching the birds.

Questions concern "who did it," and "what they did." Gestures, used for a time, dramatize the responses as representing the NP VP.

A sentence is presented on the chalkboard.

In the NP subject of this sentence, there are two words, *the robins*. One of these words will be the *N*, the noun. Which word is the noun?

There are noun phrases in the predicate too, in fact, two noun phrases. Find these noun phrases in the predicate.

Which word is the N in the noun phrase *a nest?* In the noun phrase *our tree?* So there are three places in this sentence that noun phrases occur.

There is the NP that is the subject of the sentence, and two places for NP's in the VP. Look at the noun phrase *our tree.* I will ask you:

Where are the robins building a nest?
So the noun phrase *our tree,* is part of the phrase *in our tree.*

Which word has the "first position" in this phrase? The word *in* is called a *preposition;* it has the "first position" in the phrase. The three words *in our tree* are called a prepositional phrase, PP.

Draw a line from the S to the NP that is the subject of the sentence. The NP that is directly under the S is the subject of the sentence. The rest of the sentence is the VP.

Find the NP, *a nest* in the VP.

Draw a line from the VP to the noun phrase, *a nest.* Draw a line from the VP to the prepositional phrase *in our tree.*

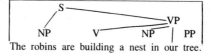
The robins are building a nest in our tree.

A VP will have a V, a verb.

Two words tell what the robins are doing. What are they doing? Draw a line from the VP to the V in this sentence.

Adverbs are introduced. A transformation, prepositioning the adverb, is considered a choice of style in writing and speaking. The referents of pronouns are identified:

Now the mother robin is finishing the nest. Soon she will lay four blue eggs.

Other transformations, including negation, the question, the negative question, the passive (a noun phrase transferred from the verb phrase to the subject position) are presented. Cleft sentences occur in the speech of the children. The NP in these sentences is identified.

Word Meanings. The structure of a sentence expresses meaning. Words expressing meaning within this structure are abstractions. These words will be class names representing clusters of features. Features are elicited as the children discuss questions such as these:

What is a tree? What is a robin? What is a bird? What is a nest?

Having a *concept* of a tree, bird, nest, means understanding the relation of inclusion of these class names within a hierarchy of superordinate classes (Anglin, 1970).

In understanding a particular sentence, it is also necessary that the words *tree, robin, nest,* be appreciated as images:

What do you "see" when you read these sentences?
How big is the tree you are imagining?
Where is it standing?
How are the robins bringing the sticks and the mud to the tree?
How high in the tree are they building the nest?

Understanding in reading and the contribution of reading to the development of intelligence will now be considered.

Cognitive Operations and Reading

The outcomes for the treatment group in the school study indicate that within a relatively brief period of instruction, progress in learning to read may be considerably accelerated. A concurrent concern in teaching children to read is the development of intellectual capacity including operations in classification and inferential reasoning.

Olson's view of the development of intelligence in a literate culture appears to support this concern (Olson, 1976). "The conception of intelligence that is dominant in our culture," he writes, "may be characterized by the terms 'abstraction' and 'rationality.'" "'Abstraction,'" he explains, "refers to the fact that an event is treated not in terms of its functional or perceptual qualities but rather in terms of its membership in some class-inclusive category. Thus a pen is 'a writing instrument' but not 'to write with' or 'for school'. . . . Classification at the level of function is universal, while classification by means of superordinates is unique to a literate culture . . . only the latter is taken as an index of intelligence. . . . Rationality refers to the quality of arguments. Thus, if a conclusion 'follows logically' from its premises it is rational" (p. 200). "Our culture," he states, "has invented two devices of extraordinary power—written statements and extended prose statements."

An awareness of the importance of the role of a literate culture, of reading and schooling, in effecting changes in cognitive structure appears to be quite recent. These changes, however, do not follow automatically from contact with the culture. There are children who "read" and do not discover the techniques in thinking offered by the culture; there are children who do not read, who may or may not discover them. But the possibility that "intellectual achievements in our time depend critically on hooking our human resources to the most powerful technologies available" (Olson, 1976, p. 199), implies that serious consideration be given to this relationship in teaching children during the elementary-school years. The influence of a culture begins early. It involves, as Piaget suggests, productive and continuing experiences with manipulable materials and the kinds of questions that encourage thinking. In a literate culture, operations in thinking will be modified and extended during schooling, as the child learns the code, and social experiences are extended. But what happens during the process of learning to read in a literate culture appears to be critical for learning to think.

If this is the case, criteria for selecting the materials children read may require rethinking. Books, articles, and stories need to challenge thinking. They should describe experiences that are new and surprising, that involve life "out there" beyond the self. Of less concern in these choices is vocabulary control (words not recognized will be pronounced on request), the repetition of "new" words (they will be pronounced again), and sentence length and sentence structure. It is sufficient if these are within the extended reach of some or most of the children. The more important criteria are the characteristics of the book or story. It should be well organized and well written; there should be questions that are not answered in the text; and the text should accurately represent conclusions from recent research. Beautiful illustrations are necessary in the book itself or available in other books. Each child requires a copy of a new book, article, or story for each reading session.

Experimental materials for introducing topics in reading are also needed: magnets for a book on magnetism; an "iceberg" floating in a bucket of water to introduce a book on icebergs; maps, photographs, and paintings of animals in presenting a series of books and articles on animals in different regions of the world—on the tundra, in the deserts, and in the mountains.

A clear break will be established between "reading" and the study of word and sentence structures. Reading is a reward. It is an opportunity to meet with a new person, the author, to find out what he knows and what he does. When a word that is not recognized is casually provided, the child is free to concentrate on ideas, to hold and relate information, and to respond to what is new in a situation. Comments such as these suggest the attitude of the children. "A new book!" "A book on icebergs!" "Could I read next, please?" "It must be fun to be lost!" (The last comment is in reaction to a story about children lost on a large lake studded with islands. They were able to think cleverly and coolly about how to find the way home).

Responses to comprehension questions during the first few sessions with underachievers in the school study suggest the persistence of a literal and personally oriented pattern in interpreting what is read. When they read,

> The days grow short.
> The nights grow long.
> Winter is coming.
> The grass is dead and brown.

The explanations they gave were:

> The days are short because you have to go to bed early. You have a long time to sleep at night and it gets boring.

> The grass is dead all right. You can *see* it's dead.

Oh yes, it can come alive again. It has to come alive because it's green all summer.

Is it quite dead, all of it? How can it come alive again if all of it is dead?

But it does!

Later, however, concepts and relationships were better understood. The children had read a number of books and stories about animals in winter—animals of the northern forests, the Arctic, and the Antarctic. They had had considerable experience in classification—in abstracting criterial properties, identifying categories and describing inclusion relations. They agreed that what they had learned about animals might be presented in a hierarchical structure. Their suggestions were written on the chalkboard as they presented them. The final result is shown in Figure 2.

The children discovered they could read up, or down, or across the diagram and tell the story. Expressions such as *some-others, either-or, both-and,* were used in speaking. It was suggested that the structure could also be useful in writing. This became a group effort, each child choosing to write about one of the categories in the sequence.

An attempt was made to extend cognitive operations to include hypothesis construction and testing. Other questions required an understanding of what was implied but not expressed in the text:

What would you hypothesize would be the survival value of the sounds the Weddell seal makes in the dark under the ice? Why do you suppose the seal does this? How would you test that hypothesis?

Plants remove some 5 billion tons of minerals from the soil each year! How is it possible, after millions of years, that there are still minerals in the soil?

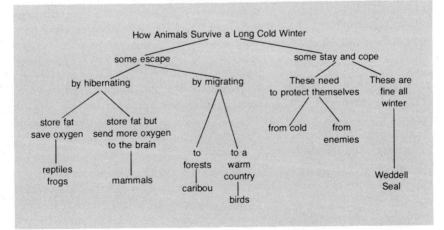

FIGURE 2.   Hierarchical structure, reading.

Find the word *so*. It's the first word on page two.

So the animals that live in the Arctic must survive the big change from winter to summer.

What does *so* mean? What does *so* suggest you are expected to do. Is it possible to remember everything that went before? In this case, what is necessary to remember?

Questions such as these anticipate the transition to the formal level of thinking.

The Transition to Formal Operations

Piaget suggests that the transition to formal operations begins with an awareness that the thinking skills of the earlier period, skills that had seemed adequate and even powerful, are not capable of taking into account all the possible combinations of interacting events that can be postulated as contributing to outcomes (Piaget, 1971, 1972). There are attitudinal changes that support this discovery: a greater respect for evidence; openness to evidence that conflicts with expectations; excitement in proposing alternative hypotheses. There will also be feelings of frustration and doubt when solutions are clearly seen to be "too simple," but strategies for recognizing and testing "all possible combinations" are not available. The transition to formal operations appears likely to involve stress as well as exhilaration.

The responses of young children who are discovering operational thinking suggest that similar experiences accompany the earlier transition. Before the discovery of operations in conservation and classification, the responses of the children appear to reflect a certain complacency:

That one's lighter. I can see a hole in it.

The cave's not really different. Those boys are just imagining things.

Like I said, more circles. There are 7 of them. I can count.

The beginnings of doubt, perhaps anxiety, may be reflected in expressions that appear from time to time in their responses, expressions such as, "I think . . . ," "I don't really know, but . . . ," and "maybe." The child seems to accept that he has a responsibility for "coming to know," and he seems to be concerned about the difficulty in doing so:

I think the water will stay up with the sugar in it, but I don't know because the sugar would all go into the water and you couldn't see it, so I don't really know how you could tell.

Well . . . a bird's alive. But it has only two feet, and it flies, and animals can't fly; so I can't say.

Something happened in the cave all right, but I don't know what. What *is* the answer?

Later, when problems such as these can be solved, the child speaks with a certainty that is neither complacent nor anxious. Expressions such as "has to be," "must be," "so... ," "if... then," and quantifying terms such as *all, some,* and *any* appear in the protocols. Proof is valued:

> They're all red, it's only that some are squares. So there's more red ones because they're all red.
>
> Well, the shape's changed. But I didn't drop any of the plasticine and I didn't put any of it from the snake to the pieces. So they have to be the same.
>
> Ducks are birds too, you know. So if all the birds left, then there wouldn't be any ducks here, because the ducks would have to go too.

Children who resist change appear to need both challenge and acceptance of their responses in order to begin to question their solutions and risk being in doubt. Correctness is not the point at issue. Rather it appears, at least in part, to involve a shift in attitude, a willingness to feel uneasy about an answer but to take a chance on being wrong. Challenge and acceptance is not an easy combination to provide. It means accepting all responses as relevant and valuable and at the same time implying that there may be more here "than meets the eye."

It may be helpful if the adult expresses doubt, and indicates a need for evidence. This child's response suggests kindly concern but it is overlooking the logic in the situation:

> He gave all the birds the same amount to eat.... Well, I just know he'd do that, because he was sorry for them out there in the cold.

The adult's response was:

> Suppose I can hardly believe you. How could there be as much for the sparrows to eat in those little pieces! The jays got the big chunks. How will you help me?

He hesitated, then abandoned the problem. Later he returned to propose a Piagetian-type experiment:

> I just thought of what I could do. I could get two glasses and put the same amount of water in each of them. I'd put the tiny pieces in one glass and the big chunks in the other. The water would go up the same in both, and then you'd have to believe me.

This indirect approach, questioning but not "telling," appears to be helpful to younger children. For older students a more direct approach may be indicated. Their responses suggest that the difficulty is still with operations characteristic of an earlier period: classification seems to be particularly vulnerable to delay. Operations in classification, not discovered earlier, are experienced at high school and college levels as difficulty in organizing and writing reports; in summarizing in an orderly way for recall; and in recognizing the complexity of word meanings. A more direct approach could be an analysis of operations in classification, deduction, induction, and probability reasoning. Doubt could be openly valued. Procedures for testing "all possible combinations" need not be remarkable or mysterious and out of reach. They may be symbolized, and demonstrated, and perhaps assigned as tasks in a variety of situations.

Society beyond books and the schools offers many experiences that urge toward responsible, creative adulthood. In our culture, however, young people who do not read intelligently and have not learned to think seem singularly handicapped in using these experiences to move toward cognitive and social maturity.

References

Anglin, J. M. *The growth of meaning*. Research Monograph No. 63, Cambridge, Mass.: The M.I.T. Press, 1970.

Baker, J., & Orne, M. *An analysis of a Piagetian and linguistic based reading program*. Toronto: The Ontario Institute for Studies in Education, 1977.

Bocheñski, J. M. *The methods of contemporary thought*. Dordrecht-Holland: D. Reidel, 1965.

Chomsky, N., & Haller, M. *The sound pattern of English*. New York: Harper & Row, 1968.

Elkind, D. Quantity concepts in college students. *Journal of Social Psychology*, 1962, *57*(2), 459–465.

Fillmore, C. J. The case for case. In E. Bach & R. T Harms (Eds.), *Universals in linguistic theory*. New York: Holt, Rinehart & Winston, 1968.

Grimes, J. E. *The thread of discourse*. The Hague: Mouton, 1975.

Halliday, M. A. K. Language structure and language function. In J. Lyons (Ed.), *New horizons in linguistics*. Toronto: Penguin Books, 1975.

Herron, J. D. Piaget for chemists. *Journal of Chemical Engineering*, 1975, *52*(3), 146–151.

Inhelder, B., Sinclair, H., & Bovet, M. *Learning and the development of cognition*. Cambridge, Mass.: Harvard University Press, 1974.

Lovell, K., & Ogilvie, E. A study of the conservation of substance in the junior school child. *British Journal of Educational Psychology*, 1960, *30*, 109–118.

Lovell, K., & Ogilvie, E. The growth of the concept of volume in the junior school child. *Journal of Child Psychology and Psychiatry*, 1961, *2*, 118–126. (a)

Lovell, K., & Ogilvie, E. A study of conservation of weight in the junior school child. *British Journal of Educational Psychology*, 1961, *31*, 138–144. (b)

Lyons, J. (Ed.). *New horizons in linguistics*. Toronto: Penguin Books, 1975.

Matalon, B. Etude génétique de l'implication. In J. Piaget (Ed.), *Implication formalisation et logique naturelle*. Vol. 16 of *Etudes d'épistémologie génétique*. Paris: Presses Universitaires de France, 1962.

Miller, G. A. The magical number seven, plus or minus two. Some limits on our capacity for processing information. *The Psychological Review*, 1956, *63*(2), 81–97.

Olson, D. R. Culture, technology, and intellect. In L. B. Resnick (Ed.), *The nature of intelligence*. Hillsdale, N.J.: Lawrence Erlbaum Associates, 1976.

Piaget, J. *Biology and knowledge*. Chicago: University of Chicago Press, 1971.

Piaget, J. Intellectual evolution from adolescence to adulthood. *Human Development*, 1972, *15*, 1–12.

Piaget, J. *The grasp of consciousness: Action and concept in the young child*. Cambridge, Mass.: Harvard University Press, 1976.

Piaget, J., & Inhelder, B. Le développement des quantités physiques chez l'enfant. Neuchâtel: Delachaux et Niestlé, 1962.

Piaget, J., & Inhelder, B. *Memory and intelligence.* London: Routledge & Kegan Paul, 1973.

Piaget, J., & Inhelder, B. *The origins of the idea of chance in children.* New York: W. W. Norton, 1975.

Rawson, H. A study of the relationships and development of reading and cognition. Unpublished doctoral thesis. Faculty of Education, University of Alberta, Edmonton, Alberta, 1969.

Renner, J. W., Stafford, D. G., Lawson, A. E., McKinnon, J. W., Friot, F. E., & Kellogg, D. H. *Research, teaching and learning with the Piaget model.* Norman: The University of Oklahoma Press, 1976.

Tower, J. O. & Wheatley, G. Conservation concepts in college students: A replication and critique. *Journal of Genetic Psychology,* 1971, *118*(2) 265–270.

Venesky, R. L. *The structure of English orthography.* The Hague: Mouton, 1970.

CHAPTER 12

Opportunities for Concrete and Formal Thinking on Science Tasks

Robert Karplus

AESOP,* Lawrence Hall of Science
University of California, Berkeley, California

Since science as process of inquiry makes demands on the reasoning ability of practitioners, science teaching makes such demands of students. It is interesting to examine science activities at various levels and in various scientific fields with the intention of identifying the type of reasoning that may occur. Consider the example in Figure 1, for instance, used with 8- and 9-year-old children in the Science Curriculum Improvement Study (SCIS) program (SCIS, 1970, p. 27). The students are to set up experiments that correspond to the pictured systems, thus translating these representations into reality. Because of the simple and direct correspondence of the pictures and the materials, it was concluded that this task requires concrete thought. A formal thinker would, it was thought, be impatient with this activity. Compare, now, another experimental activity (Figure 2), used with 11- to 12-year-olds (SCIS, 1971a, p. 21). In part B on this page, the students are invited to set up experiments, but this time they have to select the procedure and the materials themselves, with only the instruction to "investigate variables." The lack of specific instructions—the need to consider alternatives and their relationship—led to the conclusion that this task invites formal reasoning patterns. It requires the student to accept lack of immediate closure (Lunzer, this volume) since several experiments must be carried out

*AESOP (Advancing Education through Science-Oriented Programs) was supported by a grant from the National Science Foundation.

before a pattern emerges. This task is an optional activity in the SCIS program, a challenge to above-average sixth-graders. The activity outlined in Figure 1 and in part A of Figure 2 provides closure as soon as the student fulfills the explicit requirements of the task, a characteristic of concrete reasoning.

The two examples given are concerned with experimental investigations. Theoretical activities—so-called brain teasers—can also be roughly classified in the same way. Thus, the example shown in Figure 3 requires conservation of length and seriation: many small steps are equivalent to fewer large steps (SCIS, 1972, p. 38). The children tackle this problem after they measure distances by pacing. It is the opinion of this author that this is an example of concrete thought, since a quantitative analysis of the exact length of Bill's paces is not required. Still, the inverse relationship of number and size of paces suggests a little more than the simplest kind of seriation. Appropriately, this brain teaser is intended for 9- and 10-year-olds in the SCIS program. It should be noticed that the solution may involve hypothetico-deductive reasoning along these lines: if the steps are longer, as in A, then the larger number of steps will cover a greater distance; if

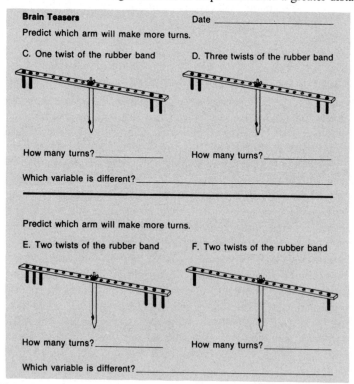

FIGURE 1. Instructions for a laboratory activity intended for 8- to 9-year-old students. (SCIS, 1970)

How does the number of turns affect the interaction
of your coil-rivet system?

A. Push the coil against the head
of the rivet. Pick up as many
steel disks as you can.

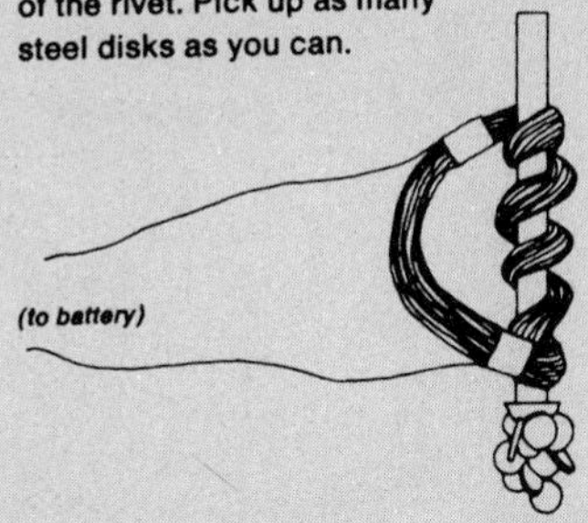

B. Investigate other variables of the coil-rivet
system. Name the variables. Draw a
picture and describe what you find out.

(to battery)

Record the number of disks
you can pick up.

1 turn _____ _____ _____

2 turns _____ _____ _____

3 turns _____ _____ _____

4 turns _____ _____ _____

5 turns _____ _____ _____

6 turns _____ _____ _____

7 turns _____ _____ _____

To put many turns on your rivet,
push them tightly together.
Put as many turns on the rivet as you can.

FIGURE 2. Instructions for a laboratory activity intended for 11- to 12-year-old students. (SCIS, 1971b)

the steps are shorter, as in C, then the larger number of steps may cover the same distance. Since the hypotheses are given by the answer choices and are not generated by the student, it would appear that they do not reflect formal reasoning.

The example in Figure 4 is used after the students have worked with a small plastic syringe at various angles to pop a rubber stopper in freely exploratory activities and in a guided investigation of the effect of varying the launch angle (SCIS, 1971b, p. 24). The second question can be answered concretely from the observations remembered by the children—using merely the idea of reproducibility of data and focusing on the angle variable only. Or the students may reason about both the angle and the stopper-depth variables, whose effects partly compensate in C and D. This would be applying formal reasoning patterns. On the first question, the crux is that whereas the flight distance is the observable outcome of the experiments, the energy imparted to the stopper is an abstraction that must be inferred by a comparison of the speed and force with which the stopper is launched regardless of the angle. Actually, the depth to which the stopper is inserted into the syringe barrel is the most important determinant of the energy transfer, and most children discover this relationship. Still, the need to distinguish the observed flight distance from the nonobservable energy transfer would classify this task as requiring formal thought.

Before we extend the discussion of science activities to the secondary level, it should be pointed out that the operation above was viewed from a theoretical base. Certain criteria were used to identify the operational opportunities in the activities. Generally speaking, concrete approaches consisted of seriation, one-to-one correspondence, conservation, transitivity, and class inclusion applied to real objects or to symbols representing them. If the subject formulated and tested hypotheses, used symbols that did not correspond directly to real objects, used a functional relationship quantitatively, planned a series of interdependent steps that covered all available alternatives, considered a general case instead of specific instances, or accepted lack of closure in other ways, then it was concluded that he applied formal reasoning patterns.

The question arises, How does the performance of students on science tasks in school relate to their developmental level as determined by standard Piagetian tasks? This matter is being investigated by Anton E. Lawson, working with John

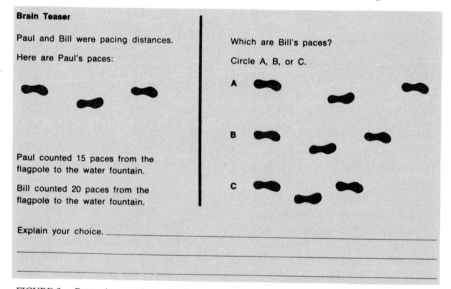

FIGURE 3. Reasoning puzzle used after a laboratory experience by 9- to 10-year-old students. (SCIS, 1972)

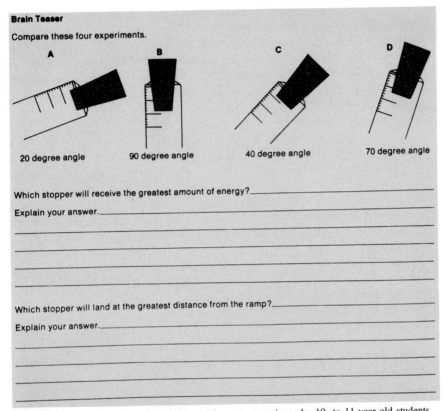

Brain Teaser

Compare these four experiments.

A   B   C   D

20 degree angle   90 degree angle   40 degree angle   70 degree angle

Which stopper will receive the greatest amount of energy?_____

Explain your answer._____

Which stopper will land at the greatest distance from the ramp?_____

Explain your answer._____

FIGURE 4.   Reasoning puzzle used after a laboratory experience by 10- to 11-year-old students. (SCIS, 1971a)

W. Renner at the University of Oklahoma in Norman (Lawson & Renner, 1973). By using floating and sinking objects, conservation of volume, and the balance beam, Lawson is seeking to identify the developmental level of a large group of secondary-school students. He has prepared tests in biology, chemistry, and physics whose content is appropriate to the respective high-school courses and whose questions have been classified by him and several others according to their operational level. By comparing the students' responses on the questions with the students' developmental level, Lawson hopes to find how reliable the classification of the questions is and what opportunities for logical operations arise in these courses. One might add that the reviewers of the questions did not agree on all items, partly because the students' unknown educational experience was expected to influence their responses. Personality variables such as impulsiveness and anxiety also will affect the outcome of this study. In this kind of investigation, one may choose to examine three quite different problems: one is to identify the reasoning used by a particular individual in responding, successfully or unsuccessfully, to a particular task; the second is to predict the degree of success on the task that will be achieved by individuals who usually reason at a certain developmental level and have a specified background of instruction and/or experience; the third is to consider the latitude of a task—what range of logical operations is stimulated by it and what range leads to success.

The following discussion now turns to additional examination questions that were taken from teacher-made tests, College Entrance Examination Board (CEEB) practice questions, and Lawson's work, with some adaptation to make them more suitable for this presentation (CEEB, 1971, 1972; Lawson & Renner, 1973). In Figure 5 are two biology questions dealing with heredity. The first of these involves crossing heterozygous individuals with homozygous recessives and requires concrete thought, in the opinion of the author. None of the biology books examined actually presented this example, but they did present a technique for predicting the outcome by manipulating the symbols D and d that represent the alleles. Three-quarters of the 45 high-school students who responded to this question predicted a 50–50 division of the two genotypes Dd and dd. Some of these students drew the diagram indicated at the bottom of Figure 5 to help them answer the question, thus giving evidence of a concrete approach.

The second question specifies the distribution of alleles and can be solved by the same type of diagram, but only if 10 alleles are indicated along each edge of the box: three A and seven a (see Figure 5, bottom). If these are matched in the square array, the relative frequencies of the three genotypes can be predicted. Even though this procedure appears to be a direct extension of the simple one used by many students, it differs in one significant respect: in the solution to Item I, the symbol Dd represents both the equal frequencies of the two alleles and the occurrence of alleles in each individual of one mating population; in the solution to Item II, the symbols A and a describe the relative frequencies of alleles in the population but have no connection to individual organisms (these may have genotypes AA, Aa, or aa). In Item II, therefore, the symbolism is more abstract than in Item I. Actually, two of the students stated the correct percentages, and one of them quoted the Hardy–Weinberg principle, which provides an algorithm that is applied in the students' text to the case of a 40% dominant allele (Biological Sciences Curriculum Study, 1963, Chs. 13, 15). Of the remaining students, somewhat more than half quoted three percentages for the three genotypes, often using figures so that the dominant genotype or the dominant phenotype had a probability of 30%. The others provided partial answers. Unfortunately—and this was a mistake—the students were not asked to explain their procedure.

Another question can be injected here: What is the operational meaning of the use of an algorithm, a standard, memorized procedure for generating a result?

I. One pair of alleles (D and d) controls a certain trait in fruit flies. When many crosses are made between Dd and dd flies, how many different genotypes will there be among the offspring, and what will be the approximate percentage of each?

II. A certain characteristic of sexually-reproducing organisms in a population is determined by one pair of alleles (A and a). The dominant allele makes up 30% of all the alleles in this population.
   A. How many different genotypes are there with respect to this characteristic?
   B. How many different phenotypes are there with respect to this characteristic? What percentage of each is present in the population?

Solution to I

	D	d
d	Dd	dd
d	Dd	dd

Solution to II

	A	A	A	a	a	a	a	a	a	a
A										
A	9	AA				21 Aa				
A										
a										
a										
a										
a	21	Aa				49aa				
a										
a										
a										

FIGURE 5. Two biology questions requiring combinatorial, proportional, and probabilistic reasoning. Item I can be solved by manipulation of the symbols, while Item II requires explicit recognition of the relative frequencies.

Does the fact that the algorithm is stated in formal terms mean that the user is necessarily applying formal thought? This is not thought to be the case, and this author would suggest that each instance be judged individually.

The next question has been selected as affording either concrete or formal thought (Figure 6). It involves seriation with respect to a tangible relationship, that of one organism consuming another, but also brings into play the food–mineral cycle. Indeed, about three-fourths of the student group successfully selected alternative C, with most of the remainder choosing D; two were undecided. In all but a very few cases, the reason for eliminating an incorrect alternative was a single objection, such as "seeds don't eat sparrows," for A. This was taken as a concrete approach. Some responses, however, showed awareness of the mineral cycle and the similarity of C and D and explained that seeds must be first because they initiate the food chain. This explanation indicates a formal operation.

The last example from biology is shown in Figure 7. In this author's view, the problem requires formal reasoning, since a quantitative analysis is requested. Actually, 3 out of 55 students selected the correct answer, E, but only one

Which of the following is the best example of a food chain?
A. sparrow → seeds → hawk → bacteria
B. seeds → bacteria → sparrow → hawk
C. seeds → sparrow → hawk → bacteria
D. bacteria → seeds → sparrow → hawk
Please explain what is wrong with each item you did not choose.

FIGURE 6. Biology question in multiple-choice format with explanation required. Seriation according to an abstract criterion is required.

justified it by referring to the 25-fold enlargement of the field of view. A second one said the field would be larger without saying how much, and the third one stated only "80 × 50 = 4000/2 = 2000." Surprisingly, 4 of the remaining students chose C, and even more surprisingly, the other 48 students chose answers B and D in equal numbers! Many explanations included arithmetic operations only, but some added qualitative comments about the enlarged field of view when the individual cells appear smaller under low power. Others justified the smaller number in terms of the lower power, however. This observation reflects many students' tendency to suppress common sense (lower power means larger field) when confronted with mathematical tasks, a tendency that has been observed all too frequently on other occasions.

When eight teacher-made biology tests were originally examined, no questions that invited formal thought were located. Even on the CEEB examples, it seemed that the wording of the questions in biology, rather than the application of biological concepts, was used to make the questions more demanding (CEEB, 1971, 1972). Clearly, there are tasks that allow formal thought, such as the planning of experiments that involve the identification, separation, and control of variables or the evaluation of the consequences of man's interference in the interlocking cycles in the ecosystem. In efforts to make up examples, however, it was found that these tasks, when stated verbally on a written test, lost most of their challenge because all of the conditions have to be specified explicitly. In a laboratory or real-life situation, this would not be the case, and tracking down

A microscope has objective lenses of 10× and 50× power. Under high power, 80 evenly distributed bacterial cells can be seen in the field of view. About how many cells can be seen in the field of view under low power on the same slide?
A. 3
B. 16
C. 30
D. 400
E. 2000
Please explain how you found the answer.

FIGURE 7. Biology question requiring application of a functional relationship: the number of cells is inversely proportional to the square of the magnification.

sources of error or inconsistencies among data can be exceedingly demanding in biology as well as in other fields. It is the author's view that teachers should challenge their students without requiring all to perform on the same high level of reasoning.

We shall turn now to high-school chemistry. Here, problems were found everywhere requiring formal thought. There was difficulty in locating items that could be solved on the concrete level and that did not depend on recall of facts concerning the properties of specific elements and compounds. The atomic theory, of course, is the main conceptual framework in chemistry and affords ample opportunity for formal thought when chemical phenomena are being interpreted and explained. At the same time, it has some aspects of a language that, once learned, can be applied in simple situations (e.g., conservation of atoms in a reaction) by the use of concrete operations. In many applications of atomic theory, proportional reasoning, an aspect of formal thought, is exceedingly important. It occurs in applications of the ideal gas laws, the calculation of the ratios of reactants and reaction products, and the use of equilibrium constants. Other tasks requiring formal thought have to do with the application of energy conservation and energy transfer, where energy has to be discriminated from observables such as temperature and pressure (see also Figure 4). Finally, there are problems of deductive logic, when data about precipitates, color of ions, and weight ratios have to be used to identify the reacting compounds. Since this last process requires chemical tables or a great deal of empirical information, we decided not to investigate it.

The first example relates to the use of chemical symbols to represent atoms (Figure 8). Here, the manipulation of symbols according to well-defined rules makes use of concrete thought. Seven of nine students counted the atoms successfully, one made a counting error, and the last omitted the three atoms in water.

A second task involving chemical symbols is the balancing of chemical equations. Here one has to apply conservation of each atomic constituent in the participating molecules. Two examples are included in Figure 9. In Item I, the atoms of the water molecule become separated and the coefficients are equal to 1. All students arrived at this conclusion and explained it in terms of the available atoms. Item II is much more difficult in that four steps of reasoning are needed, one for conservation of each atomic species. None of the students answered it correctly, and only three referred to the balance of one or two specific elements;

How many atoms are in one molecule of the substance

$$(NH_4)_2TiO(C_4O_4)_2 \, H_2O?$$

Please show your calculation.

FIGURE 8. Chemistry question requiring only manipulation of symbols.

I. Balance this chemical reaction:
   1 Ca + (a) H_2O → (b) CaO + (c) H_2
   The coefficient (a) is
   A. 1   B. 2   C. 3   D. 4   E. 5
   Please explain your choice.

II. Balance this equation involving the new elements X and Z:
    2 H_2XO_3 + (a) H_3ZO_3 → (b) HX + (c) H_3ZO_4 + (d) H_2O
    The coefficient (c) is
    A. 1   B. 2   C. 3   D. 4   E. 5
    Please explain your choice.

FIGURE 9. Two chemistry questions requiring identification and solution of linear equations. In Item I, the equations are independent, but they have to be solved simultaneously in Item II.

the others said that they guessed or merely asserted that the equation was balanced. It was concluded, therefore, that the need to keep track of the four atomic species demanded a systematic overall approach and lack of premature closure that are characteristic of formal rather than concrete thought.

Actually, the students could have solved both problems in Figure 9 by an algorithm, by stating the conservation of each atomic species in the form of an algebraic equation and then solving the resulting equations. In Item I, the result is three equations for calcium, hydrogen, and oxygen, which can be solved in sequence. In Item II, the result is four equations (for hydrogen, X, Z, and oxygen), and two of these have to be solved simultaneously. From the author's knowledge of high-school courses, it is believed that this algorithm is not taught and that students balance equations by inspection and a trial-and-error process, achieving closure immediately after each trial.

Still another task involving the manipulation of chemical symbols is presented in Figure 10. Here the student has to determine how the third reaction can be represented as a composite of the other two and then use the composition relationship to compute the required heat of reaction. Out of 11 students, 7 were able to do this; the other 4 put the two reactions together but did not apply the factors for the molecular ratios involved. The question arises as to whether or not this task requires formal thought. Associating a reaction energy with each pro-

Consider the reactions

$$2\,Fe + (3/2)O_2 \rightarrow Fe_2O_3 \qquad \Delta H = -191\,kcal$$
$$3\,Fe + 2\,O_2 \rightarrow Fe_3O_4 \qquad \Delta H = -266\,kcal$$

From this information, calculate the H of the reaction

$$2\,Fe_3O_4 + (1/2)O_2 \rightarrow 3Fe_2O_3, \ \Delta H =$$

Please explain how you found the answer.

FIGURE 10. Chemistry question requiring propositional and proportional reasoning.

cess and operating mathematically on these energies would seem to be a formal operation. Yet the class had practiced extensively on this type of problem, though the particular example was novel. Regardless of operational level, it may be reassuring to find out that some students can learn something.

The next example involves application of the kinetic theory of gases, a powerful model for understanding chemical and thermal phenomena (Figure 11). Complete understanding of this model certainly requires formal thought, especially insofar as the particles of the model have idealized properties rather than being "ball bearings." In the problems of Figure 11, only the motion of the particles is involved. Item I needs only quantitative serial ordering but does require two inversions from the data given (high weight ↔ slow rate and slow rate ↔ long time) to the ultimate result of a direct correspondence (low weight ↔ short time, high weight ↔ long time). Out of 13 students, 11 selected answer A successfully and quoted the information given to eliminate the other choices. Only 3 of the students, however, gave evidence of formal reasoning by selecting the correct answer B in Item II and justifying it through the inverse square-root relationship. Most of the others took answer A, applying the inverse proportion without taking the square root, a concrete approach; a few guessed various answers (Wollman & Karplus, 1973). As in the biological example on microscope magnification, the nonlinear function was found to be much more challenging for the students than the direct proportion.

The last example, in Figure 12, comes from high-school physics (CEEB, 1971, 1972). Even though we have not had an opportunity to use it with students,

---

I. According to the kinetic theory, the rate of diffusion of a high molecular weight gas is slower than the rate of diffusion of a low molecular weight gas. Which of the following can you conclude?
   A. Perfume vapor with a molecular weight of 360 can be smelled before onion vapor with a molecular weight of 720.
   B. The higher the molecular weight of a gas, the sooner an equilibrium state is reached in a closed system.
   C. Onion vapor is more offensive than perfume vapor.
   D. Perfume vapor with a molecular weight of 360 will be smelled after onion vapor with a molecular weight of 720.
Please explain briefly what is wrong with the other choices.

II. More precisely, the relative rates of diffusion of two gases under ideal conditions are inversely proportional to the square roots of their molecular weights. In a test comparing diffusion of onion vapor (molecular weight 720) and perfume vapor (molecular weight 360). The onion vapor is detected about six seconds after its release. How long after release would you expect perfume vapor to be detected?
   A. 3 seconds   B. 4 seconds   C. 6 seconds   D. 9 seconds   E. 12 seconds
Please explain how you found the answer.

FIGURE 11. Chemistry questions requiring serial ordering and correspondences (Item I) and functional relationships (Item II).

Linear specimens of five different materials, each of the same length at 0°C, are heated slowly; the effects of temperature changes on lengths are shown in the graph. When riveted together to form a bimetallic element for a thermostat, which combination of two materials would cause the element to curve as shown when the temperature is increased?

A. 2 on the left, 1 on the right
B. 3 on the left, 1 on the right
C. 3 on the left, 5 on the right
D. 4 on the left, 2 on the right
E. 5 on the left, 4 on the right

Please explain what is wrong with the other choices.

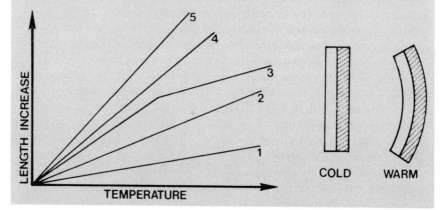

FIGURE 12. Physics question requiring serial ordering and propositional reasoning. Note the multiple-choice format with explanation required.

it is presented here because it very nicely illustrates how early and delayed closure are related to concrete and formal thought. To solve the problem, the respondent has to know that the material on the right of the bimetallic strip expands more than the material on the left, and he has to be able to interpret the graph. Yet, there are two ways of proceeding. In the first method (concrete operations), each alternative is tested in order and closure is achieved when the choice is either accepted or rejected. In the second method (formal operations), the respondent first uses the overall pattern of the graph to infer that metals with higher numbers expand more, so that lack of closure with respect to the original question is accepted. He or she then finds the final answer very quickly, however, by looking for the combination with the higher-numbered material on the right side (choice C).

The most important message in this discussion is that concrete and formal thought may be revealed by the method an individual uses to solve a problem. The answer itself indicates the level of reasoning only rarely. It would be very worthwhile, in this author's opinion, for teachers to use few questions on their tests and to require explanations. This approach would provide valuable diagnostic information and feedback for the teacher, even though it would not be so suitable for rank-ordering the students according to their achievement.

ACKNOWLEDGMENT

This material is based upon research supported in part by the National Science Foundation under Grant No. SED74-18950. Any opinions, findings, and conclusions or recommendations in this publication are those of the author and do not necessarily reflect the views of the National Science Foundation.

The author is indebted to Messrs. Gene R. Ala, Joseph Reitz, and Joseph E. Davis, and to their students at Campolindo High School, Moraga, California, for assistance in preparing this paper.

References

Biological Sciences Curriculum Study. *Biological sciences—from molecule to man* (blue version). Boston: Houghton Mifflin, 1963.

College Entrance Examination Board. *College Board Achievement Tests, 1972–1973.* Princeton, N.J.: College Entrance Examination Board, 1971, 1972.

Lawson, A. E., & Renner, J. W. Relationships of concrete and formal operational science subject matter and the developmental level of the learner. *Journal of Research in Science Teaching,* 1975, *12*(4), 347–358.

Lunzer, E. A. *Formal reasoning: A reappraisal* (this volume).

Science Curriculum Improvement Study. *Subsystems and variables,* Student Manual. Chicago: Rand McNally, 1970.

Science Curriculum Improvement Study. *Energy sources,* Student Manual. Chicago: Rand McNally, 1971. (a)

Science Curriculum Improvement Study. *Models: Electric and magnetic interactions,* Student Manual. Chicago: Rand McNally, 1971. (b)

Science Curriculum Improvement Study. *Relative position and motion,* Student Manual. Chicago: Rand McNally, 1972.

Wollman, W., & Karplus, R. Intellectual development beyond elementary school, V: Using ratio in differing tasks. *School Science and Mathematics,* 1974, *74*(7), 593–611.

Index

Empiricism, 3
  logical, 99, 100, 102-107, 109, 111
Empiricist, 99, 100, 103, 105
  logical, 102, 106, 107, 109, 111
Ennis, R.H., 77, 96, 104, 105, 111
Epistemological loneliness, 137, 138, 141,
    142
Epistemological problems, 101
Epistemological viewpoint, 3
Epistemology, 111
  biological, 101
  developmental, 78, 79
  mechanical, 105, 111
Equation solving, 60
Equation writing, 60
Equilibrated system, 37
Equilibration, 80, 82, 132
  field, 102
  model, 82, 84
Equilibrium, 102, 125
Erikson, E., 142, 144
  identity crisis, 130
Erlwanger, S., 109, 111
Ervin-Tripp, S., 13, 15
Esper, E.A., 85, 96
Etchasketch, 53
Ethical principles, 119
Ethical relativism, 133
Euclid, 103
Event structure, 22
Evolutionary psychology, 100
Evolutionary view, 111
Excitation
  of sensory functions, 38
Experiments
  Geneva, 53
  Piagetian, 166
  Pocklington, 50, 54
Explanation, 12
Explanatory behavior
  in children, 62-64
Explanatory models, 100
Extinction
  auditory, 40
  cross-modal, 31-35, 40
  electrophysiological correlates, 41
  pathology, 31-38
  phenomena, 40
  sensory, 38
  and spatial organization, 34-36
  tactile, 33

Extinction (cont'd)
  temporal dimensions of, 41
  temporal organization of, 37
Extrapersonal space, 35, 36

Faith, 143
Falmagne, R.J., 96
Feffer, M.H., 139, 144
Feyerabend, P.K., 99, 111
Figurative language, 92, 93
Figurative symbolic component, 28
Fillmore, C.J., 180
Fine tuning, 18, 19
Finkelstein, M.R., 104, 111
First-order relations, 83
Fishkin, J., 130, 136
Flexibility
  in thought, 172
Floris, V., 37, 43
Form construction, 19
Formal logic, 68
Formal operations, 49, 101-110, 125, 126,
    178
  and artistic development, 78
  see also Second-order relations
Formal problems, 12
Formal reasoning, 47-74
  in adolescents, 47, 133
  patterns, 186
  unity of, 47
  see also Formal thought
Formal thought, 57, 58, 77-95, 102, 104,
    107, 140-143, 183, 185, 189-194
  INRC group, 57
  meaning of, 82
  research, 77, 78, 91, 92
  role of logic, 57-58, 73
Formulas, 100
Four-card problem, 69, 71
Fox, L., Chapanis, 31, 35-37, 42
Frederiks, J.A., 35, 43
Friedenberg, E., 142, 143

Gallagher, J.M., 85, 89-97
Gardiner, H., 77, 78, 90-92, 96
Gates—MacGinitie Reading Tests, 165,
    166
Gelder, H.M., 105, 111
Generalization, 72
Generative mechanism
  in language, 73